Cohabitation, Family and Society

Routledge Advances in Sociology

Cohabitation, Family and Society

Tiziana Nazio

Routledge
Taylor & Francis Group
New York   London

First published 2008
by Routledge
270 Madison Ave, New York, NY 10016

Simultaneously published in the UK
by Routledge
2 Park Square, Milton Park, Abingdon, Oxon OX14 4RN

Routledge is an imprint of the Taylor & Francis Group, an informa business

© 2008 Tiziana Nazio

Typeset in Sabon by IBT Global
Printed and bound in the United States of America on acid-free paper by IBT Global

Library of Congress Cataloging in Publication Data
Nazio, Tiziana, 1971–
Cohabitation, family, and society / Tiziana Nazio.
p. cm.— (Routledge advances in sociology ; 36)
Includes bibliographical references and index.
ISBN 978-0-415-36841-4 (hardback : alk. paper) 1. Unmarried couples—Europe. 2. Domestic relations—Europe. 3. Family—Europe. 4. Family policy—Europe. I. Title.

HQ803.5.N39 2008
306.84'1094—dc22   2007026064

ISBN10: 0-415-36841-3 (hbk)
ISBN10: 0-203-02823-6 (ebk)

ISBN13: 978-0-415-36841-4 (hbk)
ISBN13: 978-0-203-02823-0 (ebk)

To Elide and Nicoletta

Contents

List of Figures

xiv *List of Figures*

List of Tables

Acknowledgments

I am deeply indebted to Professor Hans-Peter Blossfeld for his inspiration and training, and to both him and Professor Chiara Saraceno for their assistance and invaluable support with the development of this book from its very origins.

I am also most grateful to Professor John McInnes, for the challenging and valuable critiques, for steady encouragement, and, not least, for the English editing, and to Professor Anthony Heath, for his useful comments on an earlier draft of this work and the support I received.

I would like to express my appreciation to Dr. Erik Klijzing, Professor David Strang, Professor Valerie K. Oppenheimer, Professor Fabrizio Bernardi, and Professor Karin Kurz for their valuable comments on the pilot study on which this book is based, and to Professor Gunn E. Birkelund, Professor John Ermisch and Dr. Emilia Del Bono for their suggestions and stimulating criticisms.

This book was conceived and pursued during my work with Professor Hans-Peter Blossfeld on the projects FENICs and GLOBALIFE at the University of Bielefeld. It is to him that I owe my deepest gratitude for the opportunity he offered to work in an extremely productive and stimulating international environment. A special thanks goes also to Professor Anna Cabré Pla, for contributing to my fruitful stay in the Centre for Demographic Studies, where the first draft was completed.

A special acknowledgement goes to Nicoletta Varani and to my friends Zarife Soylucicek, Helga Faletti, Patrizia Nazio, Stefano Claus, Maria José González, Stephanie Montalvo Halfvarson, Luca Curatolo, Andressa Tezine, Lucía Gil, Klemens Keindl, and Sevillen Demirkaya, as well as to Beatriz Fernández, Karin Sommer, and Paola Dalmasso, for their encouragement, love, patience, and steady support.

Grateful acknowledgements are also due to the Advisory Group of the FFS Programme of comparative research for the permission granted to use the Family and Fertility Surveys data on which this study is based.

All the faults are mine.

1 Introduction

I: *Why do you believe people enter into partnership later and marry less?*

R: Maybe because now there are not so many problems, I mean . . . the fact that you do not marry is . . . I imagine that before they looked upon you more badly. I do not know if . . . if they had looked at me very badly. No, to tell the truth I do not care, but well . . . maybe if I would have been brought up differently. . . . At home they are . . . my mother at least, used to be more religious, now she has lost a bit her faith but (*laughs*) . . . Poor woman! But . . . how can you know if . . . I believe that nowadays . . . in former times it was true, ten years ago, . . . you would have moved in together with someone and it was something else than today, today there are many, many couples that go to live together, or maybe. . . . The truth is that I do not know, I do not know. (Inés, 28 years old, cohabiting; my translation from Domingo, 1997, p. 209)

1.1 THE TRANSFORMATION OF PARTNERSHIPS

No longer than 40 years ago, marriage used to mark the start of a first union for most couples in Europe, the overwhelming majority of children were born and reared in marital unions, and a spouse's death (rather than dissolution) was the far most common reason for the termination of a union (Festy, 1980). Since the late 1960s and early 1970s, however, family living has undergone profound transformations with marriage postponement, rise in cohabitation (particularly since the beginning of the 1980s), lowering fertility, and increasing divorce rates (Kiernan, 2000), which have impacted the prevalence and meaning of marriage (Axinn & Thornton, 2000; Manting, 1996; Cherlin, 1994). Nowadays, in many European countries cohabitation has increasingly become a common way to start a first union. Together with cohabitation, nonmarital childbearing rose to unprecedented levels (Ermisch, 2005; Kiernan, 2001) while lifelong marriage has been progressively postponed and eroded by divorce. All these changes have important implications for the demographic structure of the population as well as for the private and public domains of people's life. The spectacular rise in cohabiting unions has impacted not only the forms of living arrangements as such, but may also have long-term consequences for individuals. Indeed, though involving a shared living, cohabitation—unlike marriage—is generally characterised by a lower degree of commitment, lower fertility, and a higher risk of disruption (Mills, 2000; Wu, 2000; Praint, 1995). Cohabitation also legally implies fewer entitlements (e.g., tax allowances, some welfare benefits such as transfer of pension rights or the right to occupancy/inheritance of the dwelling upon death of the partner) but also involves fewer responsibilities towards the partner (e.g., maintenance, support, a shared living) and none towards his/her kin. Furthermore, it contributes to the process of marriage postponement because it is in itself an experience that takes time to make, especially when it is not later converted into marriage (Oppenheimer, 1994). Because cohabitation implies the postponement of marital commitment and it is characterised by a lower (nonmarital) fertility, it might indirectly contribute to the lowering of fertility through the postponement of first child-birth and consequent reduction in the time available for parity progression (Wu, 2000). The distinctive characteristics of cohabitation also imply, for example, a profound change in the intergenerational relationships as well as in the transmission of care and familial resources (a still much unexplored domain), and—upon disruption—in the prevalence of 'reconstituted' families and of single-headed households. The transformations in the family structure and prevalence of nontraditional living arrangements, which come along with increasing levels of cohabiting unions, are of high substantive interest and policy relevance. This is because of their effect on individuals' current and later life chances because 'families' are still the locus where most of individuals' well-being is being produced and secured.

The great deal of intra-European diversity in the extent of cohabiting unions is also of high interest. Why has cohabitation risen much slower in southern Europe? How do individuals strategically choose between cohabiting and marrying within different, and changing, contexts? In other words, what is the relation between macro-level context and micro-level individual actions? This book describes and accounts for the dramatic, and uneven, rise in cohabitation across European countries. The idea presented in this book is that people's choice to adopt cohabitation in their first partnership is (also) influenced by what they perceive other people are doing. In this framework, the investigation of the emergence of cohabitation—its driving mechanisms and differences between countries—should contribute to a better understanding of the dynamics of change in the process of family formation over time. It will shed light on some of the recent modifications in family formation, such as declining marriage rates, later family formation, and subsequent declining fertility rates. This is a relevant issue because the timing and nature of women's partnership decisions have played a crucial role in the demographic changes that have characterised recent decades. Indeed, forming a partnership is a choice whose effects are likely to spill over to subsequent events in the transition to adulthood (e.g., by affecting the timing of entry into motherhood and/or the spacing between children) but also in relation to the risk of dissolution. But, first of all, how often is cohabitation practised in Europe, and how large are the differences between countries?

1.2 PREMARITAL COHABITATION AS A RECENT PHENOMENON

The growth in premarital cohabitation, as a way to form a new family, can be considered as one of the most dramatic changes in family life over the last 40 years. By cohabitation we mean here a co-residential union of two partners in an intimate relationship[1] without being legally married. Cohabitation, together with out-of-wedlock childbirth, has increasingly become more widespread all over Europe (Ermisch, 2005; Kiernan, 1999, 2002, 2004a). However, this has happened at different speeds and reached different levels in different countries. In the early 1960s, premarital cohabitation was exceptional in most European countries (Blossfeld, 1995) and was rare even in Sweden, a country where cohabitation has old roots (Hoem, 1995; Trost, 1979). Today, cohabitation has not only fundamentally changed its social meaning (Manting, 1996; Rogoff Ramsey, 1996; Seltzer, 2004) but has become commonplace in most European countries, particularly among the younger generation (Ermisch, 2005; Mills, 2000; Kiernan, 2006a). There are, nevertheless, great differences in the extent, significance, and meaning of cohabitation across Europe (Cherlin, 2004; Kiernan, 1999, 2002; Prinz, 1995).

In Southern Europe, cohabitation is still rare and mostly an urban phenomenon, or, in the case of Italy, found in the northern parts of the country (Barbagli, Castiglioni & Dalla Zuanna, 2003; Castiglioni & Dalla Zuanna, 1994, Dalla Zuanna & Righi, 1999; De Sandre, 1997, 2000; Pinelli & De Rose, 1995). In other European countries, three different trends in cohabiting unions can be detected. In some Central European countries like West Germany and the Netherlands, cohabitation has become a kind of a socially accepted, short-term prelude to marriage, and it is typically transformed into marriage when couples have a child (Blossfeld et al., 1999; Blossfeld & Mills, 2001; Jong Gierveld & Liefbroer, 1995; Mills, 2000; Mills & Trovato, 2000). In other countries, such as (the former socialist) East Germany, Austria, France, Great Britain, Finland, or Norway, cohabitation has developed into an accepted alternative to marriage and begins to be connected with a high rate of extramarital births (Huinink, 1995; Leridon & Toulemon, 1995; Toulemon, 1997). In other words, cohabitation experiences tend to last longer and are increasingly the locus where childbirth may take place. And finally, the third trend can be seen in Denmark and Sweden, where cohabitation and marital unions seem to have normatively and legally converged to such a degree that for young couples the choice between marriage and cohabitation seems to be solely a matter of private taste, even when children are involved (Duvander, 2000; Hoem, 1995; Leth-Sorensen & Rohwer, 2001). In these countries cohabiting unions are the far most common partnership form, and a succession of cohabitation experiences may characterise the life course of individuals. Here, furthermore, the highest proportion of cohabiting unions is eventually never converted into legal marriages.

These differences in both the social meaning and extent of cohabitation practice in Europe raise the following questions: What are the reasons behind this uneven rise of cohabiting unions? How can these cross-country differences be explained? How did the current levels come about? Or, to put it more generally, *what drives the diffusion of cohabitation?* This question has not been convincingly answered yet, although some descriptions and tentative accounts of the phenomena have been given at both macro and individual levels, as we see in the next chapter.

Macro-level explanations of cohabitation as a diffusion process have so far distinguished a series of successive stages in the diffusion of cohabitation, resulting in three to four clusters of countries (Hoem & Hoem, 1988; Kiernan, 1993, 1999; Prinz, 1995; Roussel, 1992; Roussel & Festy, 1978; Trost, 1979). They argue that there is a common pattern of change in which cohabitation is to be observed first in the north and later diffused to the south of Europe[2]. In the first stage, cohabitation emerges as a rare practice by a selected group of forerunners who adopt it for a specific interest and particular reasons, whereas most people marry without first living together. This stage is found in Southern Europe today, or in the Swedish case, could be seen until the end of the 1960s (see Trost, 1978). In the second stage, cohabitation becomes a more widely practised form of living arrangement. Into this cluster fall Austria, Finland, France, Germany, Great Britain, The Netherlands, Norway, and Switzerland. In these countries cohabitation emerged in the 1970s and it tends to be a temporary phase preceding marriage, which can either be associated with a significant or a negligible rate of extramarital births. In the third stage, cohabitation is well established and constitutes an institutionalised form of union. This latter group of countries comprises Denmark and Sweden, where cohabitation emerged in the mid- to late 1960s and is now the far prevalent norm, also with respect to the birth of children:

> During the 1960s those couples starting a cohabitation without being married chose to cohabit instead of marrying. . . . From 1972 or 1973 or so cohabitation without marriage is the 'normal' behaviour and is in no respect at all a deviant phenomenon. Everyone does it and are obedient to the informal social norm knitted to the social institution

of cohabitation without marriage. In today's Sweden and Denmark couples do not choose to cohabit instead of marry. They just cohabit. (Trost, 1978, p. 186)

These macro analyses provide sound country typologies but are neither the different paces of spread in cohabitation accounted for, nor do they explain much about the mechanisms at play in fostering the diffusion process. Unfortunately, they do not deal with expected convergence or continued divergence between countries and they do not include any micro-level data analysis (Prinz, 1995). Such a macro approach to diffusion offers some good insights but does not specifically address through which mechanisms the diffusion process can exercise pressure by limiting or supporting specific individuals' choices (Palloni, 2001; Reed, Briere & Casterline, 1999). Existing explanations do not address how the diffusion process can intervene in the definition of behavioural options available to individuals, especially through time, when decisions are taken. Indeed, in previous studies there is an implicit assumption that all partnering options are *potentially always available to all individuals to the same degree across time and space*. This assumption means both a perfect knowledge about the functioning and consequences of cohabiting (absence of uncertainties) and an absence of constraints, or (moral) resistances as regards its choice. It is an especially improbable assumption at the beginning of the diffusion process when cohabitation is an innovative practice with a high content of uncertainty and is associated with moral stigma; thus, when ongoing practices, attitudes, and behavioural norms are being challenged. For example, it is unlikely that a young French woman considering the option of cohabiting in the late 1960s would face the same degree of uncertainty about the potential costs and consequences of her choice, as a similar age woman taking the same decision 20 or 30 years later. The same would be true for the first woman if she was 10 or 15 years older, thus taking her choice in the late 1970s or mid-1980s. Both personal characteristics and contextual circumstances are subject to change, as is the meaning of cohabitation and its degree of acceptance, along with its becoming a more common and established partnership option (Seltzer, 2004). Following this hypothetical example, another criticism that could be addressed to the macro approaches defining typologies or phases in the diffusion process is their leaving unspecified the reference to a temporal or spatial trend, whereby all countries would be following the same path (although with differing tempo and speeds). In other words, does the Swedish case simply illustrate what will be Spain's future in the long run?

Building on these critiques, in this study we relax the assumption that societies comprise completely free 'isolated actors' by describing and modelling the mechanisms through which *social influence* may affect individuals' decision processes. Stemming from social psychology, *social influence* is the term most commonly used to describe that what others say and do affects much of individuals' behaviour[3]. It is within this broad meaning that we intend to make use of the term in this work; with reference to how, when facing uncertainty about decisions on engaging in a certain type of behaviour, others' models may alter the balance between restraints and desires by raising or lowering either or both. We argue that the more common is cohabiting, the less is the perception of social stigma attached to doing it and the higher the perceived advantage it entails in the eyes of young people[4]. Social influence, which can be generically defined as the tendency to conform to the conduct of other individuals, is the effect on individuals' conduct played by their perceptions of each others' values, beliefs, and behaviour (see Aronson, 1999; Cialdini, 1984; Coleman, 1990, Jones, 1984; Kuran, 1995). Accounting for social influence is done here by introducing theoretically informed, nation-specific and time-varying (macro) contextual factors in the study of the adoption of cohabitation at the micro level, as we see in chapters 3 and 5. These contextual factors are used to account for the degree of cohabitation 'contagiousness' produced by social influence with the unrolling of the diffusion process.

1.3   GOALS OF THIS STUDY

Explanations given so far to the rise in cohabiting unions have focussed on the influence of individuals' characteristics on the individual rate of adoption, or on (cross-sectional) aggregate measures in explaining aggregate levels of adoption. However, none has yet taken account of individuals' embeddedness in a social context, wherein the easiness and meaning of cohabitation change over time and where individuals can be influenced by others' behaviours. By missing out the contextual characteristics in which individuals' frame their choices, previous analyses of the rationale of cohabiting unions have failed to investigate and explain whether, why, and how the transformation from low to high levels of premarital cohabitation has taken place (Casterline, 2001). We believe, instead, that individuals' reciprocal influence, beside the institutional contexts and individuals' characteristics, is yet another extremely important factor to be added to the analyses of the influences on individuals' decision to adopt cohabitation. This is the process that we wish to study here.

   We will do so by focussing on the individuals' decision to enter a partnership, and try to explain how others' *previous* behaviours can influence their choice to do it by adopting cohabitation rather than marrying. We will take into account both individuals' specific characteristics (by using individual-level survey data and longitudinal models), the effect of different institutional contexts (by adopting a comparative case study approach), and that of individuals' reciprocal influence through enacted behaviours and previous examples of the new practice by other individuals in the social system (through our diffusion account). To capture the social and normative change across time, this book studies the diffusion of cohabitation across successive birth cohorts[5] of young women.

This field of research has only partially been addressed. We already know something from previous studies about the influence of women's socioeconomic circumstances on the decision to enter cohabitation (Blossfeld, 1995; Kiernan, 1999, 2000, 2001, 2004b; Klijzing & Corijn, 2002; Kravdal, 1999; Wu, 2000; Xie et al., 2001), but paradoxically almost nothing is known about the effect exercised by the social context in which individuals make their choices and that changes over time. This is a surprising fact because of the long and general recognition at a theoretical level of the influence played by the cultural and normative contexts on individuals' behaviour[6].

Our aim is thus to explain the diffusion of cohabitation by filling in this gap between micro-level and macro-context of action with respect to young women's decision to adopt cohabitation instead of marriage. This study endeavours to determine whether a diffusion approach could enhance our understanding of the recent changes in union behaviours, in a positive attempt to bridge the divide between diffusion theory and the empirical examination of the life course. We are going to focus on the dynamic shift of cohabitation from a rare and deviant form of partnership to a common and socially accepted union (Prinz, 1995; Trost, 1979), and on the concomitant transformation of marriage from a socially prescribed choice to a mere option. The specific aim of the analyses presented in the following chapters is thus to explore the nature and relevance of the mechanisms responsible for changes over time in women's likelihood to initiate their first partnership by cohabiting rather than marrying.

This work aims to contribute to diffusion theory through an empirical and comparative exercise. For this reason, the results obtained are also important in that they provide strong support for the hypothesis that a mechanism related to social influence does indeed affect individuals' choice to adopt cohabitation, and thus its spread. In this respect, we are concerned not only with the development of indicators for the description and empirical test of the diffusion process of cohabitation in itself, but more generally with the understanding of diffusion processes and social change. On the one hand, this is a study of the particular social phenomenon of cohabitation, but on the other, this can also be seen as one example of the more general social processes of diffusion.

To this general interest, a more specific research question is added. This second question relates to the characteristic time-related structure of the diffusion process of cohabitation (detailed in chapter 3). We argue that an individual's relative advantage entailed in choosing to cohabit will depend, amongst other things, on the following factors: others' experiences with cohabitation, the general opinion concerning this practice, and the level of social approval associated with doing so (see also Ermisch, 2005). This general level of social acceptance in turn is a function of the population of individuals who already have adopted it in previous generations, or amongst an individual's peers. One of the issues we investigate here is whether the behaviour of previous generations or of peers is more influential. As discussed in the following chapters, in analytical terms this means testing two different mechanisms of social influence that potentially affect individuals' willingness to adopt cohabitation: *knowledge-awareness* (people's perception about the general prevalence, rationale, and meaning of cohabitation in the society), and *direct social modelling* (more direct examples of adoption of cohabitation from 'similar' others). In the empirical analyses we explore the shape and relative influence played by these two mechanisms related to the diffusion process, beside the role of socioeconomic factors.

To avoid raising unfulfilled expectations, let us make clear from the very beginning what this book will *not* deal with. In this study, we only focus on premarital cohabitation experiences, as those partnerships comprising the sharing of a living space, requiring a sexual relationship beyond friendship, and lasting a minimum duration[7]. We do not explore or compare cross-sectional measures of aggregate levels of cohabitation for women and men in European countries because the diffusion of cohabitation is a complex dynamic process unrevealing over time. Nor does our analysis include repeated experiences of co-residential unions in women's life course or focus on their duration because we aim at capturing and explaining the mechanisms and differences in the takeup process across countries.

To better capture the innovative content of cohabitation, this study concentrates instead on women's *first* adoption of cohabitation (before marriage if it ever occurs) in six different European institutional contexts chosen as case studies: the conservative-corporatist West Germany and France, the former socialist East Germany[8], the social-democratic Sweden, and the familialist Italy and Spain (Esping-Andersen, 1999; Ferrera, 1993, 1996). These countries were chosen to comprise the highest degree of variability in institutional contexts, welfare regimes[9], and family cultures, as well as in the pace and tempo of the diffusion process. Some attention is also devoted to the transition to residential independence (first exit from the parental home) and to the alternative option to marry.

These choices have both theoretical and empirical rationales. First, the selection of countries covers the entire spectrum of European welfare regimes with the exclusion of the liberal (United Kingdom[10]) but the inclusion of a former Eastern context. This choice allows us to distinguish and compare the effects exercised by different institutional contexts as well as to capture different stages and speeds in the process of diffusion of cohabitation. The high degree of variation also means setting a severe empirical test with respect to the mechanisms linked to social influence, which are thought to drive the diffusion process.

Second, we have concentrated only on the experiences of women for both theoretical and practical reasons. On the one hand, different life events and individual characteristics influence men and women very differently. The gender division of labour, for example, creates gender specific relationships between explanatory variables and the choice to partner[11]. On the other hand, it also arises from data availability for such an ambitious longitudinal comparative project covering a 30-year time span. In fact, we conducted the analyses on the (retrospectively collected) life histories of a common sample of women between 15 and 39 years of age from the Family and Fertility Surveys (FFSs). These national surveys represent an extremely rich and highly comparable source of data, comprising retrospective records of individuals' educational, occupational, partnership, and fertility careers (Festy & Prioux, 2002). However, the underrepresentation of men in the FFSs surveys samples does not leave enough events to allow us to investigate men's sensitivity to social influence. The selection made includes women born between 1954 and 1973. These birth cohorts have been recognised as the main protagonist of the changes in partnership formation brought about by the Second Demographic Transition (Lesthaeghe, 1995; Surkyn & Lesthaeghe, 2004; Van de Kaa, 1987). Thus the chosen strategy allows us to capture the main changes in family formation along different stages of the diffusion process from the perspective of women's experience.

Third, the decision to study only the first ever adoption of cohabitation is based on the need to capture the innovative content of nonmarital unions in the eyes of its adopters. The aim is to depict the factors and mechanisms behind the diffusion of cohabitation as a means to initiate a co-residential union amongst young people. The innovative character of a newly introduced practice, and the uncertainty that it involves, can be better captured by the study of its *first* adoption by each individual. Moreover, subsequent cohabitation may be affected by different mechanisms and constraints (Wu, 2000), like the legal inability to marry or the relative convenience not to marry (to prevent the loss of welfare benefits, like housing or pension, or entitlements to alimony).

In turn, some attention is instead paid to the treatment of events in parallel careers[12], which may exert a direct influence on the adoption of cohabitation: the acquisition of residential independence from the parental family and the experience of a pregnancy. Furthermore, because marrying represents an alternative option to cohabitation when deciding to enter a first partnership, the transition to marriage is also explored.

To sum up, the research question that this book attempts to answer is the following: What can explain the different pace and levels of the practice of cohabitation across Europe? Particular attention is given to testing two possible mechanisms driving the diffusion process of cohabitation.

1.4 THE THEORETICAL AND EMPIRICAL APPROACH FOLLOWED

The first specificity of this study is its focus on individuals' *social embeddedness*. The choice to begin a partnership as a cohabitation is seen here as an individually taken 'contextualised' decision, by which we mean a choice nested within a set of constraints (whether perceived or not) affecting individuals' action. For this reason, it is not sensible to study young women's choice to adopt cohabitation independently from the presence of 'situational' opportunities and constraints, obligations and conditionings with which they are confronted. This set of constraints is not only individual specific, like for example the amount of individual resources available over the life course, it is also moulded by specific national contexts, which define the available (or 'proper') behavioural options and opportunities. Indeed, in the definition of the situation in which individuals develop their strategies, the legal framework, the value system and normative pressure are important intervening factors (Boudon, 1981). A large body of sociological and psychosociological research has already shown the relevance of actors' social embeddedness in shaping individuals' behaviour via the influence of other actors' behaviour (Åberg, 2001; Cialdini, 1984, 1993; Cialdini & Goldstein, 2004; Coleman, 1990; Jones, 1984; Kahan, 1997; Kuran, 1995; Palloni, 2001). In line with this previous research we argue that the decision of *when* and *how* people enter their first partnership is influenced by the social and cultural context to which individuals are tied, although they remain mostly unaware of it.

We argue that '*social influence*' is the engine of the diffusion process. Social influence is linked to the current level of practice of cohabitation in a society. It is a factor exogenous to individuals but it is endogenously determined in a social system as a function of all previous individuals' adoptions (both in an individual's peer cohort and in past generations). In other words, social influence is not related to individuals' own characteristics but is internally produced within the social system by others' previous experiences with cohabitation. The more people cohabit, the lower the social stigma associated to doing it, the more it is know about its consequences, and the more it is believed to be an efficient choice, so that the easier it is for subsequent individuals to do the same. Thus the prevalence of cohabiters in the past is thought to determine the degree of social approval those choosing to enter cohabitation at a later time perceive they enjoy. Through the role of social influence, diffusion models are deemed to account for how exogenous changes in individuals' behaviour in a given moment (e.g., cohabiting brought about by an increasing uncertainty for young people in the labour market or a prolonged education) can increase the level of its social approval in subsequent times. This, in turn, may further increase the advantage of cohabiting and induce yet larger numbers of individuals to decide to cohabit, which will, in turn, further influence the level of social acceptance in the future. Through this self-reinforcing mechanism, the process of diffusion fosters new adoptions while at the same time the increasing levels of cohabitation change the meaning associated with its practice.

In this respect, this book contains an innovative theoretical and methodological approach. The approach adopted is embedded in a macro-sociological argument about the effect of social influence—together with structural and institutional changes—on the adoption of cohabitation in a micro-sociological dynamic framework. In other words, by attempting to bridge the micro-macro dimension, our model aims to account for the development of the process of change at the societal level by explaining it through factors affecting individuals' decision-making process (Cleland, 2001; Palloni, 2001; Reed Briere & Casterhine, 1999). Thus the approach chosen allows us to disentangle the different dimensions of the diffusion process of cohabitation at the level of young women's life course. A new concept (social influence) is introduced in chapter 2 and a suggestion for its empirical operationalisation is discussed and tested. This approach enhances the comprehension of the diffusion process through the evaluation of the influence played by the mechanisms proposed (*'knowledge-awareness'* and *'direct social modelling'*) on the timing of entry into cohabitation while also leaving room for the interpretation and assessment of other important effects.

Similarly, individuals' choices to cohabit are also not independent from institutional contexts and welfare systems, in that they promote or hinder specific family forms by allocating citizens different amounts of rights and responsibilities (Daly, 1994, 1996; O'Connor, 1993, 1996; Orloff, 2002; Saraceno, 1988). By setting the range, generosity, and conditions of entitlement to provisions and benefits, they also shape familial obligations. It can be argued that ultimately specific national contexts and welfare models can be more or less conducive to the spread of new family forms such as cohabitation. We thus also adopt a comparative focus to analyse the extent to which the institutional and normative contexts affect the rate and the form of the diffusion process of cohabitation and lead to a path-dependent development in each nation (Mayer, 2001). This book presents results using highly comparable data and models from six different institutional contexts, offering a wide range of variation both in terms of diffusion of cohabitation and of other important variables such as labour markets, educational and political systems, cultural and family traditions, and of historical legacies. The high degree of standardisation achieved[13] enables a systematic and direct comparison of the results across countries.

We also provide a detailed description of the changes in some domains of the various institutional contexts over the last three decades. In particular, the development in labour markets, housing markets, and law on cohabiting unions are documented and discussed in relation to their effects on the relative advantage offered by cohabitation over marriage. Furthermore, a wider range of influences has been taken into account than in previous research, particularly, in addition to social influence, the effects of parallel events on two interrelated careers, namely that of pregnancy and the subsequent birth of a child, and that of gaining residential independence from the parental home. In the comparative framework adopted, these aspects are especially interesting for exploring the effect of the institutional contexts.

Because *both individual* and *contextual* characteristics change *over the life-course and across birth cohorts,* there is a need for an approach that can take into account both these time-related dimensions. To capture the complex and dynamic nature of the diffusion process of cohabitation, the study presented in this book makes use of the most recent comparable survey data available, and the process of entry into partnership is described on the basis of a continuous succession of birth cohorts. This allows us to examine the long-term impact of several mechanisms on the growth of cohabitation, including that of social influence. In an event history analysis framework (Allison, 1984; Blossfeld & Rohwer, 1995b; Blossfeld, Hamerle & Mayer, 1989; Yamaguchi, 1991), a diffusion model at the individual level is developed and implemented[14]. Through this new approach it is suggested that a more complex mechanism may be at work in driving the diffusion of cohabitation than that envisaged by traditional models.

A big advantage of a life-course approach is that it allows us to detect and reconstruct the complex time-dependent structure of the process in more than one dimension. Through the chosen models it is possible to distinguish different calendars: historical time along individuals' life courses and the process of change across a succession of birth cohorts[15]. This allows us not only to get a better grasp of the underlying process but also to unravel its temporal patterns (Mayer, 2000). In this framework women's choice to cohabit is explained by their changing position in a developing social context, combined with their time-varying individual characteristics. This approach stresses the need to combine the changing macro (increasing rates of cohabitation and its acceptance) and micro (women's characteristics) elements, which allow women to act and plan their lives strategically while being simultaneously constrained by their embeddedness in a social context.

1.5   OVERVIEW OF THE STUDY

This book comprises seven chapters, including the present introduction. In chapter 2 the differences in the practice of cohabitation across Europe are documented. Current theories dealing with the phenomena are discussed and a new theoretical approach is introduced. A diffusion account is put forward as a possible explanation of these trends and is argued to be appropriate theoretically. Drawing on diffusion theory, we suggest that young women's decisions to adopt cohabitation depend both on their personal characteristics and on their social embeddedness. In particular, we argue that in conditions of uncertainty brought about by the introduction of an innovative practice, it is rational for individuals to draw information from others' previous experiences for conducting their behaviour. To conclude, the role of *social influence* in the diffusion of cohabitation is discussed.

In chapter 3 the current debate on the diffusion processes and their specificity is developed. It is argued that combining a traditional structural account with a diffusion explanation is the best approach to follow. The role of endogenous feedback effects is discussed and the timeframe structuring the specific diffusion process of cohabitation analysed. We describe how, in the case of premarital cohabitation, adoption is confined to a relatively short window in the life course (transition from youth to adulthood) and the population of potential adopters is highly dynamic over time. This chapter also presents some first results of the diffusion of cohabitation as captured by the indicators developed. These results offer an innovative picture of the changes on cohabitation practice over the period studied, but in themselves they are unable to tell us about the underlying mechanisms giving rise to the observed levels of nonmarital unions.

In chapter 4 the role played by institutional contexts in making cohabitation appear attractive to young women is assessed. The institutional contexts in which the young women's choices to cohabit take place are described. The longitudinal perspective followed in this study separates considering the current conditions, from the way these conditions have changed over the historical period relevant to the study. Thus the transformations that have taken place in recent decades in each country are briefly documented. Some institutional features are particularly relevant to a rising interest in new forms of family arrangements. These settings and their changes are treated in distinct sections, namely: the development of laws and regulations framing partners' entitlements and obligations, the general cultural contexts; the effects of educational expansion; increasing female labour force participation and rising uncertainty in labour markets, and, finally; the characteristics of different housing markets. In each of these sections country-specific hypothesis are developed in relation to the specific opportunities and constraints on the decision to cohabit set by the institutional contexts and their transformations.

In chapter 5 the statistical models, data, and variables used in the subsequent empirical analyses are presented. Particular attention is given to the integration of a diffusion approach with event history analysis. Methodological and epistemological differences between the proposed individual level diffusion model and standard models are stressed. Because this analysis models the interrelated effect of two other parallel careers undertaken by individuals (residential autonomy and entrance into motherhood) on that of partnership formation, some discussion of the modelling of interrelated events is presented.

In chapter 6 the empirical findings are presented and discussed. Initially, the changes across birth cohorts in the timing of leaving the parental home are documented and their interrelationship with corresponding changes in the entrance into partnership is assessed. This discussion concludes with the presentation of the most interesting results of a hazard rate model on young women's exit from the parental home. In a second step, women's decisions to enter a first partnership are modelled in a competing risk framework. The effects of the institutional contexts are interpreted and the relative hypotheses tested with respect to the entrance into marriage and the adoption of cohabitation. The results of an additional individual-level diffusion model, specifically tailored to test the effects of the indicators of social influence thought to drive the diffusion of cohabitation, are then discussed. Finally, the relative influence of the two driving mechanisms is assessed.

In chapter 7 the results of this research are assessed with respect to the theoretical and methodological contribution of this diffusion approach. The meaning and implications of the findings on the interpretation of the dynamic change in early family formation patterns is discussed. To conclude, some suggestions are given with respect to policy making.

2 Diffusion Processes and Longitudinal Approach

2.1 A LONGITUDINAL APPROACH FOR THE STUDY OF THE DIFFUSION OF COHABITATION

The rapid rise of cohabitation as an alternative form of living arrangement for young couples has been described as one of the most dramatic changes in family life that has occurred in the last decades (Kiernan, 2000, 2002; Wu, 2000). But the onset and pace of its spread has been largely uneven across social groups, space, and time. Many previous analyses (Blossfeld, 1995; Kiernan, 1999, 2000, 2001; Prinz, 1995; Trost, 1978) have already noted a sharp north-south divide in cohabitation rates in Europe. In the mid-1990s around a third of couples under 35 were cohabiting in the UK, West Germany, and East Germany, around two thirds in France, and well over 90% in Denmark and Sweden (Barlow et al. 2001; Kiernan, 1999). In Southern European countries such as Spain, Greece, or Italy, however, cohabitation was far less common, not exceeding 3% (Kiernan, 1999). Again, whereas in the mid-1990s in Sweden, Denmark, and Norway (together with East Germany) over 40% of women had their first child in a cohabiting union, in Spain, Italy, and Greece the proportion keeps under 10% (Kiernan, 1999, 2001).

What can explain these differences? This chapter deals with the contribution that a diffusion approach can offer to the understanding of how such rates vary both over time within countries and in the same period across countries. *Diffusion* relates to a learning process where a macro phenomenon, such as the increasing spread of a new behaviour, is the result of the combination of individuals' actions at the micro level (Åberg, 2000; Cialdini & Trost, 1998; Kahan, 1997; Schelling, 1978). Diffusion, in fact, is conceived here as an individual-level process where previous adoption of cohabitation by some in the social system alters the probability of choosing to cohabit for the remaining members of the population (Durlauf & Walker, 2001; Montgomery & Casterline, 1993; Palloni, 2001; Strang, 1991). A classical definition is the following: "[Diffusion] is the process by which an innovation is communicated through certain channels over time among the members of a social system" (Rogers, 1985, p. 19).

And a more recent redefinition comes from Palloni, who states, "A diffusion process is one in which selection or adoption (rejection) of a behaviour or practice depends on an individual decision-making process that assigns significant influence to the adoption (rejection) behaviour of other individuals within the social system" (Palloni, 2001, p. 90).

In the case of cohabitation, the diffusion process seems to occur as a spontaneous, unplanned, and innovative social process. Actors in this process, belonging to different cohorts and at different life stages, comprise two groups: those who have knowledge of, or have had experience of, cohabitation, and those who do not yet have such knowledge or experience. In addition, there must be communication channels (ranging from interpersonal contacts to impersonal sources like the mass media) connecting the two groups.

In this approach we understand the ability to form a partnership as being regulated both by individuals' changing circumstances and by values and norms surrounding partnership behaviour. Although our approach as a whole considers the dual influence of the social structure (norms, legislation, social influence from previous adopters) and individual strategic action (preferences and resources) in the adoption of cohabitation, this chapter mainly deals with the first aspect[1].

This chapter begins by illustrating the main differences in the spread of cohabitation in Europe and their interrelations with the process of partnership formation and other events (section 2.2). Sections 2.3 and 2.4 discuss previous findings and, respectively, macro and micro accounts for the rise in cohabitation rates. In section 2.5 the focus shifts to the contribution that a diffusion perspective can bring about in understanding social change. It follows the presentation of a theoretical framework explaining why and how the diffusion process is driven by social influence (section 2.6). In the next section (2.7) we offer a brief clarification of the two distinct ways in which social influence can be exercised: through behavioural examples (social learning) or through normative evaluation (social pressure). The chapter concludes in section 2.8 with the suggestion that previous level of cohabitation can affect people's perception of its advantages and disadvantages and, by doing so, foster new adoptions and change the level of cohabitation in a self-reinforcing manner.

2.2   PRACTICE WITH PREMARITAL COHABITATION: DIFFERENCES IN EUROPE

As briefly mentioned, broad differences in the level and progress of cohabitation are to be found throughout Europe nowadays (Kiernan, 1999). The graphs in Figure 2.1 illustrate these differences by displaying the cumulative proportion of young women who have entered their first partnership via cohabitation rather than marriage. These graphs refer to a selected birth cohort of women born in the early 1960s. By birth cohort is meant a group of people born during the same year or period. One particular birth cohort was selected because the rising incidence of cohabitation over time has had a different impact on successive cohorts (see Figure 3.1 in the next chapter). Figure 2.1 displays the frequency of transition to a first union among young women in several Western and Eastern European countries.

Legend: darker is for cohabitation, lighter is for marriage (birth cohorts early '60s)

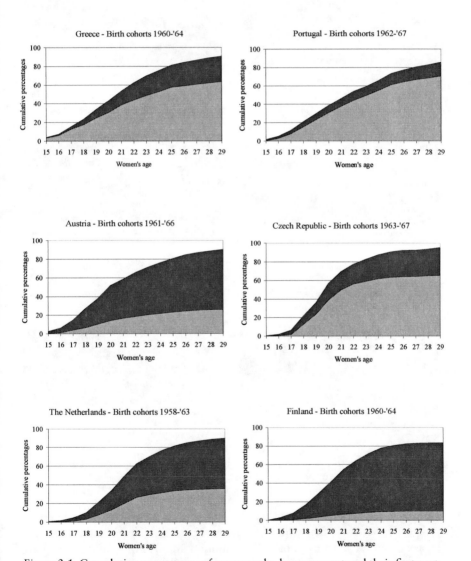

Figure 2.1 Cumulative percentages of women who have ever entered their first partnership by age (birth cohorts early 1960s). (*continued over*)

Legend: darker is for cohabitation, lighter is for marriage (birth cohorts early '60s)

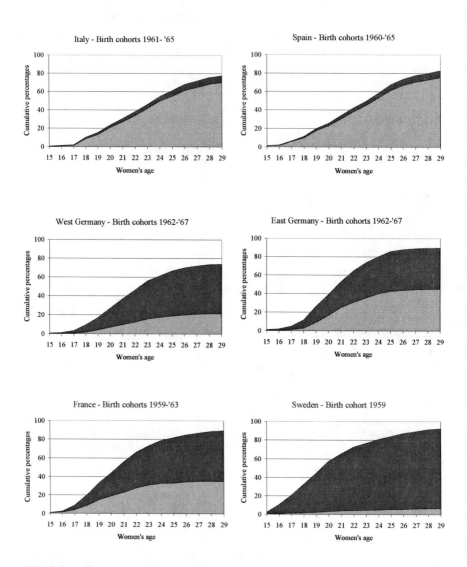

Figure 2.1 Cumulative percentages of women who have ever entered their first partnership by age (birth cohorts early 1960s).

As we can see in the first figure, hardly anybody has formed a first partnership by age 17. When women grow older, however, the figure begins to rise, so that by age 25 in Italy, for example, a little more than 60% of young people have entered a first union (almost all of whom by choosing to marry rather than cohabit). We can also see that in the Southern European countries, at any age, the bulk of partnership is mostly marriages (lighter area in the figures). In contrast in the Nordic countries, the vast majority of first partnership is by cohabiting (darker area in the figures). A common feature across the countries is the peak of the curve at the right end of the graph, which shows that by 29 years of age between 85% and 90% of respondents have experienced some type of co-residential union, be it through marrying or cohabiting. This figure is only a bit lower for Italy, Spain, and West Germany. The distinction in the type of union formed, between marriage (lighter area) and cohabitation (darker area), reveals again how the nature of this transition changes consistently by country from the north to the south of Europe. Sweden and Finland lead with a vast majority of young women opting for cohabitation as a means to entering their first partnership. France, Austria, The Netherlands, and West and East Germany follow with a relatively high proportion (up to 50%) of women adopting cohabitation first. At the other extreme are the Southern European countries, with Greece, Portugal, Spain, and Italy. Here the small proportion (not exceeding 10% to 20%) of young women experiencing cohabitation in the first partnership reveals how this is de facto a much rarer option. A further difference among countries is also the timing in which partnership decisions take place. For example, by age 22, around two fifths of Italians, Spaniards, and West Germans, up to two thirds of Greeks, Dutch, Finnish, East Germans, Norwegian, French, Belgian, and Austrian, and three quarters of Swedish young women have entered their first union in these selected birth cohorts. Thus the proportion of women who are still not in a partnership (white area) varies greatly by age across countries (see Figure 2.1).

However, to account for these differences, we must also consider that the timing of partnership formation is not independent from other events that mark the transition from youth to adulthood[2]. Finishing one's education, for example, or entering and establishing oneself in the labour market, as well as experiencing a pregnancy, are interrelated careers that may influence either the ability or desire to form a new partnership (Blossfeld, 1995; Blossfeld & Huinink, 1991; Marini, 1984, 1985; Shavit & Blossfeld, 1993; Wu, 2000); an issue we come back to in more detail in chapter 5. There are also national specific timing patterns in the experience of certain events in the transition to adulthood (often modelled by national specific settings in the educational systems and the labour and housing markets), which are related to—and we might therefore expect to influence—the adoption of cohabitation (see Figure 2.2).

Figure 2.2 uses the same countries and birth cohorts as in Figure 2.1 and shows the cumulative percentages of young women who by each age have experienced such events as leaving education, entering the labour market, forming the first co-residential partnership, and having their first child[3]. Sharp differences exist among countries, as well as across birth cohorts (not shown), in the timing of partnership formation relative to these other events. That is to say not only are there differences in the age in years at which women tend to enter their first union, but also the timing and sequence of these other events related to this.

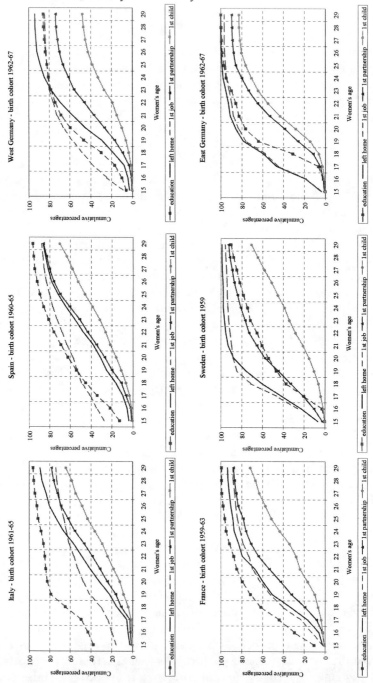

Figure 2.2 Cumulative percentages of women who have ever terminated education, left the parental home, entered the first job, entered the first partnership, and had the first child, by age (birth cohorts early 1960s).

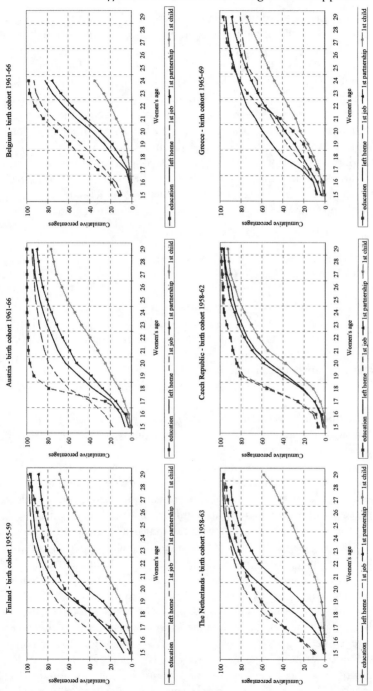

Figure 2.2 Cumulative percentages of women who have ever terminated education, left the parental home, entered the first job, entered the first partnership, and had the first child, by age (birth cohorts early 1960s).

For this reason, the multivariate analyses undertaken in this study also take into account the possible effects that these other transitions[4] may have had on the likelihood of cohabiting[5]. Moreover, there is another factor we must take into account. Cohabitation can be seen as implying a less binding commitment than marriage, which makes entry into a first partnership easier. A shift towards cohabitation from marriage would therefore increase the rate of entrance into first partnership as such[6]. If we find that a progressive postponement of the decision to enter a partnership is linked to increasing levels of young people's uncertainty about the future, cohabitation might loosen the requirement of a long-lasting strong commitment such as marriage while still allowing a partnership to take place. However, we should not forget that the measure of relative advantage of cohabiting (also) goes hand in hand with the degree of its perceived social acceptance.

2.3   WHAT DO WE ALREADY KNOW? MACRO-LEVEL EXPLANATIONS

At the macro level some explanations of the changes in cohabitation levels have been attempted, for example, on the basis of country-level measurements of out-of-wedlock births of children over time (Festy, 1980, 1985; Frinking, 1988). Lesthaeghe (1992), also, proposes a typology drawing on the relationship between levels of cohabiting unions and levels of births outside marriage, to which Roussel (1992) added indicators of divorce and fertility. A more sophisticated typology was then developed by Prinz (1995), who described a *'partnership transition'* led by changes in gender roles. In this transition an increasing number of individuals, and particularly women, would try to escape from traditional expectations and acquire a better bargaining position within the partnership by choosing to cohabit rather than marry because of the former's lack of institutionalised rules about how to live as a couple. In the course of this transition, a change in the degree of social acceptability of cohabitation and its institutionalisation is produced, the 'acceptance' of which is taken as the major indicator of the progress of the partnership transition. Prinz measures this acceptance of cohabitation through sequence ratios[7] and the computation of Gini coefficients[8], beside comparative measures of fertility of unmarried to married women in two age groups.

However, on the one hand, these explanations miss a focus on individuals as purposive decision makers, who each possess unique characteristics and are embedded in different circumstances. Another shortcoming of cross-country comparative static analyses is that they cannot easily reveal causal processes because they do not account for the individuals' decision-making processes that give rise to macro-level patterns (Blossfeld, 1995, 1996; Blossfeld & Rohwer, 1997; Blossfeld et al., 1999). Macro estimates do not clearly uncover or point to the mechanisms and 'reasons' why individuals take certain choices that lead to increasing levels of cohabitation (Boudon, 1981; Hedström & Swedberg, 1998; Pötter & Blossfeld, 2001). In a rational action theory framework[9] instead (Blossfeld, 1996; Boudon, 1998a, 1998b, 2003; Goldthorpe, 1996; Hedström, 2005; Marini, 1984, 1985), a social phenomenon is better understood as the resultant from individuals' attitudes, choices, and behaviours, and it has to be explained with reference to the 'reasons' guiding individuals' actions (Blossfeld, 1996). Because social processes are brought about by the actions of individuals, their causal explanation should not only deal with the association between aggregate-level variables but with variables that are associated through the actions of individuals. The search for causal mechanisms explaining a social phenomenon should thus evolve around the individuals, in that they relate causes and effects through their acting (according to the principle of methodological individualism; Elster, 1998). Individuals' life-history data are the only way to trace the course of action at the level of individuals over time. Rather than cross-sectional aggregate measure or aggregate longitudinal data, individual life histories constitute the most appropriate empirical evidence for the test of hypotheses about the diffusion process of cohabitation.

On the other hand, all these cross-sectional aggregate measures tend to miss the time complexity of the process. As we illustrate in more detail in chapter 3, the diffusion process of cohabitation takes place in a temporal dimension wherein a succession of birth cohorts continuously enters and exits the risk set, coexisting for a certain period. Analysing snapshots of a dynamic process may thus lead to a serious misinterpretation of the incidence and progression of cohabitation at a societal level[10].

Furthermore, because macro-level indicators are the result of the composition of the behaviour of individuals belonging to different birth cohorts, and who choose to cohabit at differing points in their life course, they are also unable to capture the effects of the changing structure of opportunities and constraints over individuals' lives (Blossfeld, 1996). Social processes, in fact, are rarely governed by a single causal mechanism but by a complex history- and context-specific set of causes (Gambetta, 1998). For this reason, the time relatedness of social processes must not be neglected, and empirical evidence of causal mechanisms must be intrinsically related to historical time. Because both purposive individuals and national specific institutions and cultures contribute to mould individuals' life courses, changing historical conditions must be taken into account (period effect) together with the different historical settings into which different generations of individuals happen to unroll their lives (cohort effect) (Blossfeld, 1996; Rogoff Ramsey 1996). In line with these observations, even the more time-aware typology developed by Prinz (by being centred on stages in the modes and levels of practice of cohabitation rather than countries) fails to capture the role played by specific institutional contexts in affecting individuals' agency and life-course outcomes. These examples show how problematic it is to use cross-sectional comparative evidence to depict the mechanisms governing processes that develop over time (Blossfeld & Rohwer, 1997).

> Any macro-micro framework must recognise that time matters in this relationship. It must identify the particular historical structures and processes which dominate the changes occurring in a given population and it has to specify the causal mechanisms that allow us to trace the encounters of intentionally acting individuals with the flow of history as a series of choice processes.
>
> (Blossfeld, 1996, p. 198)

So far we have mentioned previous studies aimed at explaining the rise of practice with premarital cohabitation across time by means of measures taken at the aggregate (macro) level. These measures refer to indicators of central tendency (average, median), rates or other indexes computed on aggregates of individuals and/or time periods. However, some of the previous research[11] has (only) recently begun to focus on cohabitation at the individual level[12]. Nevertheless, its main concerns have not been an explicit explanation of the mechanisms behind the *rise* in cohabiting levels. Instead, it has mainly focussed on the shorter lasting nature of cohabitation experiences (on their higher risk of disruption over time) or on their role as a stepping-stone into marital unions (Lillard, Brien & Waite, 1995; Rindfuss & Van den Heuvel, 1990; Thomson & Colella, 1992; Wu, 2000). Other studies have also aimed at accounting for the specific social or biographical characteristics of the women who have decided to cohabit instead of marry (Audirac, 1986; Goldsheider & Waite, 1986; Leridon, 1990; Liefbroer, 1991).

However, *explaining individuals' propensity to cohabit at a given point in time is not the same as detecting the mechanisms leading to its increasing adoption.* The latter involves unearthing the reasons behind the differences in pace and speed of the diffusion of this innovative practice over time. But without reference to the dynamic nature of the process, and to the changing structure of the opportunities and constraints facing young people, it is neither possible to account for how individuals' propensity can change over their life course nor for the factors influencing these changes. Additionally, to make progress in the knowledge of the mechanisms behind the uneven rise of cohabiting unions, we need to integrate the analysis of individuals' decisions to adopt cohabitation with an account of their being embedded in a social system (Granovetter, 1985). What is needed is thus to distinguish individuals' characteristics (micro level), from their circumstances set by the macro-level characteristics of their social contexts, such as the institutional factors or the general level of practice with cohabitation. These latter may change over time simultaneously with, but analytically quite distinct from, the development of individuals' life courses.

2.4 WHAT DO WE ALREADY KNOW?
MICRO-LEVEL EXPLANATIONS

Existing theories on the rise of cohabitation over time have suggested that its popularity might be tied to a shift in values or attitudes towards premarital sex in particular (Clarkberg, Stolzenberg & Waite, 1995; Lesthaeghe & Meekers, 1986; Lesthaeghe & Neels, 2002; Lesthaeghe & Surkyn, 1988; Rindfuss & Van den Heuvel, 1990) or more generally to changing gender roles (Goldsheider & Waite, 1986; Prinz, 1995). Yet economic circumstances have also changed substantially during the period in which cohabitation has grown. Women's educational level has risen, female participation in the labour force has increased, and young adults' working careers have become less secure and worse paid (Bergmann, 1986; Blossfeld, et al., 2005; Clarkberg, Stolzenberg & Waite, 1995; Easterlin, 1993; Oppenheimer, 1994, 2000; Saraceno, 1997). Such economic factors may well cause changes in the propensity of cohabiting. Some theories have indeed focussed on individuals' socioeconomic characteristics that could increase the relative advantage at the individual level of cohabiting compared to marrying. For example, employment and higher educational qualifications might reduce women's gain from traditional marriage, wherein wives are more likely than husbands to specialise in unpaid reproductive work rather than participate in the labour market (Becker, 1973, 1981). However, this controversial view does not make clear whether women's decreasing returns from gender-role specialisation would only undermine marriage or make *any* form of partnership less advantageous. For example, if we take the gender division of labour in housework as an indicator of gender-role specialisation, we find that although cohabiting women still tend to do more housework than their partners, this difference is smaller in cohabiting than in married couples (Clarkberg Stolzenberg & Waite, 1995). In this respect, to the extent that women's wages would reduce their incentive to enter a marital union, working women should prefer to stay single or to cohabit rather than marry. On the other hand, in a society characterised by a dual-earning couple rather than by a traditional male breadwinner model and by an increasing employment uncertainty, working women may be those facing fewer barriers in choosing marriage because they would be economically 'ready' to afford it (Xie et al., 2001). Alternatively, working women may also constitute appealing partners to men with only a precarious career, or to those who feel unwilling to support the economic dependence of a housewife as implied in a traditional model of gender division of labour (Clarkberg, 1999). Working women might also be in a better position to bargain for, and/or to have the resources to contract-out household chores, not only in a cohabiting union but also within a marriage (Major, 1993, 1994; Major, McFarlin & Gagnon 1984; Sen, 1990). Moreover, better educated and working women may be better able to negotiate both the form and the content of their partnership, and they may prefer to do this rather than choosing to remain single. As England (2000) points out, a partner may still provide some help with the household chores, whereas the load of homemaking plus paid work may be more of a problem for single women, especially if they want children. However, the feasibility and relative convenience of cohabiting is also affected by cultural and institutional barriers, or by legal entitlements and protections, which may alter its opportunity-cost balance[13].

Alternatively, cohabitation can be seen as a rational response to growing uncertainty caused by structural changes in the labour market. Indeed, the declining resources and career stability that increasingly affect younger generations might create a growing need for models of partnership that are more flexible or low binding than marriage (Barlow et al., 2001; Clarkberg, 1999; Oppenheimer, 1988, 1994). Young people, and particularly young women, are described as particularly unconvinced about the need for marriage. According to this perspective, increased flexibility in employment careers would reduce young people's readiness and ability to make long-term commitments (Blossfeld et al., 2005). Therefore, people who choose to cohabit, rather than to marry, might tend to be those less prone, or less prepared, to making lifelong commitments (Barlow et al., 2001). Their unstable careers might make them less appealing on the marriage market, or marriage an unattractive option to them, thus making the postponement of commitment through a more flexible living arrangement more attractive (Kravdal, 1999; Oppenheimer, 1988, 1994).

> Cohabitation gets young people out of high-cost search activities during a period of social immaturity but without incurring what are, for many, the penalties of either heterosexual isolation or promiscuity, and it often offers many of the benefits of marriage, including the pooling of resources and the economies of scale that living together provide. . . . However, cohabitation also provides some of the advantages of remaining single. While it may currently tie people up (though not as much as marriage), its influence on future mating behavior is much less, and the long-run financial obligations are also relatively low.
>
> (Oppenheimer, 1988, pp. 583–584)

Because of their increasingly uncertain future, young women may indeed find their circumstances more compatible with an initial period of cohabitation, which would allow them to experience and learn more about their partners' attitudes, preferences, and labour prospects (Bumpass, Sweet & Cherlin, 1991; Cherlin, 2000). Entering the first partnership through cohabitation, although translating into more time for the potential partners to establish themselves in the labour market (so as to cumulate resources and prove their earnings potentials), would also offer them the chance to gather information on the feasibility of the union. Cohabiting, in fact, is a more flexible arrangement that provides the advantages of living together but without requiring the strong degree of commitment that a marriage does (Oppenheimer, 1988, 1997a). Moreover, cohabiting unions are always open to be converted into marriage at any time. In this respect, instability in the working careers may not hamper, and, on the contrary, under certain circumstances even encourage, the transition to cohabitation. Indeed, even if the less binding character of cohabitation may be seen as less advantageous than marriage in terms of the reciprocal protections and support offered in case of adverse circumstances, such a trait might be less influential in the case of first partnership formation, at relatively young ages. It might instead become more of a serious disadvantage at later stages in life, especially for women, whose investment in unpaid work within the family tends to be higher (Breen & Cooke, 2005; Gershuny, Bittman & Brice, 2005). In addition, increasing easiness in separation and divorce could have an ambiguous effect on the relative advantage to cohabit over marrying. On the one hand, it means that cohabitation and marriage might become more similar; on the other hand, it could also decrease (to some extent) the potential advantages in terms of security and commitment offered by a marital contract. The fact that the economic and legal costs of dissolution of a cohabiting union are everywhere less than those of dissolving a marriage might be more an asset rather than a drawback for young people with uncertain working prospects, who might still prefer a lower degree of commitment to a higher degree of security[14].

To test these theories, previous longitudinal[15] studies have focussed on the effects of socioeconomic and educational resources on entering cohabitation. They stressed specific national determinants largely governing the entrance into unions by organisational rules and institutional structures in the educational and employment systems (Blossfeld, 1990; Blossfeld & Huinink, 1991; Clarkberg, 1999; Duvander, 1999, 2000) as well as by the characteristics of housing markets (Kurz & Blossfeld, 2004). For example, it has been found that norms of role transitions govern young people's willingness and capability to form a union while still studying and/or do not dispose of a stable source of income; or to engage in parenthood when they have not yet established in the labour market. These studies have provided a stable series of comparative empirical evidence on the importance of certain socioeconomic and personal characteristics in the decision to partner, like, among others, the type of job and of working contract enjoyed, the effect of enrolment in education or of experiencing a premarital pregnancy. There is now strong evidence that cohabitation is more widespread among younger generations; that more secularised individuals are more prone to cohabit, as are those who had experience of a parental divorce during childhood (Kiernan, 2002). Residing in metropolitan areas and having finished education also account for a bigger propensity to cohabit, whereas the effects played by educational qualifications and employment status tend to vary across countries (Kiernan, 2004b). Thus these recent findings also stress how the role played by socioeconomic or personal characteristics on the propensity to cohabit are affected by their location within national, differently shaped, institutional settings like labour markets and legal frameworks, as well as educational, housing, and welfare systems.

Summing up, most previous studies claim that cohabitation has emerged due to its greater flexibility, and thus relative convenience, to an increasing number of young well educated women willing to make investments in human capital and enter the labour market. Labour market changes (starting in the late 1970s and early 1980s) exposed women to both greater occupational chances and career insecurity. This element, together with increasing levels of parental divorce, secularisation, and gender-role changes, has made cohabiting relatively more advantageous than marriage. The need to cope with growing degrees of complexity and uncertainty in midterm life projects may have reinforced the willingness to cohabit. More and more young people are either not willing or not able (or both) to afford the costs implied by the highly binding and long-lasting nature of marriage (Blossfeld et al., 2005). Although these are certainly useful explanations, such arguments tend to predict especially high adoption rates of cohabitation in countries where young people face higher unemployment, where temporary jobs are most common and the costs of independence (particularly housing) are highest. However, despite the fact that the southern countries of Europe, such as Italy and Spain, have all these features, they display low rates of cohabitation. Thus such factors must be in interplay with specific cultural and institutional contexts or must be in competition with other mechanisms too.

Indeed, although these accounts can bring useful insights, there is still a lack of theories aimed at explaining not only cross-country differences in the prevalence of cohabitation at a single point in time but also the pace and patterns of change over time. Especially, there is none that tries to root explanations on micro-level mechanisms taking into account individuals' characteristics and their embeddedness in a social context[16] (Granovetter, 1985). Strikingly, the emergence of cohabitation has not been explained yet by a diffusion account at the micro level of individuals' actions. This is surprising given the large body of sociological and psychosociological research showing that many individuals' actions and behaviour are often influenced by peers' behaviour or by people with whom they interact[17]. In this respect, a diffusion account would integrate our understanding of how social influence, in conjunction with recent changes in young women's education and employment experiences, may (or may not) magnify the relative advantage of cohabitation over marriage in the eyes of its potential adopters (Ermisch, 2005; Palloni, 2001).

2.5   INDIVIDUAL SOCIAL ACTION AND MACRO-LEVEL DYNAMICS: THE PROCESS OF DIFFUSION

As just mentioned, a critique that may be addressed to standard sociological analyses of partnership decisions is that they do not adequately focus on the mechanisms connecting micro behaviour of individual actors to macro changes at the societal level. In other words, the individualistic approach and the search for mechanisms at the individual level leaves unexplained how the combination of individual actions might result in a changing pattern of norms and behaviour at the societal level. Focussing on individuals as purposeful actors as if they were isolated, only guided by self-interests, their own values, and by the rewards and constraints imposed by their environment, fails to explore the ways in which their reciprocal actions influence each other in a recursive manner so as to produce a dynamic change in the social system (Coleman, 1986, 1990; Hedström & Åberg, 2002; Manski, 2000). To connect individuals' behaviour with macro social circumstances, it is crucial to take into account the influence that actors exert on each other by sharing the same cultural and institutional environment, into which they learn from reciprocal observation and through imitation (Akerlof, 1980; Bandura, 1977; Jones, 1984; Mead & Morris, 1934). It is thus insufficient to understand the engine for the great increase in cohabitation only in the actions of isolated individuals, whose incentives are uniquely shaped by the institutional settings in which they autonomously act as if they were alone. A more adequate understanding would rather be offered by grounding the mechanisms for this diffusion process at an intermediate level, where interactions among individuals, their peers, and reference groups take place[18]. Such a model would account for how individuals' decisions combine to bring about behavioural changes and, in turn, how the ongoing level of the innovative practice in the social system shapes individuals' adoption of cohabitation. What we aim to explain are thus the changes in partnership decisions through "describing how the social conditions affected various persons' orientations to action and how these orientations to action, given the existing structure of relations, combined to produce the system of action that resulted in community action" (Coleman, 1986, p. 1314).

We thus aim to explain the dynamic shift in the practice of cohabitation as the outcome of purposive actions of individuals, but *taken in combination* with—and thought to be subject to—various institutional and situational constraints. The latter depend both on institutional arrangements and on the subjective perception about others' experiences of cohabitation. In a search for escaping exclusively either a micro or a macro approach, this work investigates how an individual's likelihood to adopt cohabitation changes along with the changes in the propensity to cohabit from others in her social context. This is to explore how, and to what extent, the changing level of practice of cohabitation in the society at any given time affects women's propensity to adopt it themselves[19].

This book thus combines two, complementary, sets of explanatory factors. The first, more traditional, approach explains women's propensity to adopt cohabitation as dependent on the sharing of similar individual characteristics or the facing of similar institutional environments. This expresses a phenomenon not subject to the effect of social influence that comprises what Palloni (2001) refers to as 'structural explanation'[20]. However we also produce a second, more innovative set of explanatory factors by exploring individuals' propensity to act in line with others' behaviour, a factor expressing how individuals' choices are influenced by their social environment[21]. Distinguishing among the effects of these two sets of factors is not only a question of theoretical development for its own sake. Rather, it is a relevant issue for the more general understanding of the process of social change. They also produce quite different predictions about the future levels of cohabitation and the possible impact of public policy. Policies directed towards the first set of 'structural' factors may act directly on changing individuals' conditions. But if some mechanisms were at work linking individuals' action to other people's behaviours, and would this be a self-reinforcing mechanism of social contagion, even small changes in individuals' initial conditions may trigger far bigger changes (both normative and behavioural) at the societal level. Diffusion models predict that after a certain threshold had been reached, the process could progress even in absence of further changes in those initial conditions, and would begin interesting individuals who do not even share such initial characteristics (Ermisch, 2005).

For these reasons it is important to discuss the mechanisms through which the diffusion of cohabitation might occur. In the next paragraph we then argue that, in the change of normative evaluations and attitudes towards cohabitation, *social influence* is the mechanism that links individuals' behaviour to the diffusion process at the societal level (Åberg, 2000; Cialdini, 1984; Coleman, 1986; Katz & Lazarsfeld, 1955; Montgomery & Casterline, 1996).

2.6   A DRIVING ENGINE: SOCIAL INFLUENCE

Why has premarital cohabitation increased so much during recent decades? Doubts about the institution of marriage cast by increased divorce rates, secularisation, educational expansion, increased female participation in the labour force, availability of reliable contraception, and the acceptability of premarital sexual intercourse are the most studied and relevant factors. They have undoubtedly played a role, but their effect is not sufficient for them to be the only factors accounting for the wide differences in pace and levels of cohabitation observed in Europe. An additional explanation is needed.

As introduced, the complementary diffusion approach chosen here adds a dynamic focus to the changing meaning and costs that the choice to cohabit has in different countries and has had over time within the same country. The diffusion process is thought of as nationally bounded given the sharing of a common language, a culture, and a political history, together with nation-specific legal and institutional frames as well as (mostly national) mass communication. Along with the diffusion process of cohabitation, we witness indeed a country-specific development in law (or lack of it) aimed at legally framing the status, entitlements (from partner/welfare state), and obligations (to partner/children) attached to cohabitation[22]. This adaptation of the law to the changing social context is also to recognise that an effective diffusion process can in turn produce changes in the structural conditions of individuals choosing to cohabit at a later stage (Palloni, 2001, Reed, Briere & Casterline, 1999). Undoubtedly, the frequency of cohabitation creates the need for legislative intervention on new questions: "Norms and values, on the one hand, and legislation, on the other hand, are strongly related. Expectations from friends, relatives or authorities are probably equally important, but these expectations can be influenced by appropriate legislation" (Prinz, 1995, p. 85).

In our diffusion approach, individuals are seen as having to make the decision to partner (and thus also choose between cohabitation and marriage) in conditions of ambiguity and *uncertainty*, both about their future conditions and about the expected outcomes of their choices (Durlauf & Walker, 2001; Manski, 2004; Palloni, 2001). As a consequence, they are likely to be inclined to make use of all the information possible drawn from their environment to help reduce the uncertainties facing them and to clarify the benefits and costs attached to their decisions. Individuals in conditions of uncertainty can indeed increase evidence available to them by observing and/or discussing with others in similar circumstances the relevant options, as well as the costs and benefits and the appropriateness of each (March & Olsen, 1979). Because the choice to cohabit involves a certain degree of risk and uncertainty, especially in an early phase of the diffusion process, adopters tend to weigh the experience of others carefully before acting (Strang & Soule, 1998). Furthermore, while making their choices, individuals are also seen to face constraints in their behaviour, which render some decisions unfeasible or too costly for them to consider. Some of these constraints may be in the form of economic limits or other resources, whilst others may have origin in expressions of social influence, such as stigma and social pressure. Others' experiences of cohabitation are thus influential because they alter the balance of costs and benefits for the individual. They can do it by either modifying individual beliefs or by imposing rewards or sanctions to specific individuals' behaviour or attitudes.

From a diffusion perspective, a particular type of behaviour is influenced (also) by the way in which the same choices have been previously taken by other individuals in a similar situation (Coleman, 1990; Granovetter, 1985; Granovetter & Soong, 1983; Palloni, 2001; Strang, 1991; Strang & Soule, 1998). Decisions to cohabit are thus thought to interact with and reinforce each other. Indeed, when cohabitation is not yet widespread, social stigma and some moral or reputation costs are attached to it. We know that individuals' perceptions about the 'appropriateness' of innovative behavioural options are often drawn by inference from other individuals' enacted behaviour, which serve as references and examples (Kahan,

1997). Because the individuals' assessment of value and 'costs' attached to cohabitation are endogenously related to their beliefs about the attitudes and intentions of others, propensities to cohabit will reinforce each other, according to a mechanism that Cialdini (1984) names the principle of 'social proof'[23]. According to this principle, people often decide to do what others like them are doing because, most of the time, behaviour that is popular in a given situation is also functional and appropriate (see also Cialdini and Trost, 1998).

> [Rational imitation] refers to a situation where an actor acts rationally on the basis of beliefs that have been influenced by observing the past choices of others. To the extent that other actors act reasonably and avoid alternatives that have proven to be inferior, the actor can arrive at better decisions than he or she would make otherwise, by imitating the behavior of others. (Hedström, 1998, p. 307)

When adopting an innovative behaviour, it can be thought of as individuals developing shared understandings and exploring its consequences through each other's experience. Learning from the experience of others appears a sensible strategy when means-ends relationships cannot be clearly understood, outcomes are difficult to anticipate, or when individuals' considerations are subject to social normative pressure, such as in the case of cohabitation (Strang & Soule, 1998). Along with a trend of increasing adoption, as an increased proportion of individuals adopt cohabitation, the social system itself will generate pressures towards further change, and the meaning attached to cohabiting will change accordingly[24]. This happens when eventually a point in the diffusion of cohabitation is reached, at which cohabiting becomes an institutionalised and fully recognised partnership option. The norms of the system towards cohabitation will change over time together with its increasing adoption and, should the process be successful, as the diffusion proceeds, cohabitation will be gradually incorporated into the mainstream of the social system (Rogers, 1985).

2.7   SOCIAL INFLUENCE: SOCIAL LEARNING AND SOCIAL PRESSURE

A vast amount of sociological and psychosociological research has already shown the relevance of actors' social embeddeddness in shaping individuals' behaviour via the influence of other actors' behaviour (Åberg, 2001; Coleman, 1990; Granovetter, 1978, 1985; Granovetter & Soong, 1983; Kahan, 1997; Kuran, 1995). They have found that individuals conform to other people's behaviour because they think that others are better informed or have more authority or competence to judge, or else because they want these other people to like them or are afraid of being pointed at or ridiculed[25]. Certainly, when facing uncertain situations, going along with the opinion or behaviour of the majority appears as the promptest and easiest rational strategy to avoid making mistakes, to gain consent, and to spare oneself the need to clear, justify, or defend an 'unusual' choice. In front of new situations, emulation of others' behaviour appears most often as an efficient and rational strategy to pursue. The famous Italian saying "When in Rome do as the Romans do!"[26]" as well as the Spanish ones "Wherever you go do what you see is being done"[27] and "People go where Vincent goes"[28], or the Turkish one "It is by looking at each other that grapes get their colour"[29] are all good examples of popular wisdom about this social mechanism (as also noted by Hedström, 1998).

Analytically, the possible rationales of referring to the example of others as a guide for action can be grouped into *social learning* and *social pressure* related reasons[30] (Aronson, 1999), although distinctions between the two modes of social influence are sharper in the theory than in their effects (Van Knippenberg, 2000).

'Social learning'[31] is defined as "influence to accept information obtained from another as evidence about reality" (Deutsch & Gerard, 1955, p. 629) and as a guide to one's own behaviour. It has to do with the informational content of behavioural models and with the fact that, in an uncertain situation, relying on others' examples is generally a comparatively more efficient, practical, and rational solution. This influence stems from the desire to be 'objectively correct' when uncertain and leads to conformity because of the belief that others' interpretation of an ambiguous situation is more correct than that of oneself (Aronson, 1999). It is determinant when a situation is new, ambiguous, or individuals presume they lack important information others may have instead. Others' previously enacted choices can provide an informational shortcut to what is considered 'normal' or 'optimal' to do in a given situation (Conlisk, 1980). When appropriate behaviour is unclear, the more people who respond to the same situation in the same way, the more correct their behaviour will be perceived to be[32] (Cialdini, 1993; Cialdini & Trost, 1998). Wide adoption of cohabitation will thus motivate further adopters by providing implicit evidence as to what is likely to be an effective and adaptive type of behaviour[33]. Others' behaviour thus provides a valid and valuable heuristic, or simple decision rule, about how to best act in an uncertain situation. For this, the evidence that a substantial number of other individuals have judged cohabitation as an appropriate and beneficial mode of partnering can be in itself a valid motivation for its adoption. Especially after a certain acceptance is reached, relying on others' enacted behaviour appears to be a rational and parsimonious strategy not to have to engage in the recognition and analysis of all aspects and implications involved in the choice of whether or not it is 'proper' and more (potentially) advantageous to marry or to cohabit.

Furthermore, we very routinely learn about a particular behaviour, its functioning and consequences by merely watching others enacting it (Klein, 1991). New practices are normally learnt through observation and imitation of examples from which information can be extracted (Bandura, 1986; Bandura, Ross & Ross, 1963; Tudge & Winterhoff, 1993). From a very young age, the most varied activities, from the simplest tasks to complex routines such as how to use specific tools or equipment, how to perform a new dance, or how to behave 'properly' in different social settings, are all learned through imitation of examples. This fundamental way of learning saves the time and energy entailed in a trial-and-error learning process (Bandura, 1977). Languages, familial customs, norms, and educational and social practices are all learned through the imitation of given models in countless situations. In much the same way, individuals can be easily thought to adopt cohabitation as the result of a learning process about its practice, its perceived working and expected consequences. This learning process is driven by the observation and imitation of examples provided by previous adopters (see also Manski, 1993a).

'Social pressure'[34] is defined here as the "influence to conform with the positive expectations of another" (Deutsch & Gerard, 1955, p. 629). It originates from the desire to be 'socially correct' when uncertain about a course of action (Asch, 1951). It is expected to increase in relevance when individuals' reference groups control the material or psychological rewards to which they aspire[35]. According to this rationale, conformity or imitation is directed towards the avoidance of disapproval, sanction, and punishment or, vice versa, aimed at the gain of consent, approval, and others' esteem.

Sociologists routinely assume that individuals seek to maintain their status and a good opinion of themselves by managing their presentation of self (Mead & Morris, 1934). Because the feelings of self-worth and appropriateness are developed in interaction with others, a good perception of oneself is closely tied to the perception of being accepted and liked by others. In this process of identity building, people routinely try to guess about others' attitudes and preferences from what they see being done by others in their environment (Goffman, 1959, 1967). Others' attitudes can be generally inferred from their behaviour because they can be passively expressed and understood via nonverbal communication and imitation (Cialdini, Kallgren & Reno, 1991; Cialdini, Reno & Kallgren, 1990). Subjective beliefs or individual perceptions of what others may think can already be sufficient to affect behaviour (Ajzen, 1988, 1991; Mead, 1964; Mead & Miller, 1982). Conforming one's own behaviour to that of others is thus rational in that it minimises the risk of being perceived, and thus perceiving oneself, as deviant, as well as avoids conflict (Moscovici, 1985). Normative pressure may originate 'internally' from the perception of relevant others' preferences, and by the motivation to comply with their expectations (Festinger, Schachter & Back, 1950). Furthermore, conformity to general behaviour provides a sense of trust that facilitates interdependence among group members (Aronson, 1999; Cialdini & Trost, 1998; Hatfield, Cacioppo & Rapson, 1993) and, in turn, the acceptance by others that accompanies behavioural conformity can enhance the individual's own sense of worth and self-esteem (Cialdini & Trost, 1998; Erickson, 1988).

There is another way in which social pressure may influence people's perceived advantage in cohabiting as tied to others' previous behaviours. Mostly, rational individuals also seek to avoid the negative consequences attached to social and legal sanctions. And the more a type of behaviour is enacted and widespread, the lower the degree of sanction that tends to be associated to that behaviour. Often, the way to determine what is regarded as a correct behaviour is to find out what others think it is correct in that given situation (Goffman, 1963). A type of behaviour is indeed generally perceived as legitimate to the degree that others are seen to perform it[36] (Cialdini, 1984). It follows that the perception of peers' or more generally of social approval or disapproval, can sustain or deter from adopting cohabitation, especially at the beginning when living together without being legally married is still a rare and deviant option. The perception about the degree of 'appropriateness' or acceptability of one's own behaviour may be easily generated, either by external (as in the case of normative or legal sanctions) or internal pressure to conform to what is perceived others think or do. Furthermore, it is not necessary for this kind of influence to be consciously perceived to display an effect[37].

Summing up, through *social learning*, as more women adopt cohabitation, each succeeding potential adopter will face less uncertainty about its functioning and potential consequences. Through *social pressure*, a greater adoption of cohabitation in the society will signal its acceptance and the lowering of social sanctions against cohabitation, thus lowering its psychological costs. Whatever the mode of social influence, the choice to cohabit in conformity to an increasingly widespread adoption of cohabitation allows the potential adopters to believe that they understand things more accurately, to gain the consent and approval of their desirable others, and to avoid one's self-perception as different or deviant. The diffusion of cohabitation, being an innovative behavioural practice, is subject to both the modes of social influence. In fact, its innovative character simultaneously induces in its adopters the need to search for more information and exposes them to social pressure, depending on the changing level of the new practice and its degree of acceptability. Observation of vicarious experiences[38] not only informs, it can also motivate or dissuade by arousing the expectations in potential adopters that they will receive similar benefits, or incur similar sanctions, for comparable choices[39].

However, empirically assessing the distinction between 'social learning' and 'social pressure' would be a hopeless task without adequate information on both network characteristics and individuals' attitudes and expectations over time. And, even if we had such information, problems would arise from neglecting other impersonal sources of influence (e.g., mass media, and other often unmeasured sources of 'verbal or symbolic modelling'); from the lack of consciousness that accompany these sources of influence and from the self-selection of individuals into specific networks across time[40]. Because both forms of (social) influence operate, often simultaneously, in the same direction, in the practice of empirical research a formal distinction is not strictly necessary for detecting a diffusion process and proves extremely difficult to pursue. Here it is important to notice that, whichever the prevailing mode of social influence may be, these two sources are not mutually exclusive in motivating individuals to look at each others' responses when they consider adopting cohabitation themselves. In both cases, conformity results from uncertainty and a general desire not to (or be seen to) be wrong. In either circumstances, the diffusion of new ideas or innovative behaviour does not need to occur through close friends; it may spread equally well through weak ties (Granovetter, 1973) or heterophilous relations (Rogers, 1985). In the process of diffusion it need not even be the case that interpersonal relations are always more important than abstract modelling (Bandura, 1986; Bongaarts & Watkins, 1996; Chaffe, 1982; Kohler, 2001; Montgomery & Casterline, 1996): "Social learning may also take place impersonally, when the information set is shaped by communications emanating from impersonal sources, such as the mass media, markets, and other aggregate social structures" (Montgomery & Casterline, 1996, pp. 154–155).

This implies that face-to-face interactions are not a necessary prerequisite to the spreading of information or to the exercise of social pressure, and that both rationales of social influence may nevertheless be at play in driving the diffusion process beyond the effects linked to network structures and direct interactions. In the words of Bongaarts and Watkins (1996), the innovative behavioural models can be potent stimuli for behaviour even if "[They] may be [. . .] as distant as Western images of the family spread through school textbooks (Caldwell, 1976) or even 'local' versions of soap operas displayed in *telenovelas*. (Farìa & Potter, 1994; Hannerz, 1992)" (Bongaarts & Watkins, 1996, p. 659).

Thus the various channels of diffusion—involving either direct or indirect contacts—are not only strictly interrelated but also mutually reinforcing (Marsden & Friedkin, 1993; Briere & Casterline, 1999).

In sum, we argue that individuals' propensity to adopt cohabitation varies positively with its prevalence in their social context (Granovetter, 1978; Merton, 1957). Because people are embedded in various structures of social relationships (Granovetter, 1985) and are exposed to the behavioural models of other social actors, these latter exert influence—whether by constraint, example, or persuasion—which contribute to shape individuals' beliefs and guide their actions.

2.8   A STARTING ENGINE: RELATIVE ADVANTAGE

The literature on demographic change highlights three preconditions for the successful diffusion of innovative behaviour: individuals' *readiness*, *willingness,* and *ability* to adopt it (Coale, 1973; Lesthaeghe & Vanderhoeft, 2001). The first refers to the need for the innovation to be advantageous to the adopter, for its perceived costs to outweigh its perceived benefits. In the case of cohabitation, the degree of advantage depends both on the individuals (changing) personal characteristics and on the changing conditions laid down by the institutional settings in which they act. The second refers to the legitimacy of the new practice. It depends on the level of conflict with established traditional beliefs and on the individual's willingness to overcome moral objections and fears. However, the current norms of conduct, the set of institutional arrangements, and the severity of sanctions attached to the transgression of normative prescriptions are all subject to change depending on the current level of practice of cohabitation in a society[41]. The third precondition refers to the accessibility of the innovative behaviour, not just in material but possibly also in psychological or informational terms. In the case of cohabitation, accessibility is rarely hindered by institutional features beyond accumulating the material resources needed to enter a partnership (e.g., there no longer exist norms that impede the renting of a house to a nonmarried couple).

The extent to which these conditions may hinder the diffusion process is not only individual and context specific but also changes continuously. Cohabiting as a prolonged trial-and-error procedure in partnering, for example, may be perceived as a negative feature in the marriage market in those countries where a high value is attached to women who have not previously been in a couple relationship. However, social norms, attitudes and thus expectations are subject to change, although with a greater or lesser amount of resistance. This is a factor that helps to explain why the process started more easily in some countries than in others. This 'contextual' responsiveness to behavioural changes highlights again the prominent role of social influence in determining choices and in redefining values and attitudes through the illustration of 'vicarious examples' of innovative practices. Once more, this reciprocal influence between individuals' choices and institutional settings, which is characteristic of the diffusion process, requires the sociologist who wants to understand it to undertake a dynamic analysis capable of taking into account this aspect of reciprocal determination.

Because individuals, in their decision processes, tend to choose the 'best they know' among what they see as available alternatives (Boudon, 1998b; Mills, 1999; Montgomery & Casterline, 1996; Lesthaeghe & Vanderhoeft, 2001; Rogers, 1985), the perception of a relative advantage entailed in the innovative practice is a relevant precondition for the start of the diffusion process. However, individuals' motives for preferring cohabitation to a direct marriage may take many different forms. Next are listed some of the most commonly mentioned reasons for cohabitation's greater desirability with respect to marriage, which can be thought of as the specific individuals' interest in its adoption (Barbagli, 1989, 1990; Kaufmann, 1995, 1996):

1. Co-residence. Cohabitation can combine the sexual and emotional closeness of marriage with a degree of independence and autonomy more similar to that of the single state.
2. Less-binding commitment. Refers to the belief that marriage involves a higher degree of commitment than the individual is yet (or possibly) ready for. It comprises the belief that unpredictability of future circumstances does not (yet) allow for lifelong commitments. With cohabitation there are fewer restrictions on when and how the relationship can start and end (i.e., flexibility of duration).
3. Fewer 'traditional' expectations. Being an innovative practice, the kind of expectations about the gender division of roles is less codified and thus more open to negotiation by the partners (i.e., flexibility of content)
4. Economic (or material) considerations. For example, when tax regulations favour unmarried couples or do not explicitly favour married ones; or the economy of scale of sharing a single flat relative to living independently or the cost of the wedding relative to marrying; or the lower responsibilities towards the partner upon disruption entailed by cohabiting.
5. Trial marriage. Sustained by the belief that a period of cohabitation prior to marriage can be a preparing phase for it. Cohabiting can be perceived as helping the couple to closely explore each other's attitudes and adjust to one another before marrying.
6. Absence of a legal contract. It draws on the belief that a deeper quality of relationship can be enjoyed outside marriage. Maintaining a certain degree of uncertainty in the relation would encourage the partners to concentrate more on the maintenance of the couple relationship.
7. Fear of an unsuccessful marriage. This belief especially applies to those individuals who have had a close personal experience of unhappy marriages (e.g., witnessed a parental divorce), or who feel uncertain about their capabilities to maintain a satisfactory relationship.
8. Inability to marry. Refers to the legal inability to marry due to existing marriages to other people. Being focussed on the first partnership, this case is excluded from this study, and it might only refer to the condition of the potential partner.
9. Ideological rejection of marriage. For those who do not recognise or welcome any state intervention in regulating individuals' relationships. It may comprise a resistance to the (originally) religious character of the marital institution.
10. Institutionalised practice. Cohabitation is enough widespread to be perceived as the 'proper,' 'usual,' 'normal,' or 'more advantageous' thing to do either before marrying or instead of marrying.

To summarise, individuals' relative advantage in adopting cohabitation instead of marrying depends on (any combination of) three broad sets of factors. First, the degree of *specific interest* in—or appeal of—the practice (1 to 3). For example, cohabitation's higher flexibility allows for a prolonged search of optimal mating and a redefinition of reciprocal responsibilities, commitments, and relational contents. These characteristics make it a better option, especially for women, to redefine inadequate traditional gender models (Baizán, Aassve, & Billari, 2003; Blossfeld & Drobnič, 2001; Nazio & Blossfeld, 2003; Prinz, 1995). Second, cohabitation is more convenient because of an *increasing demand* or need for less binding relationships produced by uncertainties about the future (4 to 9) when difficulties arise over engaging in long-term commitments to others (Mills, Blossfeld & Klijzing, 2005; Oppenheimer, 1988, 1994). Third, individuals may be prone to cohabit because of the *increasing acceptability* of this way of forming a partnership (10) (Mulder & Manting, 1994; Prinz, 1995; Trost, 1979). This latter effect depends on the current levels of practice and on the sensitivity of potential adopters to social influence, it being an expression of informational learning about cohabitation or of lowering social pressure.

3   The Diffusion Process of Cohabitation and Time

Diffusion processes only become manifest over time. To investigate how the diffusion of cohabitation occurs, we need to understand these time-related characteristics. To do this, and given the specific characteristics of the process, we also need to think sociologically about time. We have already suggested that in a diffusion perspective, an individual's rate of adoption of cohabitation is subject, among other things, to the influence of its prior adoption by other actors in the social system (Rogers, 1985). The overall shape and speed of the diffusion process of cohabitation at the macro level results from the aggregate pattern of adoptions at the micro level of individual decisions. We can easily think of these individuals as decision makers who are in an uncertain situation (Burt, 1987; Durlauf & Walker, 2001; Manski, 2004; Palloni, 2001; Strang & Soule, 1998; Strang & Tuma, 1993) and who are embedded in a developing social and institutional context. As argued in chapter 2, the adoption of cohabitation is the result of an individual's choice. The decisional process is influenced by both individual-level risk factors and by the social context in which individuals frame their actions. When it first emerges within each national context, premarital cohabitation can be thought of as an innovative behavioural option for entering into a partnership. Its innovative character for the individuals is captured by our focus on young women's first experience with cohabitation before (if ever) entry into a marriage. In each country its degree of 'innovativeness' is allowed to vary with the accumulation of experiences across time for different birth cohorts of individuals and according to their age.

This chapter is organised as follows. Sections 3.1 and 3.2 offer an account of the recent debate on the nature and distinctive characteristics of diffusion processes. The complex time-related structure of the diffusion process of cohabitation is then disentangled in section 3.3. In sections 3.4 and 3.5 we propose two mechanisms related to social influence as potentially driving this specific diffusion process and introduce their empirical operationalisation. The results of these first analyses are presented in section 3.6. A discussion of the role of these mechanisms on the decision-making process to adopt cohabitation, together with that of other sources of influence, concludes the chapter (section 3.7).

3.1 'STRUCTURAL' VERSUS DIFFUSION ACCOUNTS OF SOCIAL CHANGE?

In chapter 2, we argued that *both* socioeconomic conditions *and* others' behaviour may influence individuals' propensity to adopt cohabitation. The former source of influence is generally dealt with in traditional analyses, whereas only diffusion approaches take account of the latter. Traditional analyses understand the causes of an increasing adoption of a new behaviour in terms of the alteration of individuals' preferences and opportunities resulting from changes in their social structural position (e.g., Oppenheimer, 1988), or from changes in their material or symbolic resources and values (e.g., Lesthaeghe & Meekers, 1986; Lesthaeghe & Surkyn, 1988; Mills, 2000). The adoption of cohabitation would thus be seen as solely dependent on the characteristics associated with the individual, regardless of others' behaviour. Diffusion approaches, by contrast, investigate a different cascading mechanism, driven in part by social influence. Diffusion explanations centre on a broader class of contextual and environmental processes, where conditions outside the individuals contribute to shape their behaviours (Strang & Soule, 1998). Through social influences exercised by previous adopters, an increasing adoption of cohabitation can occur even when potential adopters' characteristics and resources remain unaltered or hardly change. In Palloni's words,

> In diffusion models, the behaviour 'spreads' and is adopted by individuals irrespective of their socioeconomic positions, even among those whose social or economic positions are hypothetically associated with cost-benefit calculations that do not necessarily require the new behavior. Adopting the new behavior occurs as a result of reevaluation of one's own choices in light of other people's behavior, not as a strategic response or accommodation to a realignment of resources associated with one's social position in the social system. (Palloni, 2001, p. 68)

Diffusion models thus focus on the reciprocal influence of the behaviour of different individuals. Through this social influence, changes in the attitudes and behaviour of some individuals (past and current adopters) can induce modification of other individuals' later behaviours (potential adopters). This change in attitudes occurs as a consequence of the inclusion in individuals' decision-making process of others' perceived preferences and of the observed outcomes associated with others' previous adoption. In this respect, a diffusion explanation of cohabitation takes account of a social dynamic that, at the aggregate level, can contribute to alter both the social norms around partnership formation, its timing and the pace, and thus can also be treated as a causal factor of change.

As described in chapter 2, different sources of social influence may be responsible for such a causal effect[1]. Firstly, it may be that 'social learning' brings about more instances of adoption and, together with it, each succeeding cohort of women will face increasingly less uncertainty, thereby lessening the 'cost' of adoption for others in the future. According to this mechanism, individual's experiences with cohabitation serve as vicarious examples and/or provide mainstream role models. Beside, it may *also* be that a greater adoption of cohabitation may signal its increasing acceptance and the lowering of moral and social sanctions against cohabiting (less 'social pressure'). In this second case, it is normative pressure that directs young women away from feelings of shame, inappropriateness, and potential conflicts, which could result from deviating from what is normal or typical in one's own reference group. In particular, the more common it is to either be cohabiting or have cohabited in a society, the weaker the normative pressure towards the 'need' for a formal marriage is likely to be, thus the lower will be the social and psychological costs of adopting cohabitation.

Whatever the rationale of social influence driving diffusion, there is no theoretical reason for setting the traditional ('structural') and diffusion explanations in opposition to each other because they are neither mutually exclusive nor single accounts of social change[2]. In fact, they can both contribute to explain the causal mechanisms responsible for the spread of cohabitation (or its absence) over the last few decades. However, to disentangle these two types of explanations, diffusion processes cannot be simply indirectly deducted from the amount of change not accounted for by structural explanations solely based on individuals' own characteristics (Palloni, 2001). It would not be very convincing to build a 'structural' model and then claim that everything it could not explain must be down to 'diffusion.' By the same token, a diffusion explanation cannot do away with the need to account for the structural conditions that create different costs and benefits to the cohabitation choices of individuals in different circumstances. Because diffusion processes take place in social environments that are institutionally and culturally structured,

> [I]n order to be analytically useful, diffusion models require theorising about social structures, about the positions that individuals occupy in them, about individual decision-making processes that accompany adoption of a behavior, and about the constraints these individuals face. . . . Well-defined diffusion hypotheses and models must be built on assumptions about social and economic conditions that constrain individual actors' preferences and resources, and rely on these assumptions. (Palloni, 2001, p. 67)

We thus need both approaches, structural and diffusion explanations, as complementary accounts of normative and social change (Durlauf & Walker, 2001). Furthermore, they are also intertwined because of the role of 'endogenous feedback.' That is to say, the process of diffusion itself can also play a part in altering the structural conditions for individuals. For example, the increasing diffusion of cohabitation may itself lead to changes in the institutional and normative contexts. This combined approach is the one chosen here[3].

3.2 CONDITIONS FOR THE IDENTIFICATION OF A DIFFUSION PROCESS

Unfortunately, until recently, most diffusion analyses have been based on aggregate rather than individual data[4] (Kiernan, 1999; Prinz, 1995; Trost, 1979; and for a review of diffusion approaches, see Rogers, 1985, and related to fertility, Cleland, 2001). However, this weakens such analyses because it leaves unidentified the mechanisms that drive diffusion by affecting, for example, the balance between expected costs and benefits of cohabiting in the individuals' rational decision-making process. Although it is not possible to distinguish empirically which source of social influence has been operative in a particular instance[5], both social learning and social pressure relate to the effect of individuals' exposure to determined levels of practice of cohabitation in the population. Both influences operate in the same direction and often in combination: The more widespread cohabitation is in a social context in a given moment, the easier it is for any successive individual to adopt it. However, the effects of the social influence related mechanism is also dependent on cultural and institutional contexts (Cleland, 1985; Lesthaeghe, 1977; Lesthaeghe & Vanderhoeft, 2001, Watkins, 1991). Cohabitation 'compatibility' with existing norms and 'structural' conditions contribute to the relative convenience of the practice in the eyes of potential adopters.

Besides the lack of individual level analyses, we are going to take definite account of other important elements of diffusion processes that tend to be overlooked (Cleland, 2001; Palloni, 2001; Strang & Meyer, 1993): the assumption of rationality of decision-makers; the possible resistance to the diffusion of an innovation; the role and weight of social and economic structures and; endogenous feedback[6].

A.   Individuals as Rational Decision Makers

A common denominator between structural explanations and diffusion models is their focus on individuals, thought of as rational decision makers (Carter, 2001; Palloni, 1999, 2001; Reed, Briere & Casterline, 1999; Strang & Meyer, 1993; Strang & Soule, 1998). Diffusion occurs because individuals decide to adopt (or not) cohabitation after having observed (or having got to know about) others choosing it before. They would normally decide after having included the choices and (possibly) observed outcomes derived by others' previous experiences into their own evaluation of the relative advantages expected by the new practice. This is how the evaluation of behavioural examples from previous adopters produces a change in the payoff in the choice of potential adopters to enter cohabitation. We thus argue that individuals' decision to cohabit is affected by the spread of new information, ideas, beliefs, or social norms that occur through social interaction and social influence, either at the personal level or originated from impersonal sources of information and behavioural example such as the mass media.

B. Possible Resistance to Adoption

Actors differ in their individual general propensity or reluctance[7] to engage in innovative practices (Easterline, 1975) as well as specifically in their choice of whether or not to cohabit. That is, there might be individuals who are more (or less) risk adverse and thus adopt less (or more) easily than others. Rogers (1985), Coleman (Coleman, Katz & Menzel, 1967) and Burt (1987) distinguish between groups of individuals ('forerunners' and 'laggards'[8]) depending on the timing of their adoption. But in the case of cohabitation it is difficult (and not even sensible) to distinguish the two groups, given that the population at risk changes continuously over time and that the choice to take a partner can take place at any time over the life course. Rather, in the case of cohabitation, such heterogeneity in individual propensity must be accounted for at the individual level. Empirically, through a multivariate analysis it is possible to control for factors that are already known to affect an individual's propensity to cohabit, which may frustrate or foster the diffusion process[9]. These are individuals' educational attainment, religious beliefs, their labour attachment, the characteristic of their local environment, whether they experienced a parental divorce, or similar characteristics. For this reason, the approach to diffusion we propose, instead of estimating the process of adoption at the population level, models the risk of entering a cohabitation over time at the individual level. In fact, in our model there is no assumption that the diffusion process must lead to a specific, previously defined, shape and/ or level of cumulated distribution of adoptions over time. Nor is there the assumption that the diffusion process must necessarily have the same effect in each country. On the contrary, beside the estimated effects of personal characteristics, the role and shape of social influence from previous adopters on the individual likelihood to adopt cohabitation is empirically investigated. This empirical test leaves room for resistance to, and even failure of, the diffusion process. In this model, individuals' calculation of cost benefits under uncertainty in the choice to enter a partnership can result any time in either following the lead of others' previous adoption of cohabitation or alternatively in resisting it, by opting for the traditional alternative of marrying. And even in the case of those who eventually decide to cohabit, their choice might either display sensitivity to social influence (a significant effect) or rather simply result to be a product of their socioeconomic circumstances and personal dispositions.

C. Role of the Social Structures in Affecting the Relative Convenience to Cohabit

Adoption of cohabitation takes place in differently shaped social settings in which (heterogeneous) individuals are to be found at different points of their life course. They also differ in their socioeconomic circumstances, their preferences, and their personal characteristics. Some of these differences may be related to the propensity to cohabit rather than marry (as discussed earlier). However, the degree to which a group of individuals displays a common given characteristic also depends on the shared circumstances established by their respective institutional settings. For example, their chance of having a certain educational level, or of having reached that level by a given age, is strongly determined by the organisation of the school system in the country where they live. In the same way, their employment status is also determined by the characteristics of their respective labour markets. Institutional and cultural contexts not only influence the differences in the prevalence of a given characteristic within a population, but also the effect that the same trait may have on the adoption of cohabitation. As it is for education and working circumstances, so it is with the regard to the prevalent cultural norms and models of behaviours. Diffusion processes are thus affected by the cultural and social structures of the systems in which they occur. These can either facilitate or frustrate the diffusion process:

> Social structures determine the content and shape of the repertoire of feasible behaviors ('Is the behavior within the realm of conscious choice?'), individual's preferences ('Is the behavior advantageous at all?'), and individual's resources ('Can individuals adopt at low costs?'). (Palloni, 2001, p. 73)

The ease with which a cultural setting can respond to, and assimilate, new practices can speed up or slow down the diffusion process. In particular, sociocultural factors are considered to be an important determinant of the overall diffusion pace and level in a given setting (Cleland, 1985; Cleland & Wilson, 1987; Coale & Watkins, 1986; Lesthaeghe & Vanderhoeft, 2001). For example a 'common law' legal tradition, where actual practices leads the formulation of norms, may integrate and foster new practices more rapidly than a 'top-down' legal tradition (Rosina, 2001) where citizens have to conform to laws that generally lag behind social change. The degree of traditionalism and religiosity of a society is another important aspect. When the social structure, rather than individuals' risk aversion, is what explains the observed delays and lags in the diffusion process, institutionally driven effects can still be distinguished with an individual-level model through the comparative framework adopted. For example, we might find that individuals' religiosity negatively affects their propensity to cohabit, and that it does so with different strength depending on the country. However, even when the effects were to be equally strong across countries, religiosity would affect the takeup of the diffusion process more strongly in the less secularised countries (where there is a bigger number of religious individuals). In the same way, it could be that the enrolment in education decreases individuals' likelihood to cohabit (Blossfeld & Huinink, 1991), but that this effect differs between countries in a way that is consistent with their differently organised school and labour markets.

D.   Endogenous Feedback

It is also worth noting that personal and environmental factors do not function as independent determinants but rather determine each other. The changes that individuals cause in environmental conditions, in turn, affect their behaviour and the nature of future contexts of action (Palloni, 2001; Tudge & Winterhoff, 1993). This 'endogenous feedback' further complicates the analysis of the underlying process of adoption. Diffusion processes, in fact, are distinctive also in their self-reinforcing character. Because innovations involve uncertainty and a certain degree of risk, their takeup tends to be initially slow, when little information about the consequences of their adoption is available. The incidence of takeup then accelerates (or not) driven (also) by the social influences on potential adopters (Cleland, 2001). This self-reinforcing process is supported by reductions in the perception of risk and uncertainty attached to cohabiting as it becomes more common and familiar. Additionally, as the process of adoption progresses, the social and economic environments are—with some time lag and to a varying degree—modified by the process of adoption itself. This happens because the diffusion process may change the initial conditions leading to adoption (for example, by a change in laws and regulations), and this transformation feeds back into the diffusion process. Thus, as the process evolves, the cultural and institutional contexts in which the decision to cohabit is taking place will be modified accordingly. These progressive cultural and institutional adaptations will result in a change in the elements that enter into the decision-making process of everybody, including nonadopters eventually preferring a direct entry into marriage. For example, the initial expansion of education, combined with the increasing participation of women in the labour force and flexibility in young people's careers, could have produced an increasing need for a less-binding form of partnership. In turn, the less traditional gender-role division of labour brought about by more cohabiting couples could favour women investing in a paid job and increase returns from educational credentials, which would strengthen further the aspiration to educational achievements and, in turn, also the propensity to cohabit. Alternatively, an increasing number of couples cohabiting without marrying might encourage a change in the legal regulation and recognition of these relationships from the point of view of rights and obligations. In fact, for a cohabitant couple to be acknowledged as a household may be crucial for access to social security and social assistance benefits, as well, depending on the taxation system, to more or less advantageous tax treatments, and to inheritance entitlements. Both the legal recognition of unmarried cohabitant partnerships, and the conditions under which it operates, will thus change the payoff in the choice to cohabit or marry for *all* individuals about to enter a partnership in a subsequent time.

These four characteristics of the diffusion processes make it necessary to study the phenomenon longitudinally, taking into account the changes in individuals' conditions and resources, *both* along their *life course* and *across birth cohorts*. This is to say that in the course of the diffusion process, we have to pay attention that in each point in time individuals' characteristics will tend to differ systematically from those of people belonging to different birth cohorts. These latter are to be found in either earlier or later stages of their life course with respect, for example, to the level of education achieved as well as to the completion of schooling, or to the entrance into the labour market. For the same token, by growing older, the same individuals within a single birth cohort will also experience changes in their own characteristics and circumstances over time. Figure 3.1 provides a simple illustration of this.

In Figure 3.1 are sketched the hypothetical cumulative proportions of individuals entering their first cohabitation or marriage by age, for a selection of four fictitious birth cohorts (in line with the actual figures we have shown in Figure 2.1 for a single birth cohort). We can observe immediately two things. First, the lowering of the higher curves profile, from the top to the bottom of the graphs, shows that the process of partnership formation tends to be postponed across birth cohorts. So, for example, we can see that by age 20 a decreasing proportion of people have ever formed their first partnership (marked with a dotted line on the Y-axis) in the cohort born in 1970 than that born in 1965, 1960, or 1955. In absence of a complete recuperation of this progressive delay (there seem to be no sudden increase in the steep of any of the curves), we can see that across cohorts by the end of the observation (let's imagine age 35), an increasing proportion of people has not partnered yet (area above the curves). This phenomenon translates into a decreasing proportion of individuals entering a partnership across birth cohorts in *absolute* terms for each given age: Overall, people will form their partnership later and later. Second, in Figure 3.1 we also notice that within these lowering levels, cohabitation becomes increasing more popular than a direct entry into marriage across cohorts. Thus, we can also see that by the end of the observation of each birth cohort, the *relative* proportion of individuals who have chosen cohabitation increases with respect to those having married. Depending on the magnitude of the postponement process relative to that of the increasing rates of cohabitation across cohorts, we might not necessarily be able to distinguish such a relative increase in cohabiting unions, would we only look at a single point in time. Overall, in fact, a much smaller proportion of individuals from younger birth cohorts will have formed a partnership by a certain date (because they are younger)

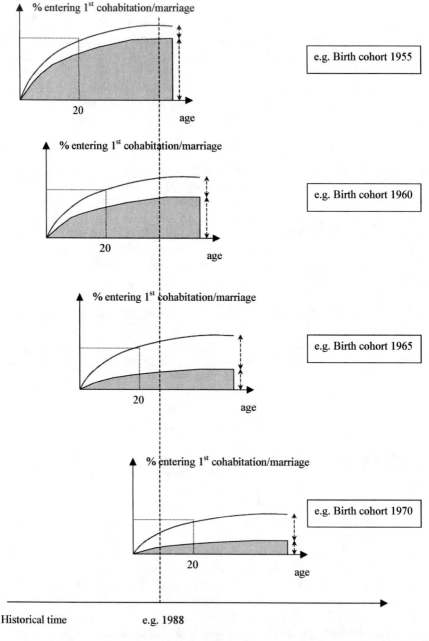

Figure 3.1 Cohabitation along the life course and across birth cohorts.

than in older cohorts (where individuals are older). As we can see, by any calendar date (let's focus, for example, on a fictitious 1988), we will find the coexistence of a certain proportion of members belonging to each of the birth cohorts who still have to partner. In a cross-sectional perspective the overall proportion having cohabited or married by a certain time will depend on the composition of the behaviours of individuals at different ages.

How will individuals' characteristics differ from one birth cohort to another, at a certain time? And will such characteristics differ over time (by growing older)? Will these differences help explain why some individuals are still to partner in their own birth cohort at certain times? And to explain why some of them will eventually choose to cohabit rather than marry? Which will be the characteristics of the institutional environments (and their effect) experienced over time by this heterogeneous composition of individuals? A longitudinal perspective, by observing individuals over time, can help shedding light on these issues in a way that is precluded to cross-sectional observations.

Insofar, the diffusion of cohabitation among young women is not only a process intertwined with institutional features but also marked by its highly complex time-related structure. A specific characteristic of cohabitation before entry into marriage (if it ever occurs) is that the time span of potential adoption for each generation is highly concentrated within the period of transition from youth to adulthood. Those who might potentially adopt cohabitation are individuals at a certain stage of their life course that we could call 'ready for partnership formation.' Over time there is a continuous inflow of birth cohorts who are entering into this life stage and thus are becoming members of the risk set of potential adopters[10]. At the same time, there is also a continuous outflow because some young individuals adopt cohabitation or marry and therefore also leave the group at risk. This means that, in the case of premarital cohabitation among the young, potential adoption is typically confined to a specific window in the life course and the population of potential adopters is highly dynamic over time.

Thus, to depict diffusion processes, one needs to shift the analytical focus to individuals' choices (Strang & Tuma, 1993) and to what determines them, in relation to their *timing*. Studying individuals' likelihood to cohabit in a longitudinal framework allows one to take into account individuals' heterogeneity both within the population *and over time*, thus allowing a clearer assessment of social influence. By applying appropriate (time-varying) controls for changes in individuals' characteristics together with theoretically informed measures of possible sources of social influence, we can attempt to distinguish 'structural' effects and 'social influences.' The proportion of individuals having had *previous* experience with cohabitation will thus directly take part in the explanation of future individuals' choices to cohabit, alongside socioeconomic factors. Once parameters are estimated, hypotheses testing will determine whether the estimates are consistent with those to be expected when social influences were operating as part of the individuals' decision-making process (for a discussion of the results, see chapter 6).

What we propose here is an integrated theory and model, which leaves room for both structural factors (individuals' changing social and economic characteristics) and previous adopters' behaviour to influence potential adopters' choice to cohabit. This model acknowledges the role of social influences in the decision to adopt cohabitation while allowing for the effects of structural determinants. While allowing for impersonal sources of influence to affect individuals' behaviour, it also allows all parameters of the model to be estimated from available data. Moreover, as detailed in the next section, the complex time-related nature of the diffusion process of cohabitation allows us to describe and empirically test two different mechanisms related to social influence. The proposed indicators of the diffusion process will thus capture the dynamic interplay between changing levels of practice of cohabitation witnessed by individuals belonging to different birth cohorts and individuals' decision to cohabit, as the diffusion process progresses. This is why the next section is dedicated to a more precise investigation of the time-related structure of the mating process.

3.3   TIME FRAME AND THE MECHANISMS DRIVING THE DIFFUSION PROCESS

The diffusion of cohabitation among young women is a highly complex time-related process. A characteristic of cohabitation before entry (if ever) into marriage is that the time span of potential adoption for each generation is highly concentrated in the period of transition from youth to adulthood. There is then a continuous succession of birth cohorts over time moving through this life-course window.

Past research has shown that in modern societies the readiness of young women to enter a first marital or nonmarital union over the life course is governed, to a large extent, by organisational rules and institutional structures in the educational and employment systems (Blossfeld, 1990, 1995; Galland, 1986; Klijzing & Corijn, 2002; Marini, 1985; Nilsson & Strandh, 1999). At specific ages, women typically move from one institutional domain to another (e.g., from secondary school to vocational training, or from school to the labour market) and these transitions often serve as markers for the beginning of a life stage where women form partnerships (Blossfeld & Nuthmann, 1989; Corijn & Klijzing, 2001; Huinink, 1995, 2000; Settersten & Mayer, 1997; Klijzing & Corijn, 2002). It is well known, in fact, that completing education and establishing oneself in the labour market are among the most important transitions in the process of getting ready for entry into marriage (Blossfeld, 1995; Blossfeld & Huinink, 1991; Oppenheimer, 1988, 1997b).

Figure 3.2 presents a stylised picture of the complex dynamics involved in the diffusion of premarital cohabitation among young women. The two horizontal dotted lines describe the inflow to, and outflow from, the risk

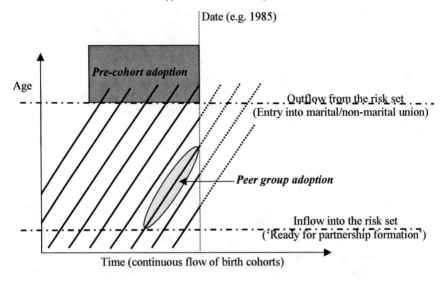

Date (e.g. 1985)

Figure 3.2 Time-related dimensions of the diffusion process of premarital cohabitation.

set given the variable ages at which these entries and exits take place for each individual. The succession of oblique parallel lines shows how there is a continuous inflow of birth cohorts entering into the life stage 'ready for partnership formation' and thus becoming members of the risk set of potential adopters; and, at the same time, there is a continuous outflow of women from this risk set. They leave the risk set not only because some young women adopt cohabitation but also because others choose to marry and therefore are not anymore exposed to the risk of entering their *first* partnership. Thus a continuous succession of birth cohorts will be passing across this window where the historical time at entrance and exit for each woman will depend respectively on her 'readiness' and age at formation of her first partnership (by either cohabiting or marrying).

In other words, in the case of premarital cohabitation, the choice to cohabit instead of (or before) marry is typically confined to a specific window in the life course through which a dynamic population of potential adopters transits over time. These peculiarities of the adoption process have significant consequences for the mechanisms that drive the diffusion process of premarital cohabitation among young women over time.

At each individual age[11], a young woman will be experiencing a certain prevalence of cohabitation in her environment, depending on the rate of adoption of those who have previously chosen to cohabit by that time. Here a distinction could be made between earlier adopters among older birth cohorts or among her peers who have already entered their first partnership through cohabitation. Will this woman be more susceptible to the influence from the example of her peers or will she draw information from the overall rate of experiences with premarital cohabitation of previous generations in her society by that time? This distinction is what characterises the two mechanisms linked to social influence, which are proposed in the next paragraphs.

The coexistence of several birth cohorts of individuals at different ages in each point of the historical time in which we happen to observed the diffusion process, and the dynamic process of learning from past cohort experiences is also a main concern in Manski's recent study (2004) because:

> Youth deciding whether to initiate risky behaviour such as drug use may draw lessons from the experiences of their peers. These and many similarly recurrent decision problems generate dynamic processes of social learning from private experiences. The member of each new cohort of decision makers attempt to learn from the actions chosen and outcomes realised by past cohorts, and then make decisions that produce new experiences observable by future cohorts. (Manski, 2004, p. 443)

He also observes that the kind of inference that individuals can make about the prevalence of a type of behaviour in the social system depends on the position from which they happen to observe it. This consideration highlights the relevance of the time structure of the process for detecting the mechanisms conveying social influence across successive birth cohorts of individuals. Because the distinctive feature of a diffusion approach is its hypothesis about the existence and the role of social influences, a key element must be the identification of the set of 'significant others' whose behaviour is thought to affect the individual's propensity to cohabit (Casterline, 2001; Coleman, Katz & Menzel, 1967; Greve, Strang, & Tuma, 1995; Manski, 1993b, 2000; Palloni, 1999, 2001; Strang, 1991; Strang & Soule, 1998). Here, we argue that young women faced with the decision to cohabit may draw information and example from the experiences of their peers or from the action chosen and outcomes realised by *past* cohorts. As they grow older, each successive birth cohort of these women will be confronted with a cumulating bunch of previous experiences from both previous cohorts and peer groups, which are being cumulated over a longer period.

In the following sections (3.4 and 3.5) we present two ways in which others' experiences with cohabitation may convey social influence that further fosters its subsequent adoption. The specific time-related structure of the diffusion process will aid in distinguishing which others' experiences may be particularly influential in affecting women's perception of a relative advantage entailed in cohabiting and/or its 'appropriateness.' Event history analysis will then help to assess their relative weight, and the shape of their effects, along with the diffusion process of cohabitation in each country.

3.4   KNOWLEDGE-AWARENESS ABOUT THE EXPERIENCES OF OLDER COHORTS

In the course of the diffusion of premarital cohabitation within a given society, each new cohort of women who enters the phase of being ready for partnership formation will encounter an increasingly greater proportion of prior adopters from previous cohorts. Each new cohort of women will therefore gradually experience premarital cohabitation as a less deviant (or stigmatised) and more socially acceptable living arrangement right from the beginning. Television, newspapers, magazines, and radio means of communication will increasingly disseminate knowledge-awareness on the growing popularity of nonmarital cohabitation among older birth cohorts and enhance its social acceptability. They will inform the young potential adopters of each new generation about the rising incidence of cohabitation, about why people increasingly choose to cohabit, about how long their relationships last, and how they end. In other words, they will inform the young women about the likely benefits of the new living arrangement and their costs. They will also transmit information on what cohabitation means socially as well as an understanding of how cohabitation should be normatively evaluated.

Strang and Meyer (1993) term *theorisation* the process of transmission of information that may help people to understand the new private living arrangement of nonmarital cohabitation. The two authors suggest that the better theorised an innovative practice is, the less its diffusion will need to be relationally structured. Indeed, an easily communicated, eventually legitimate new behavioural model would require less persuasion and reciprocal sense making than a practice that is hard to comprehend and motivate. Theorisation shapes and accelerates diffusion in that it 'translates' new practices into abstract general models. Theorisation eases the transmission of cohabitation because it provides a clearer frame to new behavioural models, making them more salient, familiar, and compelling to potential adopters (Strang & Soule, 1998). Interpretative frames and 'theorised models' that foster diffusion can be provided by previous adopters, through a sharing of their own experience with cohabitation. But it can also be provided by any other source of information, provided it is reliable in the eyes of potential adopters (favourably) commenting on the cultural and social change that is being realised. In the case of theorised models of behaviour, the degree of influence will depend on how compelling these interpretative frames are in the eyes of the future decision makers.

This consideration highlights the relevance of cultural conditions for diffusion, which is to say the compatibility of the new practice with the dominant values. As Strang (1990) shows, practices that match with cultural understandings of appropriate and effective behaviours tend to diffuse more quickly than those that do not. Thus, in a cross-national comparison, it is to be expected that both cultural and structural factors may contribute to the shaping of the diffusion process across different institutional contexts.

In the literature it is also stressed that new practices are adopted to the extent that they appear more effective or efficient compared to their alternatives (Rogers, 1985). Indeed, the spread of cohabitation seems to meet an increasing need for more flexible family forms across generations (Blossfeld, 2000), an issue we have already touched on in chapter 2. However, better knowledge of the existence and growing popularity of cohabitation through mass media information might *also* itself create motivation for its adoption (Gantz, Krendl & Robertson, 1986; Hornik & McAnany, 2001; Kaufer & Carley, 1993, 1996). Thus the dissemination of knowledge on cohabitation can create needs as well as vice versa.

Knowledge-awareness will generate social learning in that it will offer a wider knowledge of all factors that might bear on the decision to cohabit. It can imply either direct interactions within a social network and/or the transmission of abstract information. It is a mechanism by which the relative convenience and appropriateness of cohabitation becomes intelligible through others' experiences via examples, stories, or debates. Through social learning a new understanding of the phenomena is developed and the degree of its acceptability is enhanced. Relatively distant actors[12] are thought to be more effective in carrying information on what others have done (Rogers, 1985; Strang & Soule, 1998) because new information tends to better travel via weak ties[13]. This is because strongly related actors tend to share links to third parties and thus to share little new information (Granovetter, 1973). But, as we have seen, also impersonal sources of information can contribute to a better understanding and increased acceptance of cohabitation.

We hypothesise that the cumulative experiences of earlier cohorts with cohabitation and the dissemination of their experiences through mass media serve as an important mechanism in the transmission of the new form of living arrangement. In particular, we expect that the cumulative proportion of prior cohabitation adopters from previous cohorts has a positive effect on the conveyance of cohabitation in the following generations of women. This mechanism refers to the general level of previous experience with cohabitation made by older cohorts, and thus to the rectangular area (*Precohort adoption*) in Figure 3.2.

However, it is well known that abstract information about the existence, functioning, and rationality of cohabitation is necessary but not sufficient for its adoption in practice. Adoptive behaviour is highly susceptible to reinforcement influences, in particular at the beginning of the diffusion process, when the degree of uncertainty associated to new behaviours is higher (Bandura, 1977). In the initial phase, women are reluctant to simply embark on premarital cohabitation because it still involves a high degree of uncertainty and unknown risks. In particular, women are seldom certain that a new practice like cohabitation represents indeed a superior alternative to marriage. They neither might know exactly about the possible short- and long-term outcomes of such a choice nor about the societal approval associated to cohabiting. When cohabitation is not yet widespread, its benefits and costs are not necessarily very clear cut, at least not in the eyes of the early potential adopters. In the case of cohabitation, social and moral convictions are also often violated at the beginning of the diffusion process and the practice is stigmatised. Many women will therefore only engage in cohabitation after it has been gradually redefined in more acceptable terms. We thus hypothesise that, at the beginning of the diffusion process, knowledge-awareness about the experiences of previous cohorts should have a rather small or negligible impact on the spread of cohabitation. The effect of cumulative precohort adoption on the rate of diffusion should be weak or not even statistically significant at the beginning of the diffusion while increase its effect at later stages.

At an empirical level, at each point in time (t), the ongoing level of *knowledge-awareness* (P_c) to which each individual is exposed, is measured in this study by the cumulative proportion of prior adopters from previous birth cohorts at each age:

$$P_c = \frac{\sum_{i<c} \sum_{j<t} n_{ij}}{N_p(t)} * 100$$

where c indicates the birth cohort; t is the woman's age; n_{ij} is the number of prior adopters among older birth cohorts at age t; and $N_p(t)$ is the number of women belonging to older birth cohorts at age t. In other words, we created an indicator measuring, for each age of the woman observing, the percentage rate of practice in previous cohorts *up to* that moment. This is obtained by dividing the sum ($\sum$) of events (n_{ij}) in previous cohorts ($j < c$) up to each moment ($j < t$) by the total number of woman belonging to those birth cohorts ($N_p(t)$) at each time. The same set of measures has been computed in each country for every combination of (growing) age and birth cohorts in the sample for the period of interest.

3.5   DIRECT SOCIAL MODELLING OF PEERS

Especially in an early phase of the diffusion process, young women often need to confirm their beliefs about cohabitation through more direct experience. They have to be persuaded by further evaluative information about the actual benefits and possible disadvantages of cohabitation through more concrete examples. These examples are most convincing if they come from other individuals like themselves who have previously cohabited, and whose experiences can constitute a sort of vicarious trial for the newcomers (Bernardi, 2003; Kohler, 2001; Strang, 1991). More similar individuals may be more easily and better understood, or identified with, and thus be more capable of exercising persuading influence. In this latter case social influence would operate through 'direct modelling' (Bandura, 1977), which refers to how young people learn about the attractiveness of cohabitation by observing the examples given by their peers' behaviour instead of, or next to, receiving general information via the mass media. According to Bandura (1977), in the process of social learning there are three types of modelling stimuli: (1) the live models; (2) the symbolic model, and (3) verbal descriptions or instructions. 'Live models' comprise family members, friends, schoolmates, or work associates and others with whom the individual has direct contact. The 'symbolic model' is a pictorial representation of behaviour, whereas the mass media are a source of 'verbal modelling.' The important aspect of all types of modelling is that behaviour can be acquired simply through observation. The potential adopter does not have to practice the behaviour herself to be able to explore its potential consequences. Whatever the stimuli, others' enacted behaviours achieve influencing individuals' choice through modelling via *vicarious reinforcement* [14]. Modelling reduces both the burden and the hazards of a direct trial-and-error learning process, as well as the risks and costs that might be associated with breaking social norms or choosing a less favourable option. At the same time, it also enables young women to learn from others' example what would be (potentially) more convenient for them to do, already before they attempt a co-residential partnership themselves. This way, modelling influences produce learning through their informative function. The symbolic representations acquired serve potential adopters as a guide for appropriate actions. But simultaneously, observing the consequences of others' previous choices also conveys information about rewards or sanctions they have been subject to. Others' similarity makes it easier to identify and conveys the expectation to incur in similar consequences, should the same choice being taken. Peers' examples thus alter the perception of the relative advantage entailed in the choice of cohabitation, and thus the thoughts, feelings, and actions of subsequent others (Bandura, 1971): "[B]ecause of benefits cannot be experienced until the new practices are tried, the promotion of innovations draws heavily upon anticipated and vicarious reinforcement" (Bandura, 1977, p. 52).

Studies on the effectiveness of *'vicarious learning'* (Cox et al., 1999; Kanfer & Marston, 1963; Lee et al. 1999) have shown that dialogue and reflection over vicarious experiences are essential components of learning. Thus, through observation and 'listening' of experts or peers' discussing cohabitation, young people who find themselves in a situation similar to that portrait in dialogues or reports can helpfully 'reuse' the information received. Useful models for vicarious learning can stem either from experts (such as in the case of 'theorisation' or mass media communication) or from the observed models of peers with whom identification may more easily occur. Vicarious learning has proven to be a powerful tool in influencing moral judgements towards a practice (Bandura & McDonald, 1963) and in increasing the adoption of an innovative behaviour (Bandura, Blanchard & Ritter, 1969; Rosekrans & Hartup, 1967).

However, it is not only conversation and personal contact with one's peers that count but also the perception of the practice, which is 'proper' to an individual's position within the social structure. Burt (1987) terms it *'structural equivalence.'* He argues that structurally equivalent actors, namely those possessing similar ties to others, attend carefully to each other's behaviour in order to be able to manage the uncertainty entailed in innovative practices. The driving force for social influence is then competition, where individuals use one another to evaluate the relative 'appropriateness' or suitability of cohabitation. Equivalence of roles and positions provides them with a ground for easing social comparison (Erickson, 1988). Structural equivalence is thus assumed to generate *social pressure* towards adoption. In the case of structural equivalent actors, interpersonal relationships and primary groups are not the analytical frame of reference. Rather, the channels of social influence are the entire social system and feelings of competition, or of relative deprivation, within a status. For example, an account of peers' behaviour conformity depicted as structural equivalence is that of young people's common relation to—or sensibility to the influence of—third parties: namely, mass media images of 'appropriate' youth behaviour, subcultures, or role models (Friedkin, 1984; Mardsen & Friedkin, 1993). Cohabitation of peers should therefore constitute a particularly valuable trial example of the new living arrangement.

This second mechanism for transmission of social influence draws on the degree of similarity between previous and potential adopters. Earlier studies from social psychology have also widely documented how innovative types of behaviour exemplified by similar others tend to be more effective in encouraging imitation and conformism[15]. In the words of Strang and Meyer,

> The individual's cognitive map identifies reference groups that bound social comparison processes. Rational mimicking requires prior and potential adopters be understood as fundamentally similar, at least with respect to the practice at issue. Perceptions of similarity may enhance rates of diffusion for additional reasons, as actors find themselves enmeshed in competitive emulation. (Strang & Meyer, 1993, p. 491)

Reference groups may also be culturally constructed around common status and condition rather than dense network of interactions (Strang & Soule, 1998). From these considerations originates the need for an age-defined indicator, intended to detect a possible channel for peers' influence. Indeed, belonging to the same culturally defined social category constructs a tie that is not necessarily relational but may have a direct impact on diffusion, in that it produces 'cultural' similarity and affects the easiness in the spread of information. This is not the same as arguing that age similarity fosters higher levels of interactions between individuals or that it might be a proxy for direct relations. Rather, we argue that culturally recognised similarities (e.g., belonging to the same age group that moves across the same life-course transitions around the same 'historical' and 'cultural' conditions) favour meaningful communication and influence between weakly related individuals, as between theorists and adopters (Strang & Meyer, 1993).

This mechanism for social influence suggests that at the heart of the diffusion process there is direct social modelling (Bandura, 1977) by potential adopters of their peers who have adopted previously. This mechanism relates to the oval area (*Peer-group adoption*) in Figure 3.2. Through this channel, attitudes towards cohabitation are confirmed through direct experiences made by *similar* others, who constitute concrete examples (a sort of valuable vicarious trial). Peer groups should play a particularly influential role in the diffusion of cohabitation mainly at the beginning of the diffusion process because that is when strongly held attitudes have to be changed. If young women are exposed to conflicting standards (informal cohabitation versus formal marriage) exemplified by adult and peer models, they more often adopt the new standard of conduct than if adults alone set the example (Bandura, 1977).

Thus we hypothesise that cumulative *peer-group adoption* is an important force that drives the diffusion process and is relatively more important than cumulative *precohort adoption*. And further, that the relative importance of *peer-group adoption* compared to *precohort adoption* should even increase over time. Later adopters rely even less on mass media because a bank of peer experience has accumulated over time (Rogers, 1985).

Empirically the size of *direct social modelling* (P_g) is measured as the cumulative proportion of prior adopters belonging to the women's own birth cohort at each age:

$$P_g = \frac{\sum\limits_{i=c} \sum\limits_{j<t} m_{ij}}{N_c} * 100$$

where c indicates the birth cohort; t is the woman's age; m_{ij} is the number of prior adopters within the woman's own birth cohort at age t; and N_c is the total number of women in the woman's own birth cohort. This is obtained by dividing the sum $(\sum)$ of events (m_{ij}) in the same birth cohort ($j = c$) up to each moment ($j < t$) by the total number of woman belonging to that birth cohort (N_c) at each time. Again, these measures have been computed in each country for every combination of (growing) age and birth cohorts in the sample for the period of interest.

Over the life course, the women belonging to each birth cohort will thus experience different degrees of increase in others' previous adoption of cohabitation each successive year, depending on the 'popularity' and appeal of cohabiting for each generation of women in each country.

3.6 RESULTS: THE DIFFUSION OF COHABITATION

We now present the first empirical results, starting from a description of the diffusion of cohabitation among young women across birth cohorts in the six countries under study. As discussed earlier in the chapter, we are specifically interested in two different mechanisms driving the diffusion process: knowledge-awareness (measured as the cumulative experiences of older cohorts) and direct social modelling (measured as cumulative experiences of peers within the same birth cohort).

Figure 3.3 describes the changes in the *cumulative proportions of pre-cohort adoption* across age in five of the six countries studied, for the birth cohorts from 1954 to 1973[16]. Unfortunately, given the sampling

Sweden: not computable

France

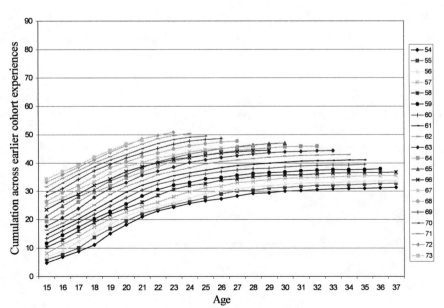

Figure 3.3 Cumulative proportions of precohort adoption. (*continued over*)

West Germany

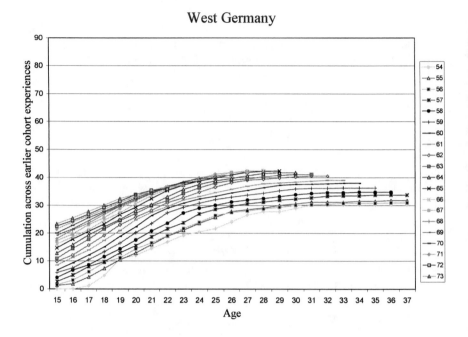

East Germany

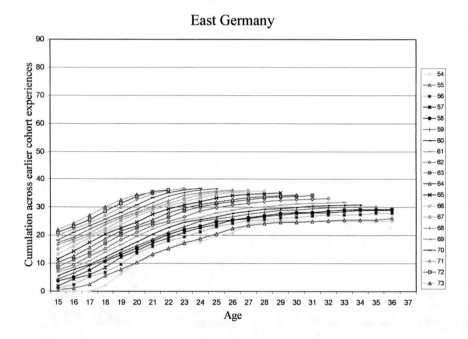

Figure 3.3 Cumulative proportions of precohort adoption.

Spain

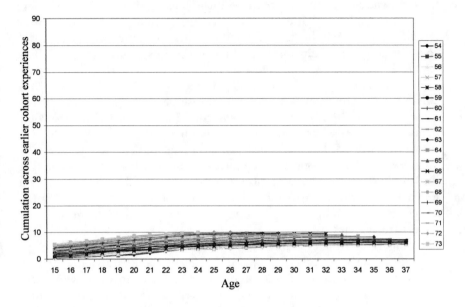

Italy

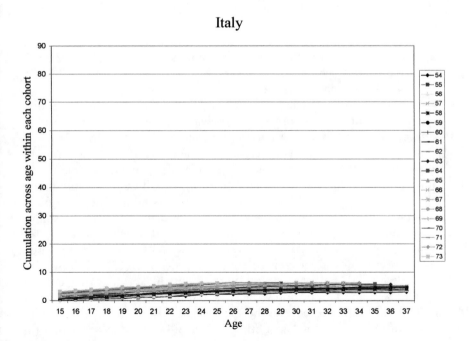

Figure 3.3 Cumulative proportions of precohort adoption.

structure of the FFS survey in Sweden, it has not been possible to compute these measures for this country. In France, East Germany, and West Germany, it is apparent that each successive birth cohort of women encountered an increasingly higher proportion of prior practice with premarital cohabitation right from the beginning of their exposure at age 15. For example, in France, women born in 1973, at their entering the window of risk exposure to partnering at age 15, witnessed a rate of practice with cohabitation around 30% higher than those perceived by women of the same age born 20 years before (see Figure 3.3). In East and West Germany, this increase across generations had been of around 20% to 25% for women age 15. In other words, across birth cohorts there seems to be an increasing level of social acceptance of cohabitation for each younger birth cohort so that cohabitation can progressively be considered as a less deviant form of partnership. This trend continues to rise during the life course of each birth cohort of women, as can be seen from the birth cohort trajectories.

Compared to these countries, the diffusion of cohabitation develops quite differently in Italy and Spain. Although there is also an increasing proportion of the cohabitation practice, the differences between birth cohorts are not very marked, and the increase of cumulative previous cohorts experience over the life course is very small. Thus, in Italy *cumulative precohort adoption* reaches its maximum at about 7%, in Spain at 11%, whereas in East Germany it reaches it at 36%, in West Germany at 43%, and in France at 50%. This description suggests that in the Southern European countries, even for younger birth cohorts of women, the adoption of cohabitation is still an uncommon practice and thus remains a kind of deviant behaviour.

Figure 3.4 displays the *cumulative proportion of peer-group adoption* for the same countries and birth cohorts, measured as the proportion of prior adopters across age within each birth cohort. Starting from zero, cohabitation is at first adopted in each birth cohort by only a few people who might serve as an example. Then it is adopted at a rapidly accelerating rate with increasing age, gradually slowing down and finally stabilising at a specific level. The resulting distribution of cumulative adoptions over age can generally be described as taking the form of an S-shaped curve. There are, however, important differences in the shapes of the curves among birth cohorts and the overall levels reached by the younger cohorts in the six countries. The maximum cumulative proportion of peer-group adoption is reached in Sweden with 87%, followed by France with 78%, West Germany with about 50%, and East Germany with 40%. Spain lags behind with 17% and Italy even further apart with about 10%. With reference to the steep of the slopes and the relative distances of the curves from each other, Figure 3.4 clearly indicates that the diffusion of cohabitation seems to have been overall slower and somehow blocked in the south of Europe, at least until the early 1990s.

Sweden

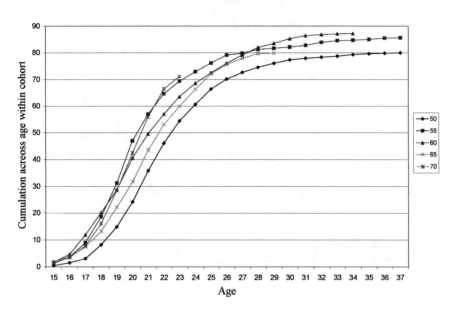

France

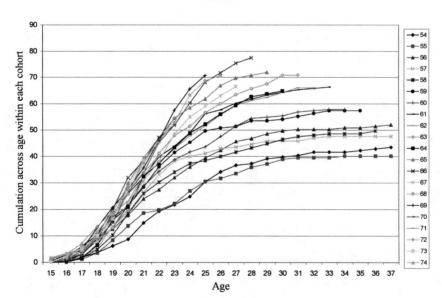

Figure 3.4 Cumulative proportions of peer-group adoption. (*continued over*)

West Germany

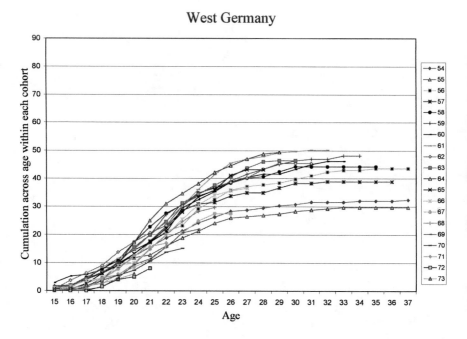

East Germany

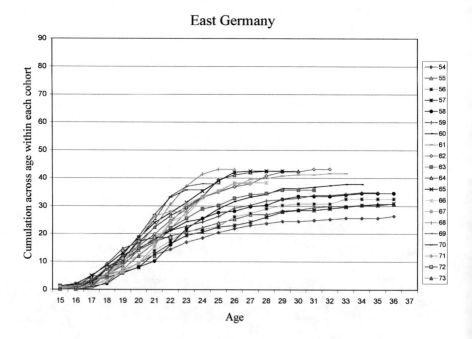

Figure 3.4 Cumulative proportions of peer-group adoption.

Spain

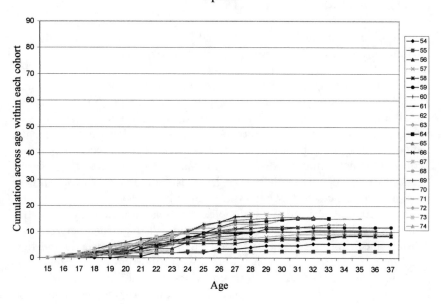

Italy

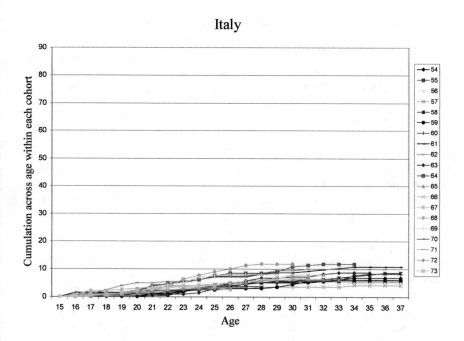

Figure 3.4 Cumulative proportions of peer-group adoption.

3.7   THE DIFFUSION PROCESS AND INSTITUTIONAL CONSTRAINTS

Summing up, we argued in chapter 2 that it is rational for individuals who are in uncertain situations to observe and refer to others' enacted behaviour to orient their actions and acquire new information. We then argued that the relative advantage entailed in adopting a new behavioural option such as premarital cohabitation increases together with the proportion of previous adopters in a social system. We proposed two rationales by which *social influence* should raise the social acceptance of a new behavioural model and the convenience of cohabiting together with its ongoing level of previous adoption, namely, influences related to *social learning* and *social pressure*.

As a further step, in this chapter we have also noted that the proportion of previous experiences with cohabitation that individuals can observe depends on their changing position in the complex time-related structure of the diffusion process of this new practice. We have thus distinguished between two possible mechanisms related to the effect of social influence: *knowledge-awareness* (P_c), measured as the cumulative proportion of adopters from previous cohorts, and *direct social modelling* (P_g), measured as the cumulative proportion of previous experiences among peers. These constructs will be used in an attempt to better understand the underlying mechanisms governing the changes in the process of adoption of cohabitation. We have claimed to expect 'similar' others to be more influential, especially at the beginning of the diffusion process when social norms have to be violated and more persuasion is required. We argued that when individuals are 'similar' in some respect, diffusion should be rapid because of the perceptions built into them. In the following phase of the study we will then test the absolute and relative strength of these two channels for social influence, in affecting young women's likelihood to adopt cohabitation. By simultaneously testing these effects in the empirical model, together with socioeconomic factors, the multivariate analyses become more than a description of the path of diffusion. They will test different hypothesis about the ways of channelling social influence. The empirical test will explore whether individuals seem to be more influenced by their peers' behaviour or by another social effect that operates across generations (see Manksi, 1993b). The test of a double specification of possible reference groups allows one to better disentangle social dynamics without assuming any specific a priori unique channel of social influence. Additionally, to investigate the shape of the effects played by the diffusion related mechanisms, the functional form of these two indicators will be flexibly specified, so as to leave room for a wide range of different possible forms (see chapter 5).

However, as discussed in chapter 2, others' degree of adoption and experience with cohabitation is only a part of the explanation of rising levels of this practice over time: the part connected to the perception of the relative advantage entailed in cohabiting. However, differently shaped national institutional structures also contribute to defining the relative convenience of the options available (and feasible) in individual choices. The legal framing of partners' and spouses' obligations and entitlements, the permeability of cultural and normative contexts to innovative behaviours and practices, housing and labour markets, educational systems, and the gender division of roles are among other factors that contribute to the making of a possible advantage of cohabiting relative to marrying. Chapter 4 is dedicated to the influences of these institutionally related factors. Here it is important to illustrate the contribution that the approach we propose may bring in addition to the classical 'structural' explanations.

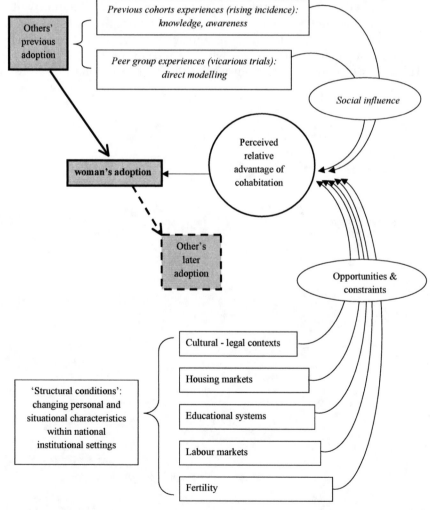

Figure 3.5 Individuals' adoption of cohabitation and institutional contexts in the diffusion process.

Figure 3.5 sketches a stylised schema of the main components of this approach. On the top-left side of the schema, is the part of reasoning linked to the diffusion process (darker areas). On the bottom-right part are represented those socioeconomic factors that contribute to influence partnering behaviours. Both of these influences are thought simultaneously to affect women's perception of the relative advantage entailed in cohabiting: the former through social influence, and the latter through the setting of 'structural' opportunities and constraints in individuals' choices. The diagonal thick arrows on the top-left part of the schema point to the diffusion process per se: The rate of previous adoption of the new practice enhances women's actual likelihood to cohabit, which in turn contributes to foster the probability that other women will cohabit in the future. In this respect, shading light on women's likelihood to adopt premarital cohabitation while taking into account also the effect of previous adopters means tackling the diffusion process at an individual level and helps predict likely future developments. The multivariate analysis will thus integrate both perspectives as explanatory factors in young women's likelihood of cohabiting.

4 Sociodemographic Factors and the Influence of Institutional Contexts

4.1 THE STRUCTURE OF OPPORTUNITY AND CONSTRAINTS: RELATIVE ADVANTAGE OF COHABITATION

As anticipated in the previous chapters, in the approach we propose the prevalence of practice of cohabitation is not the only factor affecting individuals' decision to enter it. The choice to engage in an innovative behaviour depends on the degree of its perceived relative advantage with respect to other alternative choices. Individuals' considerations about cohabiting take into account the structure of opportunities and constraints set by institutional contexts while being affected (whether consciously perceived or not) by others' behaviour. We have argued that a diffusion account (social influence) and a structural explanation (socioeconomic and institutional related factors) are two perspectives complementary to each other (Casterline, 2001; Dechter, 2001; Palloni, 2001). This chapter deals specifically with the impact of the institutional features that might affect individuals' interest in adopting cohabitation rather than marrying. In this chapter we discuss those features that might increase or decrease the advantage entailed in adopting cohabitation in each of the countries chosen as case studies: the conservative-corporatist West Germany and France, the former socialist East Germany[1], the social-democratic Sweden, and the familialist Italy and Spain.

Across Europe there are different sets of opportunities and constraints rooted in individuals' changing socioeconomic circumstances about when (and how) to leave the parental family (Jurado Guerrero, 2001) and when and how to enter a partnership (by marriage or cohabitation) in each country. They depend to a large extent on specific institutional contexts. We already know from previous studies that the readiness of young women to enter a partnership is influenced by institutional characteristics of the educational and employment systems (Blossfeld, 1990; Corijn, 2001a). The literature distinguishes several domains in which social mechanisms can influence the relative easiness in the choice made between living independently as a single person, cohabiting, or marrying[2]. In the following sections, we discuss in more detail (section 4.2) the different legal frameworks that regulate cohabiters' reciprocal duties and entitlements in each country, (4.3) the role of the general normative context, (4.4) the effect of a general educational expansion, (4.5) the different labour markets for young women, and, finally (4.6), the characteristics of housing markets.

4.2   THE LEGAL CONTEXT: LAW REGULATIONS ON COHABITING UNIONS

Among the countries analysed, France and Sweden were those in which the legal framework reacted fastest to social change, incorporating and recognising cohabitation and making it an accepted alternative to legal marriage. In Sweden, for example, cohabiting couples are treated the same way as married ones for the purposes of tax and social laws, although there is no legal duty to support the partner economically and the rules of inheritance rights between spouses do not apply to cohabiters. However, the legislation, specifically the 'Cohabitees Act' (1987), in the case of partner's death allows the surviving party to use and occupy the joint home and further protects the survivor by a special rule on the division of property (Saldeen, 1995).

In France, informal family behaviour was already regulated in the Civil Code dated 1804, according to which—beside having a chance to be granted a share in the couple's belongings—a cohabitant who had been abandoned by his or her partner may obtain a compensation similar to that a legal spouse is entitled to in case of divorce. In the case of a partner's death, where spouses share also a relatively weak position in French succession law, inheritance rights for the survivor are not granted (Glendon, 1989). Since 1948, different provisions grant a right of occupation to a cohabitant who has been living on the premises for at least one year. For the period analysed here, tax law did not take cohabitation into account[3], so each partner was taxed as if he or she was single. Therefore the tax position may have been more favourable for cohabiters than for spouses as far as tax deductions are concerned (Guimezanes, 1995). In welfare law cohabiters are instead often equalised with spouses, even though their children are deemed illegitimate children until their parentage is being established. But once parentage is proved, both parents have a duty to maintain their children in the same way as married parents.

In West Germany the protection offered by the 'Federal Constitution' (1949) to the institutions of family and marriage is denied when couples choose to cohabit and, in the absence of minor children, the relationship is not seen as giving place to a family. Instead, cohabiting partners are free to make private arrangements according to the general regulations of the Civil Code on contracts, properties, and successions. Cohabiters enjoy a weaker status, however, when they could not reach agreement on all issues or did not regulate their union through a private contract because they are not eligible for the protection and privileges connected with marriage. Two principles seem to dominate the German legal approach: protection of the institution of marriage and respect for the presumed intention of cohabiters to avoid legal consequences. These conditions still prevent nonmarital unions benefiting from a range of entitlement and rights accorded to marriage (including a far more favourable tax arrangements: the *Ehegattensplitting*; see Steiner & Wrohlich, 2004); and cohabiting unions are left free to develop in a way that in case of dissolution the weaker or economically dependent part is more exposed to adverse outcomes (Glendon, 1989). Only in 1991 an explicit reference to cohabitation (aimed at protecting marital rights) was made in the 'Federal Relief Act,' whereby relief payments to unmarried cohabiters are subject to the same reductions as the payments made to married couples (Graue, 1995). Some more legislation came into place in 2006, extending to cohabiting unions the legal obligation to support the unemployed partner economically, a period not covered in this analysis.

In Italy and Spain the contrast is still greater. Cohabitation in Italy has yet not been given any legal recognition, although public debate has recently begun about the urge to acknowledge and regulate cohabiting unions. Here cohabiters have no mutual rights and duties to live together or to provide material and moral support or to be faithful. Cohabitation is thus seen as a free and unbinding relationship, which is terminable by either party at any time and in which each partner owns and disposes separately of any property acquired during cohabitation. In presence of children recognised by both partners, both have parental authority and the same rights and duties as married parents, in that they have to provide them maintenance and alimony. However, cohabiting partners have no legal obligation to pay maintenance or alimony to each other; nor do succession rights exist under the Civil Code. Cohabitation contracts have only recently emerged, and are indirectly acknowledged by the Constitutional Court (Timoteo, 1995).

In Spain too, cohabitation is neither recognised nor regulated, cohabiters do not have the same rights as married couples, and no special family proceedings are available in courts. Unmarried parents have parental rights and duties, and since 1987 (1991 for Catalan law) they are allowed to adopt children. Cohabiters have neither reciprocal maintenance duties nor rights to a widow's pension or succession on the death of the partner, but they may be entitled to social security benefits (e.g., health assistance) when living together with a person or child entitled to such assistance (Alberdi, 1993; Roca, 1995).

This set of differently shaped legal frameworks creates advantages and disadvantages of a marital union compared to a cohabiting one. Given the lower legal constraints, the choice not to marry means, on the one hand, avoiding the responsibilities and restrictions imposed on married persons but, on the other, forgoing rights to protection and privileges connected with marriage. This might be especially important in the eyes of the weaker, because more economically dependent, partner. It is thus expected to play a greater role for women in those countries where the gender division of paid and unpaid labour is more traditional. As described, these legal restrictions are more pronounced in Italy and Spain, followed by Germany, France, and finally Sweden, where marital and cohabiting unions are made virtually identical. Such restrictions are expected to affect the diffusion process, enhancing (in the southern countries) or reducing (in Sweden, France, East Germany, and more ambiguously in West Germany) the degree of risk entailed in cohabiting unions.

Hypothesis 1: We expect legal frame of opportunities and constraints set by national laws to increase the advantage of cohabiting in Sweden, France, and East Germany, whereas to decrease its relative advantage in Italy, Spain, and to a minor extent in West Germany.

4.3   THE CULTURAL CONTEXTS

Social norms tend to define the range of appropriate and tolerable practices with respect to family formation. What kinds of 'family forms' are possible is defined at the societal level by the general normative context of a society. During the process of behavioural change that goes along with the diffusion of cohabitation, the general cultural framework serves as standard or guide for the members of a society and determines the ease with which young women can establish themselves in it. For example, their cultural norms suggest the appropriate social and economic circumstances under which young people can enter either a marriage or a cohabitation. With regard to cohabitation, beside legal norms, family cultures, traditions, and social norms can operate at the level of the *nation*, religious *communities*, and *local systems* (Rogers, 1985).

Among the countries studied, Italy and Spain are distinct in having more traditional family norms (Barbagli, Castiglioni & Dalla Zuanna, 2003), which we might expect to inhibit the early process of diffusion of cohabitation. In fact, practices that match with cultural understandings of appropriate behaviour tend to diffuse faster than those that do not (Strang, 1990), whereas cohabiting seems quite distant from a traditional vision of the family, often defined by the marital contract. The more traditional context of these societies should affect the mechanisms of dissemination of information because opinion leaders are usually a separate group of individuals from the innovators (Barbagli, Castiglioni & Dalla Zuanna, 2003). Here, the authorities are not expected to be particularly favourable to a more flexible less binding behavioural innovation and, as a result, society should remain comparatively traditional for longer. In a traditional cultural climate, early innovators will be more likely to hide or underreport cohabitation, and they are also less likely to have their experiences disseminated through mass media. As a result, in societies with traditional family systems we expect that cumulative precohort adoption of cohabitation should not be a relevant engine in the diffusion process, particularly so in its beginning phase. In traditional societies it should also be harder to get cohabitation off the ground because social forerunners engaging in the new practice are a selective group of the population, and they might not favour an immediate self-identification by the people in general. If mass media channels are not a viable means of transmission of information at the start of the process, and if ordinary people find it hard to identify with early innovators, cohabitation might rather diffuse further mainly along horizontal networks of specific innovative peer groups. Furthermore, the strong interdependence between family members characteristic of more 'familistic' countries might also add resistance to such change through more traditional parental values (Dalla Zuanna, 2004). Given the limited economic independence from their families enjoyed by young people, parents can more effectively limit their offspring's preference for innovative behaviours, even when *peer-group* information is available and has generated a favourable attitude towards the new practice in the younger and generally less traditional members of society. Accordingly, we might also expect a failure of the diffusion process of cohabitation to occur if the innovators do not effectively manage to transmit their experiences to weakly connected broader outsiders' groups (i.e., if there is no "strengths-of-weak-ties"; Granovetter, 1973).

With regard to the normative structure of societies, the contrast between East Germany and the other countries is another interesting case for the test of the diffusion argument put forward in this analysis. The German Democratic Republic was, in fact, a political system that normatively opposed social change. In this former communist country, the whole public system, politicians and bureaucrats as well as the mass media in general, did not promote social change. This normative structure should therefore have created barriers for the dissemination of knowledge-awareness and fostered a cultural climate resistant to the diffusion process. In contrast, the situation in France, Sweden, or West Germany has been different, in that the capitalistic economy, society in general, and the mass media in particular, have generally been oriented towards social and economic development. We therefore expect the rate of cumulative *peer-group* and *precohort adoptions* to have a smaller effect on the diffusion of cohabitation in East Germany than in these countries.

Hypothesis 2: We expect 'peer-group adoption' to have a positive effect on the diffusion of cohabitation. This effect should be particularly strong at the beginning of the diffusion process. The positive effect of 'precohort adoption' should be comparatively smaller and rather more influential at a later stage of the diffusion process when a general level of social acceptance has already been reached. The strength of these mechanisms should be lower in the former socialist East Germany.

An important normative context with regard to cohabitation is the degree to which people are *religious*. In fact, sexuality, marriage, and childbearing (along with contraception) have long been highly central issues for Christian churches. In particular, both cohabitation and nonmarital sex therein are highly incompatible with the Roman Catholic sacrament of marriage (Wu, 2000), which is there seen as the only possible way of establishing a new family. Even after the Protestant Reformation, most Christian churches still proscribe premarital sex. Because cohabitation acknowledges a sexual relationship and can thus emphasise nonconformity to religious doctrine, such churches firmly discourage sexual relationships within a co-residential informal union (Thornton, Axinn, & Hill, 1992). It is thus likely that nonreligious young women are the most likely to endorse premarital cohabitation, and that the capacity of religious doctrines to influence young people's behaviour is associated with the degree of religious practice in a given country. Because most religious groups discourage cohabitation and instead place a high value on marriage and procreation within a regulated family life, we expect women's religiosity[4] to decrease their likelihood to cohabit and increase that of marrying. In fact, young religious women are more likely to enter in contact with adult people who encourage marriage and thus be influenced by the teachings of their churches on marriage and cohabiting unions. In this cross-societal comparison we particularly expect that religiosity should have a positive effect on entry into marriage and a particularly negative effect on the diffusion of cohabitation in Catholic Italian and Spanish societies. But in an atheist society like the (former socialist) East Germany, religion was fairly unimportant and should therefore have neither a strong effect on marriage nor on cohabitation. Finally, West Germany should have a position in the middle between East Germany and the southern countries. It is a country with mixed religious affiliations and a lower degree of religiosity. Given the higher rate of Protestantism in West Germany, religion should thus have a positive effect on marriage and a weak negative effect on cohabitation. It is not possible instead to test any hypothesis for the French and Swedish cases because the question on religiosity was not asked.

Hypothesis 3: We expect religiosity to have a positive effect on the likelihood of marrying and a negative effect on the adoption of cohabitation. These effects should be stronger in the more religious southern countries, especially with regard to cohabitation, and weaker in the more atheist East Germany.

Social norms, values, and traditions should also play a role in union decisions in the case of the birth of a child. The event of a *pregnancy*, for women in a relationship that does not entail the sharing of a residence with the partner, is expected to accelerate the decision to enter a union (Blossfeld et al., 1999; Blossfeld, Manting & Rohwer, 1993; Blossfeld & Mills, 2001; Mills, 2000). Single pregnant women may indeed desire to offer their child the social and economic protection that accompanies a stable and regulated union. The strength of the pressure to enter a partnership is expected to be generally greater in the case of formal marriage than cohabitation (Brien, Lillard & Waite, 1999; Goldsheider & Waite, 1986, see also Baizán et al., 2003, for Spain, and Baizán et al., 2002, for West Germany and Sweden). The higher degree of commitment required by marriage[5] makes it be generally regarded as a more stable and guaranteed living arrangement than cohabitation. Thus, if a union is seen as the proper setting in which to bear children, a pregnancy may precipitate the entry into a first partnership, especially in the case of marriage[6]. Differences are expected between countries, however, depending on the meaning attached to cohabitation and marriage in each country and on the legal frameworks that define and recognise rights and responsibilities of the parents, both to each other and to their children. If cohabiting couples are no longer a small proportion of unions with a low level of social acceptance, being in a union might still be seen as an important precondition to bearing children, but there should be less pressure to marry (Mulder & Manting, 1994).

In Sweden and France, where cohabitation is widespread and its status with regard to children is legally recognised and regulated to a degree comparable to that of marriage, we do not expect a substantially different effect. In East Germany, the effect on marriage is not expected to be greater than for cohabitation because of the entitlements reserved to unmarried mothers in the socialist part of Germany (see section 4.6 on housing). The West German institutions are instead strongly committed towards marriage and fail to provide the same support to cohabiting and married couples, thus increasing the incentives for individuals to marry. In the case of the southern countries, cohabiting parents are far from being attributed the same status as married ones, and, given also the more traditional context, the effect of a pregnancy is expected to be substantially greater in the case of marriage. The effect of a pregnancy on union formation is expected to decrease after the birth of the child because the pressure on the decision to enter a union has disappeared (Blossfeld, Manting & Rohwer 1993). It may, however, be that an intended marriage or cohabitation could not take place before the birth on various grounds, and it may thus spill over into some months right after the birth. No accelerating effect is expected on the choice to leave the parental home in order to live as single.

Hypothesis 4: We expect an ongoing pregnancy to accelerate the entrance into a partnership, this effect to be generally greater in the case of marriage, and to be especially influential in West Germany, Italy, and Spain. Its impact should decrease shortly after the birth of the child.

The experience of a *parental divorce* should also affect partnership decisions because it reflects an unfavourable family climate (Clausen, 1991; Corijn, 2001b) or one with a lower standard of living (Goldscheider & Da Vanzo, 1989). Having witnessed divorced parents reentering the courtship process and confronting them with nonmarital sex and postmarital cohabitation might also modify children's attitudes towards these behaviours, with marriage becoming less important to legitimate intimate relationships (Thornton, 1991).

Furthermore, former married parents entering a postmarital cohabitation may provide behavioural role models for their children and induce a more approving attitude towards cohabitation. Parental separation or divorce may also question marriage as a long-binding commitment because the failure of the parental marital relationship constitutes an unsuccessful example and may increase apprehension about marital success. A more cautious attitude toward marriage may slow down its pace of entry and open room for cohabitation, either as a trial to gain more confidence or as an alternative form of relationship. Separated or divorced parents may also have a lower capacity to influence and exercise social control over their children's behaviours because of the shortening of time in which they can interact with, guide, and supervise them, and because of their weakened ability to reinforce each other (Thornton, 1991). A declined parental influence might then enhance children's sensitivity to peers' influences, and thus to the appeal of alternative emerging partnership models. This should be especially important in more traditional contexts where social stigma is more difficult to resist. We thus expect that young women who have experienced parental divorce or separation to be more likely to cohabit, leave the parental home earlier, and marry less (or later) than those who have not. This effect should be stronger in the southern countries, where divorce in the parental generation was still a rather rare phenomenon.

Hypothesis 5: Parental divorce is expected to have a negative effect on the transition to marriage and a positive effect on the adoption of cohabitation. We expect a particularly strong effect for cohabitation in the southern countries.

With regard to local systems, we expect ecological effects of *city size* and *region* (Lesthaeghe & Neels, 2002). Small- and medium-size cities should be more traditional with regard to family values. Cohabitation should therefore diffuse more easily in large cities than in medium ones and in medium cities more than in small ones, at least in the initial phase of the diffusion process. There might also be differences with regard to region in various countries. For example, it is well known in the literature that regional differences in countries like Italy are quite pronounced (Barbagli, Castiglioni & Dalla Zuanna, 2003; Billari & Kohler, 2002). The south of Italy is much more traditional with regard to religious and family values than the northern parts. Moreover, in the south of Italy there is a long tradition of a brief 'escape' by the young couple from the parental families for a few days ('*fuitina*'): an extremely short period of cohabitation (often under familial control) aimed at forcing a subsequent marriage or at reducing the costs of a marriage, then only seen as a necessary 'remedy' to preserve the bride's honour (Barbagli, 1989). In the empirical analysis, these differences are controlled.

Hypothesis 6: We expect large urban centres to favour the diffusion of cohabitation more than small cities. We also expect the young women living in the more traditional regions of the centre and, especially, the south of Italy to have a greater propensity to marry and a lower propensity to cohabit.

The prevalent gender-role expectations about the household division of labour once married might also influence individuals' decision to partner. Indeed, in spite of a move towards gender equalisation in the labour market, there are still significant aspects of older gender arrangements to be found within households, for nowhere has the gender division of labour disappeared (Arber & Ginn, 1995; Gershuny, Bittman & Briere, 2005; Kemp, 1994; O'Connor, 1996; Saraceno, 1993; Orloff, 2002). Across Europe there are still pressures for women to subordinate their employment to accommodate the responsibility for caregiving unpaid work (see Bernardi, 1999, 2001a, for Italy; Drobnič, Blossfeld & Rohwer, 1999, for Germany; Sigle-Rushton & Perron, 2006, for United Kingdom). So that most women (and some men) face challenges in reconciling paid work and family life (Becker & Moen, 1999; Nazio & MacInnes, 2007; Saraceno, 1987a, 1992). And indeed, part of women's identity is still built around the roles of wife and mother, which results in a gender-specific investment in reproductive and caring activities[7]. But this reproductive work within the families is generally underevaluated and is also scarcely compensated when it is paid for by externalising it in the labour market (O'Connor, 1996; Orloff, 1993). We can thus expect that younger generations of women, who have invested many years and resources in education, would want to challenge a traditional division of labour towards a new role negotiation (Huston &Geis, 1993). These young women might prefer cohabiting over marrying on the basis of a less established and more open gender-role negotiation (Bernardi, 2003; Prinz, 1995; Sweet & Bumpass, 1990). Cohabitation, moreover, may provide the room to explore and observe partners' attitudes, skills, and preferences to domestic and caregiving activities (Cherlin, 2000; Wu, 2000). It thus offers an incentive to both partners to please each other through a more equitable contribution to unpaid household labour. In this respect cohabiting may also represent an information-gathering period that might precede the decision to marry (Oppenheimer, 2000). We thus argue that the innovative and less binding character of cohabitation—by being less charged with traditional norms and expectations—can offer a better setting and more room for women to (re)negotiate the gender division of labour.

Thus in what way do young men and women combine market and family work in marital and nonmarital unions and to what extent are they able to practise more gender-equal behaviours in informal cohabitation than in formal marriage? There is preliminary evidence that gender equality in the division of work within the household is greater if couples cohabit (Huinink, 1995; for West Germany, MacAllister, 1990; Shelton & John, 1993; Baxter 2005; Wu, 2000), whereas marital unions tend to reproduce rapidly a traditional division of labour between spouses (Thiessen, Rohlinger & Blasius, 1994, for Germany). These results suggest that (in particular working) women may have an incentive to cohabit instead of marrying. For this reason, we generally expect a negative effect of women's labour force participation on the rate of entry into marriage and a positive effect on the adoption of informal cohabitation. Particularly in Italy and Spain, there might be a more substantial relative advantage of cohabitation compared to formal marriage for working women, given the importance of the male-breadwinner family model and a comparatively more traditional division of work within the family. We therefore expect a particularly strong positive effect of women's labour force participation on the diffusion rate of cohabitation in these countries. In the southern countries, however, a traditional marriage might still represent a form of reaching security for nonworking women, for those who face difficulties in entering the labour market, or those who specialise in caregiving activities within the household (England, 2000). Previous research has in fact shown that in Spain, where a marital union is still the prevalent option for gaining independence from the parental family, being in a nonworking status enhances the transition to a first union for women, although this effect becomes smaller for younger cohorts (Simó Noguera, Golsch & Steinhage, 2001).

In dual-earner societies, like the former East Germany or Sweden, women's gainful employment has been standard, and the female partner's income has become a significant determinant of the living standard and the 'lifestyle' of couples and families (Blossfeld & Timm, 2003). Under these conditions, women's labour force participation should have no effect on the rate of marital or nonmarital unions. In particular in Sweden, a forerunner country in Europe in terms of gender equality, no effect of women's labour participation is expected to influence the likelihood to enter a first union.

Hypothesis 7: Especially working women are expected to perceive a greater relative advantage from cohabiting (positive effect), the more if they belong to a country with a traditional gender division of labour. To the contrary, we expect a negative effect of women's work on the likelihood to marry. This effect should be much lower in dual-breadwinner countries, such as Sweden, East Germany, and (to a lesser extent) France.

4.4   EDUCATIONAL EXPANSION

In Europe, a major change affecting the transition to adulthood was the widespread expansion of education in the 1960s and 1970s (Müller & Wolbers, 2003). There are at least two consequences of this macro process. First, it has increased the duration of young people's *participation in education*, in particular for young women (Shavit & Blossfeld, 1993). Because attaining an education makes it difficult to take on long-term binding family roles like marriage and parenthood (Marini, 1985) and involves a high degree of economic dependency, educational expansion clearly leads to an increasing postponement of entry into marriage and parenthood across cohorts. Completion of education is an important step in the normative (and economic) conception of the transition to adulthood and in this way, becomes a significant marker for entry into marriage. We therefore hypothesise that finishing school has a strongly positive effect on women's entry into first marriage. Although this relationship should, in principle, also hold for informal cohabitation, this type of living arrangement is less binding and more flexible than marriage. It is easier for young women to enter cohabitation as an 'interim' strategy when they are still at school (Wu, 2000). We therefore expect that the positive effect of completion of education on the rate of women's entry into cohabitation is lower than on marriage.

We also expect this effect to be smaller in the case of East Germany, where educational participation was not incompatible with family formation and where educational attainment quite straightforwardly determined job placement and position. This is because, in the former East Germany, occupations in the labour market were highly structured along educational and vocational certificates (Konietzka & Solga, 1995, Solga & Konietzka, 1999), provided less room for occupational mobility, and income differences were rather small in the occupational structure (Szydlik, 1994). As a result, a postponed entry or a temporary withdrawal from employment would not have strongly harmed women's career prospects, creating little reason to postpone family formation. Furthermore, policies made it easier to combine child-rearing activities with paid employment because of a much higher provision of public day care and women-tailored working schedules (designed to allow women to combine their domestic responsibilities with paid employment, which were not necessarily shared more equitably with men), so that educational participation should not have been particularly at odds with family plans and prospects (Kreyenfeld, 2000).

Hypothesis 8: Educational expansion is expected to translate into a dual effect: an 'enrolment' effect and an 'attainment' effect. Firstly, we expect women's enrolment in education to produce a postponement of partnership formation (negative effect), which should be particularly strong in the case of marriage. This effect should be weaker in East Germany and in the case of cohabitation.

However, because more highly qualified young people postpone the beginning of family formation longer, there is a growing probability that they will then quickly 'catch up' with their contemporaries after leaving school (Blossfeld, 1995; Blossfeld & Huinink, 1991). Thus, if the 'postponement' effect produced by a prolonged educational participation is controlled in the analysis, we expect that women's rate of partnership formation should increase with the increasing level of education. Because it is easier for young women to form an informal partnership during school, we expect that this effect of educational attainment should be smaller in the case of cohabitation.

With regard to the effect of women's educational attainment level on the adoption of cohabitation, Becker's theory implies that women's growing economic independence should reduce the benefits of all types of unions, at least as long as they are based on a traditional gender division of work within the family (Becker, 1981). However, education does also imply a cultural dimension, and thus openness to new behavioural options, as well as readiness to get and process messages about the new arrangement (beside a potentially higher advantage for graduates to cohabit; see Ermisch, 2005). Thus we could also expect that (an increasing number of) women with higher educational attainment levels tend to be more liberal and would therefore be more inclined to adopt new living arrangements. Furthermore, because cohabitation is often coupled with less rigid gender-role expectations (Huinink, 1995), highly educated women should be more interested in adopting this type of arrangement. These different explanations point to both negative and positive effects of educational attainment level on the adoption rate of cohabitation. As a result, the outcome of these competing forces is an empirical question.

Hypothesis 9: Educational attainment should produce a linearly increasing positive effect (due to the 'catching up' after an increasingly prolonged postponement), once enrolment is controlled.

4.5   WOMEN'S EMPLOYMENT AND INCREASING UNCERTAINTY IN THE LABOUR MARKETS

Another fundamental change affecting family formation in Europe since the 1960s has been women's increasing participation in the labour market. However, despite women's growing investment in human capital and new job opportunities, the responsibilities for social reproduction have still remained in charge of young working women (Borchorst, 1993; Olstner, 1994; Olstner & Lewis, 1995). Saraceno (1992, 2003a) stresses how women solve this 'double-burden' conflict between ('their') care responsibilities and paid job, with lower average working hours than men, coupled instead with an overall longer time spent in paid, plus unpaid work (see also Arnalaug, 1990; Finch & Groves, 1983; Hochshild, 1989; Zighera, 1992). It is thus important to reflect on the national-specific degree to which women's paid employment is hindered by domestic and caregiving responsibilities, along with both marriage and, even more markedly, childbirth (Jenson, 1997; Lorber, 1994; Orloff, 2002; Picchio, 1992). This is especially a problem in the Southern European countries where, although new generations of women increasingly combine paid with unpaid work (Daly, 2000a; Hochshild, 1989; Marin Muñoz, 2003), they often still withdraw from employment for child rearing (Saraceno, 2003a). In Table 4.1, some indicators of women's activity in the selected countries for the period under study are presented.

   Table 4.1 shows the steep increase in women's activity rates in all the countries studied, paralleled by a relative decrease in men's rates (originated especially by early retirement). Such an increase has been correlated with

Table 4.1 Selection of Key Employment Indicators for the Period Under Analysis

	Men			Women			Total		
	'75	'85#	'94	'75	'85#	'94	'75	'85#	'94
% activity rate (15–64)									
S	88.7	85.4	80.9	67.4	77.8	76.0	78.2	81.6	78.5
F	83.1	71.9	67.1	48.5	49.3	51.7	65.5	60.4	59.3
D	87.5*	84.9*	81.8	51.0*	54.1*	62.6	68.8*	69.2*	72.4
E	92.9	80.5	77.8	33.1	34.1	45.7	57.0	44.0	46.6
I	81.6	77.1	74.9	32.9	38.2	43.1	56.6	57.2	58.8
% proportion active in the service sector (15–64)									
S	42.4	na	56.3	77.1	na	86.8	57.1	na	71.0
F	na	49.4	57.7	na	73.6	80.8	51.1	59.4	67.9
D	40.1*	44.7*	48.1	60.2*	68.1*	75.8	47.8*	53.8*	59.7
E	34.7	44.7	50.8	52.7	69.3	77.7	39.7	52.0	60.0
I	42.8	51.5	54.6	53.3	64.0	70.4	45.7	55.5	60.2
% unemployment rate (15–64)									
S	1.5	3.0	10.8	2.1	2.8	7.8	1.7	2.9	9.4
F	2.8	8.3	10.5	5.9	12.6	14.5	3.9	10.2	12.3
D	3.0*	6.2*	7.2	3.8*	8.7*	10.1	3.5*	7.2*	8.4
E	4.9	20.1	19.8	3.1	25.0	31.4	4.4	21.6	24.1
I	3.4	5.8	8.8	8.8	13.2	15.8	4.7	8.3	11.4
% youth unemployment (15–24)									
S	na	4.3	13.3	na	4	10.0	na	4.2	11.7
F	na	12.3	10.2	na	14.0	11.4	na	13.2	10.8
D	na	5.9*	5.0	na	6.4*	4.5	na	6.1*	4.8
E	na	24.3	19.3	na	19.7	19.5	na	22.0	19.4
I	na	12.9	12.9	na	13.9	12.5	na	13.4	12.7
Employed part-time (% total employment)									
S	na	6.8	9.1	na	46.6	42.2	na	25.6	25.0
F	na	3.2	4.6	na	21.8	27.8	na	10.9	14.9
D	na	2.0*	3.2	na	29.6*	33.1	na	12.8*	15.8
E	na	2.4	2.6	na	13.9	15.2	na	5.8	6.9
I	na	3.0	2.8	na	10.1	12.4	na	5.3	6.2
% Employed on fixed term contracts									
S	na	na	7.3	na	na	14.4	na	na	12.5
F	na	4.8	9.7	na	4.6	12.4	na	4.7	11.0
D	na	9.2*	9.8	na	11.1*	11.0	na	10.0*	10.3
E	na	14.4	31.4	na	18.4	37.9	na	15.6	33.7
I	na	3.6	6.1	na	7.0	9.3	na	4.8	7.3

Source: European Commission (2000), data from the Labour Force Survey since 1983 (1986 for Spain) and from National Statistics for Sweden (Eurostat).
* These data do not include East German Länder
# Data on fixed-term contract refer to the year 1987

the expansion of the service sector. The table also shows that unemployment rates have increased during the period and that they tend to be higher for women than for men, despite women's already lower participation rates compared to men (with the exception of Sweden). Although unemployment is concentrated among young people, it is here that gender differences are smaller, a first sign that gender differentiation in the labour market might be coupled with family formation. From the table we can also see that part-time employment is an option almost exclusive to women (again less so for Sweden), and that its extension varies greatly across countries, making up over 40% of women's employment in Sweden, followed by West Germany (around 30%), France (over 25%), and with much lower levels in the southern countries (well below 15%).

The generally lower levels of women's activity relative to men's, together with women's overrepresentation in the service sector and part-time employment shown in Table 4.1, suggest how caregiving work has a significant impact on women's employment choices. These figures also reveal how part of this burden may shift from the family (and here the women) to other institutions (i.e., the market and/or the state) in distinct ways in the Nordic countries favouring women's paid employment[8]. Spain and Italy stand out as the countries with the highest female unemployment rates (overall and youth unemployment, also relative to men's rates), accompanied moreover by the lowest women's activity rates. France, Sweden, and Germany, by contrast, have a higher proportion of part-time employment among women (see also Fagan & Rubery, 1996; Rosenfield & Birkelund, 1995). These crude measures already reflect how, due to their commitment to caring responsibilities and reproductive duties, women are far more likely than men to limit (interrupted employment or inactivity) or reduce (part time) their participation in paid work, so as to concentrate on more 'women-friendly occupations' (i.e., the service sector) (see also Jenson, Hagen & Reddy, 1988). Indeed, a large share of women's integration into the labour market has occurred in the service sector, through their employment in reproductive and caregiving occupations, namely healthcare services, education, and welfare (Esping-Andersen, 1993; Ungerson, 1997).

But a note of caution in reading the figures on women's employment from Table 4.1 comes in that crude measures of participation rates hide the real intensity of women's employment and their relative contributions to paid and unpaid labour over the life course (Blossfeld & Hakim, 1997; Daly, 2000a). For this reason, Figure 4.1 presents additional figures on women's labour force participation, calculated as age-based average measures[9] (Thévenon, 2003).

Figure 4.1 again shows how Italian and Spanish women are consistently less often employed, enjoy less flexible working-time arrangements, and suffer more from unemployment than their German or French counterparts[10]. In Sweden, men and women have similar rates of participation, although a substantial share of the latter work part time. Here, however, part-time jobs

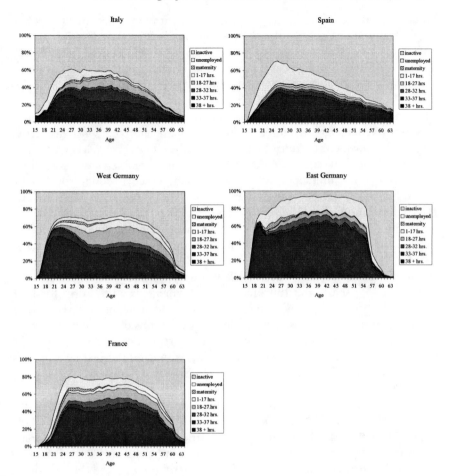

Years 1992-94, own calculations from LFS data (Thevenon 2003).

Figure 4.1 Age-based average measures of women's employment.

tend to be relatively well paid and allow for long hours, which reduces the gender-related earning gap (Borchorst, 1994a, 1994b). Although younger women increasingly work full time, occupational sex segregation is comparatively high (Borchorst & Siim, 1987; Charles, 1992, 2003; Wright, Baxter & Birkelund, 1995), but the status gap between the sexes classifies Sweden as the most egalitarian in terms of occupational prestige, suggesting that it may be easier than in other countries for women to undertake a career or enter prestigious occupations.

France is characterised by a relatively high presence of women in the labour market, just below that of the Scandinavian countries. Here, part-time work is rather frequent for women too, with long part-time hours and a generally high level of job security. Here as before, women's job attachment tends to be continuously pursued over the life course (Figure 4.1). Contrary to the Swedish case, however, in France the gender gap in pay is greater (Daly, 2000a) but occupational sex segregation tends not to be as high (Fagan & Rubery, 1996; Rubery & Fagan, 1995[11]).

West Germany belongs to a distinct cluster of countries in which medium levels of female labour force participation are coupled with distinctive women's and men's pattern of work over the life course (Arber & Ginn, 1995). These differences are due to a reduction in women's working hours (part time) and interruptions of the working career at childbirth and for child rearing (Saraceno, 1997) (Figure 4.1). Maternity leaves are comparatively long and well subsidised (Kreyenfeld, 2003), and part-time activity is strongly regulated and enjoys the same benefits and protection as full-time work, although a proportionately minor compensation (Kurz & Steinhage, 2001; Kurz, Steinhage & Jolsch, 2005).

In the former socialist East Germany, there was a statutory right to work (Kreyenfeld, 2000), and full lifelong employment was the norm for both men and women, whereby women's economic independence received strong support from the state. Women could enjoy guaranteed employment, extensive reproductive control (including free abortion), and state support for the integration of employment with family responsibilities (extensive family leave and free child care) (Adler, 1997; Strohmeier & Kuijsten, 1997). Here, the norm prevailed that all women, including mothers, should participate on a full-time basis in paid employment while responsibility for childcare was assigned to the public domain[12] (Duggan, 1993, 2003; Kreyenfeld, 2000; Rosenberg, 1991). The German Democratic Republic supported children's well-being through their mother's protection, independently of their marital status (Olstner, 2001). Motherhood was generally supported through direct and indirect assistance and incentives: that is, through interest-free loans with debt reduction for each child, housing subsidies and flat grants for each birth, housing preferences for large families and single parents, parental leave, and child allowances (see Winkler, 1990). In addition the gender pay gap was smaller than in West Germany (Sorensen & Trappe, 1995; Trappe & Rosenfeld, 1998, 2000), increasing the share of family income coming from women's employment.

The lowest levels of women's employment are to be found in Italy and Spain (Bernardi, 1999; González, Jurado & Naldini, 2000; Miguel Castaño, 1991). Here, we find the wider tradeoff between family and paid employment for women in the period studied, resulting in a polarisation of women's employment patterns: Women tend either to have a full-time job or not to participate in paid employment at all. The gender pay gap (Altieri, 1992; Daly, 2000a; Peinado, 1991) and gender segregation (Bianco, 1993; Del Boca & Fornengo, 1992; Luciano, 1992; Maruani, 1991) are high, and women's working careers are often interrupted or abandoned over the life course

(Arber & Ginn, 1995; Bettio, 1988). Moreover, Italy and Spain, together with other Southern European countries, are characterised by the highest incidence of irregular employment and self-employment (Esping-Andersen, 1995; Mingione, 1995). Via informal employment relationships, women are still incorporated into the labour market but with less social protection such as maternity leave, sickness benefit, or contribution to retirement schemes and enjoy less protection against loss of employment (e.g., dismissal when pregnant) or guarantee of reinsertion after childbirth. In this respect, the extent of informal economies in Italy and Spain further weakens women's position in the labour market relative to men's.

Some scholars emphasise and value women's *choice* and willingness to withdraw (totally or partially) from employment in order to attend to their families (e.g., Becker, 1981; Hakim, 1997, 2000). Others stress that those *'choices'* are at least in part the product of adaptive preferences inscribed in the context of opportunities and constraints still strongly structured by gender[13]. Gary Becker (1981) claims that women's rising earning power (through higher educational investments and improved career opportunities) lead to a decreasing gain from gender specialisation of work within the family. This would make marriage a setting that is less attractive for both sexes, undermine the stability of ongoing marriages (Wu, 2000), and make young men and women more cautious and reluctant to enter into a marital union. However, Becker's theory implies two contradictory expectations with regard to the diffusion of cohabitation. On the one hand, delayed entry into marriage and increasing divorce rates should increase the relative advantage of informal cohabitation as an interim or generally less binding arrangement (Oppenheimer, 1994, 2000; Wu, 2000). On the other hand, women's growing economic independence and income potential should reduce the benefits of all kinds of union relationships. Thus not only marital but also nonmarital unions should be negatively affected by women's educational attainment level and labour force participation.

However, the traditional gender-role specialisation becomes an increasingly risk-taking strategy without the perspective of a lifelong secure and satisfactory employment and partnership (England, 2000). Oppenheimer (1994) stresses how single-breadwinner nuclear unions are particularly vulnerable to the temporary (through unemployment, illness) or permanent (through separation, death) loss of a unique individual who provides an essential function—at home or in the labour market. From this perspective, women's employment can be viewed as a highly adaptive family strategy in a modern society, rather than as a threat to the union as a social institution (Oppenheimer, 1977, 1997a). And indeed, women in nonmarital and marital unions increasingly work, so that modern societies are progressively transformed from male-breadwinner into dual-earner societies (Blossfeld & Drobnič, 2001; Daly, 2000a).

However interpreted, women's lower attachment to the labour market via part-time and interrupted employment create different circumstances for women and men with respect to current and future economic status and dependence on others' familial (most often the partner's) source of income. First, it undermines women's capacities to claim employment-based benefits in the present and in the future[14]. Second, it also creates higher economic frailty, which makes women more vulnerable to the risk of poverty and dependence on protection offered by their family circumstances: a lower degree of *defamilisation*. 'Defamilisation' is a concept proposed by Lister (1997) and Saraceno (1997), and later adopted by Esping-Andersen (1999, p. 51), to refer to the degree of household responsibility for its member's welfare. Like 'decommodification'[15], defamilialisation refers to individuals' capacity to afford and maintain an autonomous living independently from their family and kin support. In this respect, the forms of partnership young women have entered—either cohabitation or marriage—can constitute very different settings for their future degree of protection against the loss of employment or of their partner[16]. Orloff (2002) identifies Italy and Spain as the countries where there is less support for women's work and where it is most difficult for women to form an autonomous household; Germany is supportive of men's breadwinner position and their wives' caregiving responsibilities (less support is given to women outside marriage); whereas France and Sweden are supportive of women's employment as the basis of household formation.

Women's relative strength and continuity of attachment to the labour market thus suggests that cohabitation be relatively more attractive in Sweden and France (where job attachment is more continuous and protected and caring responsibilities are partly externalised) and less so in the south (where women's activity is still low and their protection comes either from the family of origin or through her husband's employment; see also Daly, 2000b). West German women should be found closer to South European, given the higher legal protection enjoyed in marital unions and a tax system that favours married couples by offering the possibility of *Ehegattesplit-tung*, a (lower) joint taxation (Steiner & Wrohlich, 2004), in the most common case of one partner earning a lower income than the other.

Hypothesis 10: Because low activity and high unemployment means strong dependence on the partner's income, we expect more convenience for Italian and Spanish women for the 'protection' offered by marriage. This effect is expected to hinder the diffusion process in the southern countries, and it should be lower in the case of West Germany because of unemployment benefits and welfare protections. We expect no difference between working and nonworking women's willingness to adopt cohabitation in France, East Germany, and Sweden, where double breadwinning arrangements are the norm.

Yet, what happens when young people's careers begin to be increasingly fragile? Over recent decades, employment careers and opportunities have suffered from growing instability for both men and women, particularly among young labour market entrants (Blossfeld et al., 2005). This has been due to several structural changes that have occurred in the labour markets of modern societies since the mid-1970s and have affected the patterns of female activity described earlier (Blossfeld et al., 2005). Although changes in economic and social life have become faster and less predictable (Sennet, 2001), young people seem to feel the consequences of this growing uncertainty more directly (Mills & Blossfeld, 2001). On the one hand, they are much more exposed to them because they are still unprotected by seniority and working experience. On the other hand, they are also in a formative life phase where they have to make several long-term self-binding commitments (Blossfeld, 2003).

Based on these increasingly conflicting demands on young people, Oppenheimer (1988) interprets the increasing tendency among young adults to opt for cohabitation as a rational response to growing uncertainty. Women's feelings of general economic insecurity and their difficulty envisaging their potential partners' future career prospects may affect their decision making. This uncertainty may render women more reluctant to commit themselves to a long-term binding partnership such as marriage, thereby increasing the perception of a relative advantage entailed in a more flexible living arrangement such as cohabitation.

Recent research has shown that uncertainty in early careers has grown particularly sharply in Italy and Spain (Blossfeld et al., 2005; Mills, Blossfeld & Klijzing, 2005). In Italy young people have suffered the consequences of a progressive erosion of employment protection for new entrants into the labour market and a persistently high rate of unemployment (see also Figure 4.1 and Table 4.1[17]). Aiming to reduce unemployment levels, two reforms in 1977 and 1984 introduced incentives for fixed-term training contracts for young people (Gualmini, 1998), and in 1987 limitations to the general use of fixed-term contracts were relaxed (Bernardi, 2000; Bernardi & Nazio, 2005). These reforms have contributed to the emergence of an insider/outsider labour market that, to a certain extent, overlaps with a cohort division: Members of older cohorts still enjoy permanent contracts and the strong employment protection guaranteed by regulation from the 1960s and 1970s, whereas younger cohorts of entrants in the labour market are more likely to be either unemployed or employed with fixed-term precarious contracts, with lower retributions and lessened entitlements to social protection. Furthermore, in Italy first job seekers and the self-employed are not eligible for any unemployment benefits (Dell'Aringa & Lodovici, 1996).

Since the fall of the regime in 1975, Spain has experienced a fast and intense process of modernisation, accompanied by a sharp increase (and persistency) in unemployment levels concentrated among women and youth (Dolado & Jimeneo, 1997; Maravall & Fraile, 1998). Here, as in Italy, to facilitate an increasingly difficult access to the labour market since 1984, labour policies have introduced measures of deregulation and flexibility in employment. A reform of the Workers' Statute ('Ley de Estatuto de los

Trabajadores,' from 1980) introduced and allowed for a pervasive use of new fixed-term contracts (Cousins, 1994; Morán Carta, 1991) that offset the regulation protecting against dismissal. This measure facilitated a first entry into the labour market but at the price of increasing instability and precariousness, which were not accompanied by targeted measures of social protection (Iannelli & Bonmatí, 2003; Simó et al., 2000; Simó et al., 2001). Thus in Spain, like in Italy, the parental family remained the main institution responsible for supporting young adults until they reach (at increasingly advanced ages) a stable economic independence (Jurado Guerrero, 1995, 2001; Naldini, 2003).

In West Germany, the deregulation of the labour market was first introduced in 1985 by the Employment Promotion Act ('Beschäftigungsförderungsgesetz') in the form of fixed-term contracts. Kurz and others (2005) identify a phase of difficult labour market prospects in Germany during the 1980s, followed by an upward trend from the end of the 1980s up to the early 1990s, and by a tightening of the conditions for labour market entrance and establishment in the 1990s again (Kurz & Steinhage, 2001; Kurz, Steinhage & Jolson, 2005).

This general process of deregulation of the labour markets resulted in increasing uncertainty about future working prospects and economic insecurity for young women in the stage of family formation, thus potentially increasing the relative advantage of cohabitation in the eyes of young women (Oppenheimer, 1988, 1994). However, the impact of uncertain labour market on young people's capacity to form autonomous households should have been different depending on the part played by respective national institutional contexts (Blossfeld et al., 2005). We might expect that the growing economic uncertainty of young people in Italy and Spain (Iannelli & Bonmatí, 2003), coupled with the still low women's labour market participation and the rigidities of the housing market, should translate into a barrier for the diffusion of cohabitation as well as for one-person households among the younger generation (Jurado Guerrero, 1995), a barrier further increased by the governmental shift of the responsibility for the support of the youth to families and kinship networks (Esping-Andersen, 1999; Hobson, 1990; Jenson, 1997; Naldini, 2003; Saraceno, 1994, 1997, 2003b). This lack of defamilisation, by producing a postponement of young people's autonomy from their parental families, should restrain the diffusion of cohabitation among the younger generation. In West Germany and France instead, where affordable housing is available for the young generation and female employment is almost universal among young women, cohabitation should turn out to be an increasingly attractive living arrangement, which allows for the postponement of a long-term self-binding decision such as marriage (Oppenheimer, 1994).

With regard to labour market uncertainty, the situation in the former East Germany was different in the 1970s and 1980s. In the period studied, the socialist German Democratic Republic was characterised by a comparatively high level of individual certainty and life-course predictability (Adler, 1997; Dahlerup, 1994; Rosenberg, 1991; Szydlik, 1994). Secure and permanent employment allowed East German citizens to marry at comparatively younger ages (Huinink & Wagner, 1995; Hullen, 1998, Kreyenfeld, 2000). Because the risk of unsubsidised unemployment did not especially threaten East German women's perspective of their future circumstances, we expect that the fact of being currently employed or not should have been quite an unimportant factor for the adoption of cohabitation or marriage in East Germany, at least up to the German unification.

Unemployment has been quite low (not exceeding 3.5%) in Sweden too, up to the beginning of the 1990s. Here, the rise in women's participation in the labour market took place from the late 1960s and, despite strong gender segregation in employment, women's and men's participation rates have become very similar. Previous results have shown that in Swedish dual-earner society, uncertainty relates more to women's first entry into the labour market or inactivity during the early phase of a working career. In Sweden, it is a lack of attachment to the labour market, more than unemployment, which results in a lower propensity to start a first union for women (Bygren, Duvander & Hullen, 2005). It follows that the effect of being employed before the formation of the first union is expected to have a positive effect on entry into cohabitation, it being the most common form of union.

Hypothesis 11: Employment uncertainty is expected to increase the relative advantage of cohabitation in France, Sweden, and West Germany. It should have no effect in the former socialist East Germany and is expected instead to hinder the diffusion of cohabitation in Italy and Spain.

4.6 AFFORDABLE HOUSING: THE RENTAL MARKETS AND HOME OWNERSHIP

Because independent housing is generally a basic asset for household formation, it can have a strong impact on partnership decisions (Ermisch & Di Salvo, 1997). The choice to take a partner, for example, might be postponed when couples cannot yet afford to buy a house and there is scarce availability of dwellings for rent. In particular, the relative attractiveness of the choice to cohabit as opposed to marry is strongly influenced by the size of financial investment and degree of commitment required by house rental or purchase. Whereas a rental contract can be rescinded at any time, buying a house means a consistent shared long-term financial investment, which is scarcely compatible with a more flexible form of partnership such as cohabitation (Baizán, 2001; Barbagli, Castiglioni & Dalla Zuanna, 2003). It is more marriage than cohabitation, in fact, that encourages the accumulation of pooled savings and joint capital investments by providing greater long-term economic security (Oppenheimer, 2000). Moreover, when familial financial aid is required for young people to afford the purchase of an autonomous dwelling, the decision to marry may be also influenced by the greater parental willingness to help in the case of a formal marriage.

At the individual level, therefore, the relative convenience of different tenure modes is influenced by institutional factors such as the relative size, degree of regulation and control of the *rental sector*; the trends in real *prices* of houses and the circumstances of national *mortgage markets*; as well as by the existence of *tax incentives* and the availability of '*social housing*' for newly formed young families.

With respect to the prevalent tenure mode in the housing market, in the early to mid-1990s the proportion of owner-occupiers varied substantially across the selected countries, ranging from 39% in Germany (43% in the West, 31% in the East in 1999), up to 85% in Spain, with Sweden (53%), France (58%), and Italy (69%) in the middle of the continuum. Conversely, the share of rented dwellings in the total stock of housing in the same period accounted for 14% in Spain, 25% in Italy, 40% in France, 44% in Sweden, 58% in West Germany, and 74% in East Germany, respectively (Direction Générale de l'Aménagement du Territoire, du Logement et du Patrimoine [DGATLP], 2002, p. 34). 'Social' housing[18] in those years accounted for a 2% and 6% of the total housing stock in Spain and Italy, respectively, followed by France and West Germany with 17% and Sweden with 22% (DGATLP, 2002, p. 35). In France and Sweden, 'social' housing is thus a relevant share of the rental sector as opposed to Italy and Spain, where the percentage of social housing in the rental sector in the early 1990s was the smallest (Consejo Económico y Social, 2002). However, all these cross-sectional figures are only the outcome of a falling trend in the supply of rental over owner-occupied accommodation, which has taken place in most European countries over the past 40 years (see Figure 4.2). Exceptions to this pattern are Sweden, West Germany, and, to a lesser extent, France. In the cases of Italy and Spain, this decline has been rather sharp and is mainly attributable to the strict regulation of rental regimes until the late 1980s (European Central Bank, 2003). Thus, particularly in these southern countries, the weight of the rental market is now rather marginal and, we argue, this affects both the timing and mode of access to dwellings for newly formed families. That is to say, that young Italians and Spaniards are confronted with a housing prospect where a squeezed and expensive rental market, together with low and decreasing capital interest rates, makes the option of buying a far more attractive option. In fact, when the rental price to pay exceeds the amount due for the down payment of a mortgage for the same dwelling, it seems rational to opt for purchase. When, moreover, an increase in real housing value is foreseeable (as it has been over recent decades), purchase appears as an active form of investment, despite the degree of commitment that it involves, even when renting would incur much the same, or slightly lower, costs.

Indeed, Spaniards and Italians usually buy property at the very beginning of their autonomous life, in most cases directly after having left (or by

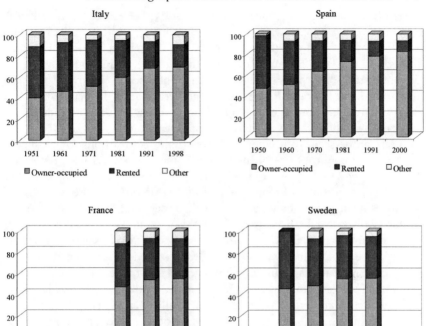

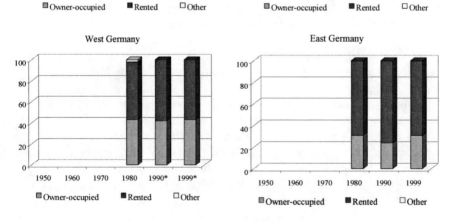

Figure 4.2 Housing tenure of occupied dwellings (Census data, time series 1950–2000).
Sources: Statistics Sweden (Sweden), CES 2002 – INE: Censo de Poblaciòn y Viviendas (Spain), Bernardi and Poggio 2002 – ISTAT (Italy), Housing Statistics in EU 2002 (others).

leaving) the parental home (Chiuri & Jappelli, 2000), an investment generally supported by familial economic aid (Baizán, 2001; Bettio & Villa, 1998). This appears as a distinctive feature of the Southern European housing system (Cabré Pla & Módenes Cabrerizo, 2004; Ferrera & Castles, 1996), in which young people wait longer to acquire a dwelling and to form a new family, through extending their stay in the parental home (Barbagli, Castiglioni & Dalla Zuanna, 2003; Naldini, 2003). Spain and Italy share a similar history of strong regulation of the rental sector, followed by a late and progressive liberalisation, which (together with tax deductions and low interest rates on mortgages) favoured home ownership and resulted in a particularly tight and expensive rental market.

As it can be seen from Figure 4.2, this trend toward home ownership in the Southern countries is a phenomenon of the last few decades. Before the 1960s, homeownership was out of the reach of most families in Spain, when a law ('Ley de Propiedad Horizontal,' 1960) created the legal basis for massive investment in new buildings to be sold as separate flats and apartments. In the 1950s, other legal measures were taken to allow for the sale of a big share of publicly owned dwellings to their permanent tenants at very attractive prices. Since then, home ownership has been boosted by rural migration, lack of effective regulations on urban planning, and substantial price inflation that facilitated mortgages or down payment of loans. To dampen the trend towards purchase, terms and prices for rentals were totally liberalised in 1985 ('Decreto Boyer'), resulting in a steep increase in rental prices. At the same time, the generalisation of direct income taxation to the whole population introduced the possibility of tax deductions for mortgage payments (Cabré Pla & Módenes Cabrerizo, 2004). Tax systems, traditionally more favourable to owner-occupied houses[19], are partly responsible of the shrinking of the rental sector across Europe, especially in the southern countries. In Spain, for example, there are substantial fiscal advantages that encourage home ownership, reduced only recently[20]. Under these circumstances, it is clear that young families will find home ownership (supported by tax deduction) more attractive than renting.

In Italy too, owner-occupation incidence increased from 40% in the early 1950s to about 70% in 1998 (ISTAT, 1999), growing remarkably during the 1970s and 1980s until stabilising during the 1990s (see Figure 4.2). Again, one explanation behind this pattern is the substantial lack of urban planning constraints during the economic boom of the 1950s and 1960s when extensive activities of new house building took place (Bernardi & Poggio, 2004). Only from the 1980s onwards, the common practice of unauthorised self-developed building was strongly restricted. Like the Spanish case, public investments contributed to the expansion of home ownership by means of public dwellings' privatisation throughout the 1950s and 1960s (Bernardi & Poggio, 2004). Moreover, as in Spain[21], in 1978 the Fair Rent Act introduced a regime aimed at controlling rent increases ('Equo Canone,' then completely abolished in 1998) that initiated the collapse of private rental. Some of the unintended effects of this law were to produce numerous evictions at the end of contracts[22], reduce the supply of houses for rent, and promote an informal, unprotected, and rather expensive rental market (Tosi, 1990). As a result, nowadays, only about 20% of the housing stock is rented (4% to 5% of which is in the social sector), and around 10% is occupied free of charge, mainly allocated within the family or informal networks (see Figure 4.2, last column). In Italy, social housing supply has always been marginal in the period analysed here, and targeted in recent decades only to extremely poor households, when little investment has added to its already small size[23]. As a result, young families have completely been excluded from this option (Bernardi & Poggio, 2004; Bernardi & Nazio, 2005). In both these southern countries, despite the presence of regulatory mechanisms and a recent general liberalisation, rental markets have remained effectively segmented and rationed with a part of the market, mainly new prospective tenants, facing increasingly tighter conditions and rapidly rising rents.

In contrast, in France, the proportion of homeowners has remained consistently stable until the 1990s, after having only slightly grown in the 1970s and 1980s. During the 1950s, tax advantages were responsible for favouring ownership[24], but by the 1990s, access to home ownership became less attractive. France also enjoys a generous system of housing allowances paid to tenants as the product of different policy measures[25]. Overall, around a quarter of households are entitled to some type of housing benefit (Balchin, 1996). Here the 'public' rental accommodation represents a big share of the total rental sector (DGATLP, 2002). This country has a long history of strong state involvement in housing, both in renting and owner occupation, through subsidies, tax deductions, land use policies, and financial market controls, which has produced a varied amount of types of grants and benefits (for a detailed treatment, see Balchin, 1996). Social housing was estimated to host around 18% of households in 2000, whereas sales of social dwellings increased significantly only after the mid-1990s (after the period covered in this analysis). Here, rents of existing dwellings are not 'free' to grow, in that they must not exceed a level established by the comparison to similar dwellings[26] (Donner, 2000). This feature has kept the increases in both the private and social rental sectors to a moderate level and helps explain the limited growth of owner occupation. Here, in fact, average real rents have been increasing at about the same rate as general price inflation, in contrast to the owner-occupied sector where prices have risen far more rapidly. To younger generations of French people facing increasing economic uncertainty, the convenience (often subsidised) of renting offers the advantage of flexible, fairly priced accommodation without having to incur the expense and long-term commitment of buying (Meron & Courgeau, 2004). Despite housing prices not having risen dramatically, and the presence of certain fiscal advantages, buying a dwelling does not seem to be particularly attractive in the French context, characterised by a housing system in which many households have a convenient rental alternative to ownership.

In the former socialist East Germany in the 1950s and 1960s, it was very difficult for young people to get access to housing if they were not married. Public housing was planned on the basis of the population needs and provided in accordance to the needs of newly formed families. Formerly, marriage was a precondition to apply for housing so as to leave the parental home and to form an independent household. However, this policy changed in the early 1970s when the German Democratic Republic suffered decreasing fertility rates and launched a programme of social policies that included special measures for lone mothers (Huinink, 1995; Huinink & Wagner, 1995). To increase fertility, the socialist state increasingly allowed unmarried couples to get access to housing and generously supported young unmarried women with children (Huinink & Wagner, 1995; Konietzka & Kreyenfled, 2002; Kreyenfeld, 2004; Kreyenfeld, 2003, quoting Trappe, 1995, and Cromm, 1998), thus creating some incentive to postpone or avoid marriage in the 1970s and 1980s. It is understood that these measures contributed to an increase in the proportion of nonmarital births, the large majority of which occurred indeed among cohabiting couples (Konietzka & Kreyenfled, 2002).

In Sweden, substantial subsidies and tax breaks were given to all tenures between the 1950s and the 1990 to promote new house building and to enable all households to live in their chosen tenure (Ball, 2003). The housing market, however, is still limited by state constraints, specifically related to land supply and rent regulation. Sweden, in fact, has one of the most restrictive systems in rent control, allowing no place for individual negotiation with prospective tenants (European Central Bank, 2003). Here the rents in the private sector (only half of the rental) are freely negotiated but set in the context of average local rents, which are generally determined in the social sector through collective negotiation[27]. In the 1980s, the home ownership rate expanded a little in the context of a newly liberalised mortgage finance market, but—as in France—the rental sector still accounts for a major source of housing for Swedish citizens. A peculiarity of the Swedish housing system is its four-tenure option: private owner-occupation (houses), cooperative ownership[28] (apartments), and private or public rental[29]. The slight increase in owner-occupied dwellings has mainly concerned the cooperative segment, which now constitutes around a third of the stock of owned dwellings, and a similar share to social housing (around a fifth of the total dwelling stock). In addition, low-income households may receive allowances towards the payment of their rents, a measure mainly provided to support young people and families with children. In sum, thanks to state support and a strongly regulated housing market, young Swedes enjoy an affordable and easy access to independent dwelling.

West Germany has one of the most active and liberal rental markets, with no appreciable difference between total rent change charged under (regularly updated) sitting tenants' contracts and new contracts. Here, social housing does not refer only to a specific set of nonprofit housing providers or accommodations but also to a specific subsidy system. In addition to housing provided by publicly owned property companies[30], belonging to social housing are all those receiving both means-tested rent allowances and support to low-income home ownership. Social housing institutions are treated as profit-making entities since the early 1990s, and as their housing stocks gradually stop receiving social subsidies they will expand the private rental stock[31].

Given the high financial investment that house purchase requires, how can young families about to be formed finance their residential independence? The European Mortgage Federation (1997) estimated 'outstanding mortgage loans as a share of GDP' on average between 1986 and 1996 as 56.5% for Sweden, 40% for Germany, 22% for France, and, respectively, 15% and 5.5% for Spain and Italy[32]. These figures point to how the mortgage market has not traditionally been a relevant source in funding home ownership in the southern countries as compared to Central and Northern Europe (DGATLP, 2002). The relatively low mortgage taken up at the national level in Italy and Spain seems to contradict the evidence of a much higher proportion of home ownership. It is counterintuitive given that a sizeable share of the property value must be reserved for down payment by those couples who want to buy themselves a dwelling. This is a relevant amount of money, especially for younger couples who have hardly saved up enough for the down payment[33] and are confronted with an increasingly uncertain labour market where longer time is required to establish the conditions to afford a loan. The capability of young couples to nevertheless access housing, despite a low takeup of mortgages and a progressively weakening position in labour market conditions and chances of entrance, suggests the existence of financial help coming from parents. In Italy and Spain, it is intrafamiliar exchange that most often provides economic support (Barbagli, Castiglioni & Dalla Zuanna, 2003; Bettio & Villa, 1998). It is so that in Southern Europe increasing house prices (Banco de España, 2002; European Central Bank, 2003) translate into a higher dependence by young people on familial financial aid, which in turn may produce partnership postponement and a difficult takeoff for cohabitation. Conspicuous familiar resources are, in fact, more easily activated to support children's decision to ground a 'secure' and 'stable' family, which is to say a marriage (see also Barbagli, Castiglioni & Dalla Zuanna, 2003, pp. 94–104). Parental pressure to marry may indeed be higher in Italy and Spain because it is often accompanied by children's financial dependence for reaching residential autonomy. Incentives toward marital union would thus not only be exercised by parents' (possibly) more conservative views (Castiglioni & Dalla Zuanna, 1997; Dalla Zuanna, 2004) but also by the contractual nature of marriage, which constitutes a better guarantee for the parental investment in their children's housing.

Summing up, a high incidence of home ownership in Southern Europe was the product of institutional characteristics, which made the rental sector unattractive while favouring investment in housing purchase. The most important institutional characteristics have been the functioning of the housing and credit markets, the (lack of) effective housing policies and social housing, and the role played by family support. The outcome has been a reduced rental market that, we argue, acts against the early emancipation of young people and produces a decrease in the degree of advantage of more flexible forms of partnership such as cohabitation. Thus a major barrier for the diffusion of cohabitation in Southern Europe has been the difficulty with which young people could establish themselves in the housing market. Because of extended educational participation and growing difficulties on the labour market, more and more young people therefore stay longer in the parental home (Billari & Ongaro, 1999; Billari et al., 2002; Jurado Guerrero, 2001). In other words, in Italy and Spain living longer in the parental home while striving for a secure position in the labour market and saving for the purchase of a dwelling seems to be more advantageous compared to its alternatives (living independently, cohabiting, or entering a formal marriage). In fact, buying a house involves a huge shared investment and represents (both psychologically and financially) a long-term binding commitment that is not only better disciplined in a marital contract but is also highly inconsistent with more a flexible and reversible arrangement such as cohabitation (Baizan, 2001; Rafóls Esteve, 1998; Saraceno, 2003b; Tosi, 1994). Thus, especially in Italy and Spain, the lack of alternatives to the buying of a dwelling, in combination with the prevalence of a more traditional view of the family, mutually reinforce each other in making marriage a more convenient option for young people.

In West Germany, France, and Sweden, as in other countries of Northern Europe, a significant increase in the number of single households and cohabitation has been observed when young people are attending upper secondary school and universities as well as immediately after graduation (Kuijsten, 1996). In countries with a strong control on rent increases and a high share of social housing, such as France and Sweden, home ownership has not been generally favoured, and affordable rental alternatives are easily available. Here, finding independent housing that is financed through parental support, own (part-time) work, or with the help of subsidies of the welfare state seems to have been less of a problem for young adults (Bygren, Duvander & Hultin, 2005, Corijn, 2001b; Galland, 1997). We therefore expect that in these countries starting informal cohabitation in an independent flat has been comparatively easy, so that the relative advantage of cohabiting compared to marrying should have been substantial.

Furthermore, residential independence should have two other positive effects on the diffusion of cohabitation. First, living apart from the parental family lowers social control, especially in the first phase of the diffusion process when the behaviour is still stigmatised or barely accepted. Second, it signals having already overcome housing obstacles, such as the rent or the purchase of a dwelling. In this sense *living independently* is expected to have a positive effect on entry into cohabitation and should score particularly strong in the Mediterranean countries. On the contrary, residential independence is expected to have a negative effect on marriage entry, insofar as marriage is no longer seen as a means, or a necessary step, for reaching autonomy from the parental family.

Hypothesis 12: Having acquired residential independence from the parental home ('living independently') is expected to have a positive effect on the diffusion of cohabitation and a negative effect on the entry into marriage. Due to the much tighter conditions of the southern countries' housing markets, this effect should be particularly strong in Italy and Spain.

4.7 SUMMARY OF MAIN HYPOTHESES

To summarise, we have suggested a set of 12 hypotheses regarding the effects of individuals' characteristics and the institutional contexts on the adoption of cohabitation rather than marriage. Given the articulated nature of the hypotheses formulated, in Table 4.2 we provide a summary of the expected effects.

Table 4.2 summarizes the effects for the different countries. Positive effects are signalised with "+," "++" when their magnitude is expected to be bigger and "(+)" when they are expected to exercise a moderate or weaker effect. The same convention applies to expected negative effects "–." When no effect is expected a "=" sign is found in the table, whereas "n.a." is used when an indicator for the testing of the respective hypothesis was not available.

Table 4.2 Summary of Research Hypotheses with Regard to the Diffusion of Cohabitation

	Italy	Spain	West Germany	East Germany	France	Sweden
H1: Legal frameworks	--	--	-	=	+	++
H2: Peer group adoption	++	++	+	(+)	+	+
Pre-cohort adoption	(+)	(+)	(+)	(+)	+	n.a.
H3: Religiosity	--	--	-	=	n.a.	n.a.
H4: Pregnancy	++	++	++	+	+	+
H5: Parental divorce	++	++	+	+	+	+
H6: Residence (rural) Region	- - Centre/ South	-	-	-	-	-
H7: Gender roles (employed women)	++	++	+	=	=	=
H8: Educational enrolment	--	--	--	(-)	-	-
H9: Educational attainment	+	+	+	+	+	+
H10: Employment	-	-	(-)	=	=	=
H11: Employment uncertainty	-	-	+	=	+	+
H12: Housing markets	--	--	+	++	+	++

5   Research Design
Combining Micro and Macro in a Comparative Perspective

5.1   TIME AND DIFFUSION PROCESSES

The methodology chosen for empirical research strictly depends on the theoretical approach and the object of study. Given the nature of the research questions, we employ a comparative case study approach that includes six countries[1], chosen for their differences both in the diffusion process (timing, development, and stage) and in institutional characteristics. The analyses undertaken explore the transition out of the parental home, the entry into marriage, and the diffusion of cohabitation at the individual level using event history analysis. Because our focus is on the rise in cohabitation (and decline in marriage) over time in a dynamic population of potential adopters, we must adopt longitudinal methods, which can explicitly recognise and handle the complex time structure behind the diffusion process. Indeed, a key methodological problem in previous diffusion studies has been that time is an essential, although often overlooked, dimension of these processes:

> Time of adoption is often the dependent variable in an analysis, and because the influences on adoption of innovations may occur over time, researchers must deal with time-varying independent variables and covariates. An additional problem is 'right censoring,' which occurs when the data are collected before the diffusion has extended to all members of the community under study. Because of the difficulty of observing such a complex process over time, most diffusion studies have relied on cross-sectional data, which reduce confidence in their results to explain diffusion as a process through time. (Reed, Briere & Casterline, 1999, pp. 8–9)

The fundamental role of time makes cross-sectional measures and standard regression techniques unsuitable instruments of analysis. In fact, cross-sectional measures and statistical models tend to miss both the time order of the events (only previous events can possibly influence later ones) and the time complexity of the process (Blossfeld & Rohwer). We illustrate the latter point with a fictitious example.

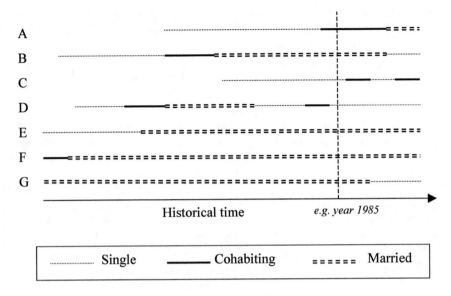

Figure 5.1 Cohabitation experiences and time frame of observation.

In Figure 5.1 we consider an ideal case in which we are interested in following the life trajectories of a set of young persons (let us imagine from 15 to 39 years of age). Let us assume that person A turns 15 and thus enters the period of interest after a few years since the beginning of the observation window. She remains single and exposed to the risk of taking a partner for a while, then meets a suitable candidate and cohabits for a short time, after which she marries. We cannot observe her until 39 because the observation window ends before. Person B follows a similar route (single, cohabiting, and than marrying) but belongs to an earlier birth cohort and thus enters our observation window earlier, takes less time to enter her first partnership (thus enters it at a younger age), and we do observe her for a longer time span. Person C is the youngest among those shown in Figure 5.1 and experiences two cohabitations with a time spell as single in between. She is still cohabiting when we stop observing her. If we are interested in a particular process, for example, entrance into cohabitation, and this event has not yet taken place by the end of the observation window, the history we observe is conventionally termed 'right censored' because we do not observe if (and when) the event of interest will eventually happen. We only know with certainty for how long this event has not happened (yet), like in the case of person C by year 1985. Case D enters a cohabiting union, later transformed into marriage, and a second short cohabitation after the dissolution of her first partnership. The last three persons observed, E, F, and G, are already older than 15 when begun to be observed, and we are not aware of previous spells of cohabitation they might have had (a case known as 'left truncation'[2]). Person E enters marriage directly, F is already cohabiting (we cannot observe for how long, which is termed 'left censoring'[3]) and converts her union into a marriage shortly after we begin to observe, and we see G's marriage dissolving in a divorce or widowhood.

To summarise, in any society by any calendar date there is a *composition* of individuals of different ages in each partnership state, who belong to different birth cohorts, some of whom partner at younger ages than others. Each individual follows a different path and remains in each state differing lengths of time. Under these circumstances, what can we say about how many persons *are* cohabiting at any given point in time? If we, for example, would interview these subjects in year 1985 (vertical line in Figure 5.1), we would observe that only 1 person out of 7 is currently in a consensual union, and 4 are married and 2 are single. Thus, hypothetically, a seventh of the individuals observed are cohabiting. What could we conclude this figure really *means* in terms of underlying processes driving the diffusion of cohabitation, when compared to an estimate taken in a different point in time? In other terms, what could we expect to happen if an increasing delay in partnership formation across birth cohorts would underlie the behaviours of the individuals observed? At the aggregate level this would result in a higher age at partnership entrance, thus in a lower proportion of individuals to be found in a partnership at any point in time. But what would be if this phenomenon was to affect marriage differently than cohabitation? Probably a relative increase in the rate of cohabiting union was to be expected among the younger individuals, which would result in a higher relative proportion of cohabitations over marriage in the figure to be estimated. Or, as a resultant, both partnership forms might be delayed, but with differing strengths, which could obscure or make more pronounced individuals' likelihood to enter cohabitation over marriage, net of the postponement process. Along these lines, what would be instead if cohabitation would increasingly be an option for younger people at any point in calendar time? Or if the age structure of the population would change across time, affecting the age composition of the individuals at risk of entering a partnership? In general terms, it is very difficult, if not impossible, to disentangle these phenomena with cross-sectional data.

It is also important to notice the distinction between how many *are* or have *ever* been cohabiting between 15 and 39 years of age at any point in time. Observing Figure 5.1 in this different perspective would lead us to answer 'at least' 5 out of 7 by year 1985, not knowing entirely the previous history of the bottom three cases. This is the direction in which this work will move, concentrating on the experiences with cohabitation as a way to form the *first* (if ever) partnership. We will concentrate on the first partnership to better capture the novel character of premarital cohabitation and the uncertainty associated to its first adoption by each women. Thanks to retrospectively collected data, which allow a complete reconstruction of respondents' partnership histories, this study also avoids the problem of left censorship and left truncation (like in the case of the last three bottom cases in Figure 5.1).

With some important exceptions and until recently, previous analyses have tended to miss the dynamic nature of cohabitation and have made use of cross-sectional multivariate techniques. However, such techniques may produce biased estimates because they do not take account of the way the length of time that individuals spend cohabiting may vary. At each time individuals with long-term spells of a given behaviour have more probability than others (with short- or medium-term spells) to show up in a cross-sectional sample (Allison, 1984; Blossfeld & Rohwer, 1995b; Duncan, 2000; Duncan & Kalton, 1987). As we saw in Figure 5.1, at any single point in time (whatever chosen) it is more likely to observe people married than cohabiting simply because marriage spells generally have a longer duration. The shorter the duration of cohabiting unions with respect to marriages, the less likely to capture them through aggregate measures computed on cross-sectional observations. This is a bias that cannot be avoided by pooling together different cross-sectional data samples, which do not capture the evolution of a process for the same persons across time. Adding together independently taken 'snapshot' observations allows more robust inference by enlarging the sample size (see Kiernan, 1999, 2004a, reporting estimates on a pooled sample of a series of Eurobarometer data) but does not help reducing the bias of those estimates. Because marriages tend to last longer than consensual unions, a cross-sectional analysis tends to underestimate the real number of cohabitations by capturing fewer of them at any point in time.

Additionally, longitudinal data are much better able to capture social change than cross-sectional data (Blossfeld & Rohwer, 1995b, 1997; Mayer, 1997, 2000; Mayer & Müller, 1996). Cross-sectional data lack variables whose values may change over time and of controls for which event precedes or follows which other. As we have illustrated, this renders them inappropriate to assess theoretical connections accurately between the statistical tools and causality in the social world. In this respect, the advantages of event histories techniques' ability to deal with time varying variables and censored processes[4] help us to draw causal inference. Their properties facilitate explanation by unearthing the mechanisms behind the changes being observed (Blossfeld, 1999; Blossfeld & Rohwer, 1995b, 1997; Hedström & Swedberg, 1996a, 1996b). Indeed, "[T]he explicit aim of life course research is to capture the processes by which social change operates to influence the development and life chances of individuals and by which these developments fit into the reproduction and change of whole social systems" (Diewald, 2001, p. 21).

Longitudinal analysis is required to understand the dynamic relationship between dependent variables and covariates that exists in the diffusion process being studied. In doing so this analysis wants to provide "a bridge between quantitative and qualitative social research" (Mingione, 1999).

This study thus attempts to exploit time-varying covariates and the time order of events along time-depending processes across birth cohorts and over a long period of time to better address causal analysis (Mayer, 2000).

Time dependence is also intrinsic to the process of cohabitation itself. Firstly, the decision to enter a partnership can potentially be taken at any point time in the life course, which means that the pool of potential adopters is highly dynamic over time. Secondly, the length of individuals' exposure to others' practices grows along with their growing older, so that, for example, they observe increasing levels of cohabiting unions over their life course (as we observed in Figures 3.3 and 3.4). Furthermore, often censored histories[5] can be observed in the empirical data. And finally, what are thought to be the 'explanatory variables' are also subject to change with time: for example the progressive educational upgrading and school leaving, the transitions in and out of the labour market, the (possible) transition to residential independence, the (possible) event of a pregnancy, which are considered to be among the most influential factors conditioning women's choice to either marry or cohabit.

Thus a specificity of the analysis presented here is its highly *dynamic* approach that allows for changing in individuals' characteristics and their contexts and comprises a changing population of potential adopters. In this book an individual-level diffusion approach within an event history framework[6] is taken because of both the theoretical approach and because of the dynamic nature of the process under study. Only with a dynamic approach is it possible to disentangle the complexity of the intertwined effects of changes on the micro and macro levels of individuals and contexts that influence young women's choices to cohabit. As we argued, indeed, institutional and social changes at the macro level, together with the system of values regarding the practice of cohabiting and its degree of legitimisation, change as its adoption becomes more widespread. In turn, this makes the decision to cohabit easier for women as this practice becomes more and more widespread.

In sum, several elements point to the need of event history analysis techniques: namely, the existence of time-varying variables capturing individuals' changing characteristics and positions in their social context, the right censoring of the process, the key role of temporal ordering in the life course, and the focus on individual decision making. This framework specifies both individual and aggregate characteristics as time-varying covariates. Their relationship to individuals' risk of adoption of cohabitation is time dependent because both individuals' characteristics, the population at risk of adoption, and the prevalence of the practice with cohabitation do change over time.

5.2   TIME AND VARIABILITY IN INDIVIDUALS' CHARACTERISTICS AND CONTEXTS

A further aspect already touched on in chapter 3 is that 'structural' and 'diffusion' explanations cannot be considered as separate accounts of the phenomenon. This is a point that has obvious implications for the choice of an analytical model, which should be able to disentangle these effects from one another. In chapter 3 we argued that the (uneven) rise in cohabitation could be attributed to both structural changes and to the diffusion process. Structural transformations are the engine of an increasing need for an alternative (and more flexible) partnership form such as cohabitation. Diffusion may sustain and speed up its emergence and spread by altering the degree of perceived advantage at the individual level, raising awareness about its being a viable or more convenient alternative option to a direct marriage (through social influence), as well as by setting the ground for further structural transformations in adjustment to its prevalence (feedback effect).

As illustrated in chapter 3, the adoption of cohabitation (before entry into marriage, if it ever occurs) is a very specific type of diffusion process for two reasons. First, because it takes place in a relatively short life-course window into which different generations co-transit at differing ages. Second, because the pool of potential adopters is highly variable: Younger birth cohorts progressively enter this life-course window while older cohorts exit it, each cohort with different speeds and proportions, depending on their mating processes. In particular, we hypothesise and test two different mechanisms that drive the diffusion of informal cohabitation in the population: 'knowledge-awareness' and 'direct social modelling.' At each point in time, *knowledge-awareness* is measured by the cumulative proportion of prior adopters from previous birth cohorts at each age, and *direct social modelling* is measured as the cumulative proportion of prior adopters belonging to the women's own birth cohort at each age (as described in chapter 3).

Detecting and testing the mechanisms driving diffusion processes is a challenging task. The first major difficulty arises from the presence of feedback effects[7], which require the disentangling of the distinct roles of social influence and structural changes on the adoption of cohabitation. This problem is also connected with the difficulty of observing, and measuring, the impact of social influence on people's behaviours directly[8] (Palloni, 2001). Thus a first methodological obstacle in the analysis of the diffusion processes lies in the measurability and in the interdependence of the various elements that may have an effect on the rate of adoption of an innovative practice over time (Rogers, 1985). In the model proposed, we tackle this issue through taking into account the complex time structure of the diffusion process and link it to individuals' changing characteristics in predicting their behavioural choices. We model individuals' likelihood to adopt cohabitation through time-varying variables capturing their (changing) individual characteristics, interpreted in the light of their respective institutional contexts. In a second step, we than test the effect of behavioural models and reinforcement influences through the two diffusion covariates illustrated, which describe what might be relevant others' *previous* experiences with cohabitation on individuals' decisions.

A second recognised difficulty in the study of diffusion processes is the role of unmeasured heterogeneity in producing a negative effect on the time dependence of the process[9]. This means that those women whose unmeasured characteristics are associated to a lower propensity to cohabit (or marry) will tend to stay longer in the risk set while others will progressively exit. Staying longer in the pool of potential adopters translates in an increasing proportion of "more resistant" women. This reads as if the risk of cohabiting would decrease over time, rather than a progressive concentration of women within the risk set who were less likely to cohabit in the first place. However, this is a concern that affects more those transition rate models trying to account for individuals' heterogeneity while estimating the hazard rate of the population-level diffusion process within a fixed population of potential adopters. Instead, in the diffusion model proposed here, it is *individuals'* changing likelihood to adopt cohabitation over time that is modelled as being (socially) influenced (also) by others' people previous behaviours. In the case of the diffusion process of cohabitation, which is characterised by a highly dynamic pool of potential adopters and is modelled in a competing risk framework[10], the bias caused by unobserved heterogeneity producing a negative time dependency on the hazard rate should be much less severe. In fact, those women more resistant to opt for cohabitation may nevertheless exit the risk set by marrying while new potential adopters will increasingly enter the risk set with the inflow of new birth cohorts getting ready for partnering across time.

We thus argue that a dynamic event history analysis covering a seemingly long time span, comprising several consecutive birth cohorts and framed in a cross-countries comparative study, may help in overcoming at least some of these difficulties. Indeed, the proposed model offers the capacity to account adequately for the complex time structure of the process while maintaining the focus on individuals' decision-making processes and incorporating the effects played by both different (and changing) institutional contexts, social influences exercised by other's behaviours, as well as differing individuals' characteristics.

5.3   SELECTION OF COUNTRIES: SAMPLE AND DATA

This cross-national comparative diffusion analysis is based on retrospective life history data from the Fertility and Family Surveys (FFS) project (Festy & Prioux, 2002; Klijzing & Cairns, 2000; Klijzing & De Rose, 1999), which contain information on the timing of recorded past life histories of sampled individuals. These databases cover 24 industrialised countries and provide internationally comparable data, which are to a large degree based on a common questionnaire (Klijzing & De Rose, 1999). Common problems in retrospectively collected data are that information is collected only on survivors and nonmigrants, and that misreporting might result from memory or recall problems of past life events. However, despite retrospective collected information suffer from a higher recall bias than panel data[11], we believe this drawback is more serious with respect to short spell duration (like job careers) than the partnership histories that are the object of interest here. We do so because the low number, the psychological meaning, and the organisational impact on people's lives, as well as the ceremonies attached to family-related events, play an important role in remembering the date of these events[12]. Checks with external data sources have shown that FFS data are quite reliable in producing estimates about fertility rates (Festy & Prioux, 2002). Overall, retrospective collected information offer the great advantage of providing comparable information on an entire set of birth cohorts for the period of interest across different countries covering a rather long spell of time (around 30 years).

We separately reconstructed the different parallel careers of each woman (i.e., partnership, fertility, educational, and working histories) in a way that rendered them comparable across countries[13]. The different careers were merged together in the creation of a single file for each country, in which all the histories and trajectories contributed to the making of a unique episode file with time-varying covariates capturing variation in women's circumstances along all dimensions of interest (Table 5.1 reports the number of spells[14] created after the splitting in this last file.) The age- and cohort-specific diffusion measures developed were then correspondingly matched to the records of this file. In other words, we created a series of data sets that tracked sequentially all the key educational, partnership, fertility, and labour career events in respondents' lives. We than matched the diffusion indicators to each of the records of these data sets correspondingly to the country, age, and birth cohort of the individuals in each spell.

As already mentioned in the previous chapters, six different institutional contexts are studied making use of the national FSS data sets: West Germany, East Germany, Italy, Spain, France, and Sweden[15]. The period covered in the analysis ranges from the late 1960s to the early 1990s, a time span when major changes in family formation through cohabitation took place in Europe with the exception of the Nordic countries, where the diffusion of cohabitation began somewhat earlier.

A common sample of women born between 1954 and 1973 was selected in each country, whose educational, employment[16], fertility, and partnership histories were observed for each birth cohort from age 15 up to an event of entry into cohabitation or, for right-censored cases, up to the date of entry into a marital union or the date of interview or age 39, whichever occurred first. East and West Germany were treated as two distinct countries because of their different political history between 1949 and 1990.

The fieldwork took place in the early 1990s in all the selected countries: between May and September 1992 in Germany, between October 1992 and May 1993 in Sweden, between January and April 1994 in France, between June and October 1995 in Spain, and between November 1995 and January

1996 in Italy. The age span of the national samples also vary a little (Festy & Prioux, 2002), which led to the selection of a common sample of women aged 15 to 39 and born between 1954 and 1973 in each country. After birth cohort selection, cleaning and consistency checks, the histories of 2,597 Swedish, 2,144 French, 2,497 West German, 2,555 East German, 2,735 Spanish, and 3,234 Italian women were retained for analysis (Table 5.1).

In each column of Table 5.1, the number of events experienced by the selected common samples of women are shown (columns 2 to 4), for each destination state in the two transitions analysed. In between brackets, in the second column, are also shown the number of spells created for the analyses. The second column reports the number (and percentage) of transitions to the single state when leaving the parental home (between brackets, in the last two columns, are the absolute numbers of direct moves into a partnership). The right-hand columns report the number and proportion of entries into cohabitation or marriage. So, for example, of the 2,597 Swedish women in the sample, 1,500 (62%) exited the parental home by the time of interview, out of which 819 for a direct entry into a cohabiting union, 97 for marrying, and 584 (the remainder) to be living independently as single. Overall, in Sweden by the time of interview, 2,133 women had entered a cohabitation (92% of the women in the sample who formed a first partnership) and 183 (8% of the ever partnered) a marital union.

Besides partnership histories, the FFS data contain detailed fertility, occupational and educational trajectories, as well as information on religiosity (with the exception of France and Sweden) and, in the case of Italy, region of residence. These data sets thus allow us to conduct a comparative individual-level study of the process of diffusion of cohabitation among successive generations of young women in these countries.

Table 5.1 Selected Sample Individuals and Number of Events for Each Destination State

	Sample (spells)	Single (% exit)	Cohabitation (direct) (% 1st part.)	Marriage (direct) (% 1st part.)
Sweden	2597 (26059)	1500 (62%)	2133 (819) (92%)	183 (97) (8%)
France	2144 (21399)	749 (39%)	1287 (697) (70%)	560 (453) (30%)
West Germany	2497 (25750)	1031 (52%)	895 (485) (58%)	638 (448) (42%)
East Germany	2555 (30068)	726 (36%)	868 (512) (44%)	1092 (788) (66%)
Spain	2735 (31369)	344 (15%)	257 (143) (12%)	1914 (1725) (88%)
Italy	3234 (37643)	374 (16%)	214 (136) (9%)	2072 (1856) (91%)

5.4 EVENT HISTORY ANALYSIS AND DIFFUSION APPROACH: THE MODELS

In the past, diffusion processes have been generally formulated in terms of population-level 'epidemic' models (Diekmann, 1989, 1992; Mahajan & Peterson, 1985). This type of analysis assumes that all members of the population are exposed to the same level of previous adoption at each point in time. It also assumes that individuals have the same chance of influencing and being influenced by each other (Strang & Tuma, 1993). However, the assumption of homogeneous mixing, whereby every individual are equally influenced by any other previous adoption, does often not hold in empirical applications (Strang, 1991; Strang & Tuma, 1993). Moreover, a dynamic population, whereby entries and exits from the risk set take place at different times, implies differing exposure to the diffusion process. In other words, not all individuals in each given year are witnessing the same levels of cohabiting unions. They will instead be exposed to different rates of previous experiences with cohabitation among different reference groups[17]. For these reasons we propose not to estimate population-level models but to turn to individual-level models of diffusion as suggested by Strang and Tuma (1993)[18]. In these models, the individual's rate of adoption of cohabitation can be estimated as a function of other actors' prior adoptions in the social system. In methodological terms, this type of model is particularly attractive for our analysis because it allows us to incorporate the effects of time-constant and time-varying individual heterogeneity that may affect the 'intrinsic' propensity of women to adopt cohabitation. Thus they allow for heterogeneity both within the pool of potential adopters and for this to change over time. We also can test ideas about structures of communication and structural equivalence (see Strang & Tuma, 1993) or, more precisely, the effects of knowledge-awareness and direct social modelling (as discussed in chapter 3). A simple individual-level based diffusion model might be formulated in the following way (Strang & Tuma, 1993, p. 619):

$$1 \qquad r_n(t) = \exp(\alpha) + \sum_{s \in S(t)} \exp(\beta)$$

where $r_n(t)$ is the propensity that an individual moves from nonadoption to adoption at time t, α represents an individual 'intrinsic' rate of adoption by effect of individual characteristics or of common environmental influences (that can alter women's willingness to adopt cohabitation), $S(t)$ consists of the theoretically relevant set of prior adopters, and β is the effect of the intrapopulation diffusion process on the rate of individual adoption. Thus this type of model combines both individual heterogeneity and the contagious influences of previous adopters on nonadopters and allows us to model diffusion within an event history framework.

As detailed in chapter 3, the decision process to adopt cohabitation (before entry—if ever—into marriage) is the resultant of a very specific type of diffusion process. A fundamental characteristic of this process is that for each birth cohort the time span of potential adoption is highly concentrated in the life phase of transition from youth to adulthood. Across historical time there is a continuous succession of birth cohorts moving through this life-course window. In our analysis the observation of the diffusion process begins for each birth cohort of women at age 15 and ends with the event of entry into cohabitation, or for right-censored cases, with the date of entry into a marital union or the date of interview or age 39, whichever occurs first.

Over the life course of young women, the readiness to enter a union is highly time dependent and governed to a large extent by women's age and by organisational rules and institutional structures of the educational and employment systems (Blossfeld, 1990; Marini, 1984, 1985). In our model these influences are controlled for with a series of time-constant and time-dependent covariates affecting the intrinsic propensity of women to partner. In particular, we take into consideration women's changing age, their time-dependent enrolment in the educational system, the associated progressive upgrading of their educational attainment levels, their changing employment participation (and acquired work experience), as well as events in other domains of their lives such as experiencing a pregnancy or gaining residential independence from the parental home. The α term defined in equation (1) is therefore substituted by $\alpha'x(t)$ in (2), incorporating time-constant and time-varying individuals' heterogeneity at the micro level, which might affect women's likelihood to adopt cohabitation.

By the combination of a diffusion perspective in the event history analysis framework, we want to allow for the combination of heterogeneity in individual-level characteristics with the social influence exercised by others' previous adoptions of cohabitation (Braun & Hengelhardt, 2002; Palloni, 2001). As described in chapter 3, we assume two different mechanisms, which are driving the diffusion of informal cohabitation in the population: knowledge-awareness and direct social modelling. At each point in time t, *knowledge-awareness* (P_c) is measured in this study by the cumulative proportion of prior adopters from *previous* birth cohorts at each age, and *direct social modelling* (P_g) is measured as the cumulative proportion of prior adopters belonging to *the women's own* birth cohort at each age. The essence of these indicators is to capture the proportion of previous experiences with premarital cohabitation made by young women's peers and by older generations. We argued that these experiences can convey social influence in that they provide information about the spread and rationale of cohabiting, the social stigma associated to doing it, and about its potential outcomes.

To allow for the nonlinearity in the relationships between these indicators and the rate of adoption over time, we made use of a third-degree polynomial[19] (see also Nazio & Blossfeld, 2003). This specification was selected among various functional forms as the theoretically most satisfying and statistically best one (in terms of likelihood ratio tests, see Blossfeld & Rohwer, 2002, p. 98). We can then replace the β term of (1) by the following combination of these two factors:

$$2 \quad r_R(t) = \exp\left(\alpha' x(t)\right) * \exp\left(\beta_1 P_g + \beta_2 P_{g^2} + \beta_3 P_{g^3}\right) * \exp\left(\gamma_1 P_c + \gamma_2 P_{c^2} + \gamma_3 P_{c^3}\right)$$

This individual-level diffusion model does not require the assumption that diffusion occurs only through interpersonal contacts. As discussed in chapters 2 and 3, it is not only direct conversation and immediate personal contacts to near peers that count but also the *perception* of what constitutes an appropriate practice for people of the same age ('structural equivalence'; see Burt, 1987). There is accordingly no assumption of a complete mixing of social members that would imply that there is a generalised, direct pairwise interaction between prior and potential adopters. Rather, a distinction between individuals is made on the basis of their age and birth cohorts in defining the diffusion covariates in the model (as detailed in chapter 3). This model also does not make the assumption that there is a constant and permanent ceiling on the number of potential adopters in the social system[20]. The number of potential adopters is rather changing over time because there is a continuous inflow of new birth cohorts of women entering into the risk set. In addition, there is no implicit assumption that the innovative behaviour does not change its meaning over the diffusion process. Instead, we assume that the meaning and character of cohabitation is subject to change along with the diffusion process (Manting, 1996) and that knowledge-awareness and direct social modelling might thus change their effects over time.

A piecewise constant exponential hazard rate model[21] was chosen, in a competing risk framework, because cohabitation and marriage constitute alternative choices in the process of family formation. This means that both women's marriage rate and women's rate of adoption of cohabitation were estimated and that women were simultaneously considered at risk of making either choice until they entered their first partnership. Using the same covariates, we can compare the effects of these variables on the marriage rate and the rate of adoption of cohabitation between transitions and across countries.

In the case of first partnership, the dependent variable is the monthly hazard rate at which a union will be entered into an infinitesimally small age interval, given that it has not yet occurred before the start of that age interval. Multivariate models, among which hazard ones, point to the effect of each variable onto the instantaneous probability of a change occurring onto the dependent variable (the event of interest), net of (taking account of) the effects of other independent variables tested in the model. A positive estimated coefficient indicates a higher risk of experiencing an event associated with a unit change in the value of that variable; the bigger the coefficient, the higher the risk of an event occurring. A negative coefficient, on the contrary, points to a lower risk of experiencing the event of interest. A higher risk might either indicate a slower entry (postponement) or a final overall lower probability of an event occurring (Bernardi, 2001b). Despite this semantic ambiguity, however, because we know the vast majority of young women will eventually enter their first partnership (see also Figures 2.1 and 6.4), we suggest interpreting the estimated coefficients as pointing more likely to postponement effects.

With respect to the adoption of cohabitation, we have chosen to present the main results in two separate models (see Table 6.4 in the next chapter). In model 1, we regressed[22] the event of entry into cohabitation on women's time-varying characteristics, without controlling for their social embeddedness through other people's examples of practice with cohabitation. In model 2, we introduced the variables capturing others' previous adoptions, thus testing for the effect of the decision to enter in cohabitation with reference to social influence. The estimates proved rather robust across the two models. The introduction of both covariates was meant to consider simultaneously both sources of social influence (Greve, Strang & Tuma, 1995) and provided an easy way to establish some evidence concerning the strength and importance of the two mechanisms onto individuals' rate of adoption. Alternative models[23] proved that results maintained robust across different specifications.

5.5   INTERDEPENDENT PROCESSES

A causal approach to data analysis seeks to determine the effect of the occurrence of an event in one career on the rate of occurrence of another event in a different career. The micro-level investigation of the outcomes of individuals' decision making under changing circumstances aids the understanding of those mechanisms and processes that, through individual action and interaction, shape the changing characteristics of societies (Blossfeld, 1999). By focussing on individuals' decisions under changing circumstances, we strive to detect those mechanisms that affect the emergence of cohabitation among groups of individuals and/or at the societal level (Blossfeld et al., 1999).

In fact, certain events in people's life, like in our case partnership formation, may be influenced by happenings in other life domains. For example, an unplanned pregnancy may accelerate entry into co-residential union with the partner or marriage (for an analysis of 'shotgun weddings,' see Mills, 2000). Indeed, nonmarital conceptions have historically precipitated marriages (Akerlof, Yellen & Katz, 1996; Brien, Lillard & Waite, 1999; Goldscheider & Waite, 1986). It is important to uncover and control for these mechanisms to reduce the bias in estimates. In the statistical models, we also control for the interdependent processes of entrance in a union and fertility by estimating the direct effect of an ongoing pregnancy on the rate of entry into a first partnership (a similar approach was implemented by Blossfeld, Manting & Rohwer, 1993; Blossfeld et al., 1999; Blossfeld & Mills, 2001; Mills, 2000). A pitfall of this approach is that it does not account for inter-dependent processes being governed by unmeasured characteristics (e.g., specific individuals' values and attitudes or constant determinants shared by the two events) or by a further intervening process (e.g., enrolment in edu-cation or participation in the labour force) on which they might be jointly dependent (Mills, 2000). A very recent statistical approach to the study of interrelated behaviours suggests the estimation of 'simultaneous (hazard) equation models' to solve this problem. These models can explicitly take account both of the heterogeneity across individuals, due to unmeasured factors, and of the correlation across processes (Brien, Lillard & Waite, 1999; Lillard, 1993; Lillard &Waite, 1993). This method accounts for the simultaneity of a set of related processes, explaining the endogenicity of each outcome in estimating its effect on the others, and it can account for processes of self-selection into specific states (Lillard, Brien & Waite, 1995). In other words, these models take into account that certain events are endo-geneity related to each other. That is to say that one event can have a direct effect on the likelihood of the other event taking place or that both events may be codetermined by (unobserved) individuals' traits.

For example, for some women an exit from the labour market may be endogenous to a childbirth event and, reciprocally, the decision to give birth may be affected by her readiness or willingness to leave the labour mar-ket. Estimating these two processes simultaneously would help account for individuals' unobserved heterogeneity and point to a potential bias in the parameter estimates of each single process[24]. In the processes of interest here, we could think that individuals more prone to early parenthood may be less strict with their contraceptive choices, more likely not to terminate an unexpected pregnancy, and also more likely to marry directly rather than cohabit. Alternatively, we could imagine those couples more keen to accel-erate entry into a union to be more willing to relax the measures aimed at avoiding undesired pregnancies or to favour less reliable methods.

However, in this study, given the already high degree of complexity of the model proposed, we only concentrate on the direct effect of a pregnancy on union formation, relying on the time order of the events to explore causal-ity (Blossfeld & Rohwer, 1997). We interpret the effect of a pregnancy on the decision to enter a union because the effect of a pregnancy on entrance into a partnership has a very limited and specific time frame (between its discovery and the birth of the child). Given the time lag from conception to the moment when a woman realises she is pregnant, and given the minimum (also legal) time required for the organisation of a marriage or adaptive housing arrangements, the coefficient estimates for these control variables for the first 2 months since conception should be read with caution because they may be biased[25].

5.6   THE VARIABLES EMPLOYED

The analyses used monthly time-varying controls at the individual level for age, being enrolled in education (before leaving the educational system), changing educational attainments, being employed (against being unemployed or inactive)[26], labour force experience (cumulated number of months of employment since first job), an indicator for the presence of a nonmiscarried pregnancy (Blossfeld et al., 1999), and a control for the state of residential independence from the parental home (*'living independently'* distinguishes the time after having left the family of origin). To introduce these time-dependent measures into the rate equation, we used the method of episode splitting (Blossfeld et al., 1989, Blossfeld & Rohwer, 1995b).

Several time-constant controls were also inserted: birth cohort, religious affiliation (not available for France and Sweden), region (in the case of Italy), size of the locality where brought up (at age 15), and an indicator for having been brought up in a broken family (Clausen, 1991; Corijn, 2001b). The following paragraphs describe the variables used in the hazard rate models in more detail.

Because age is a variable clearly related to the risk of entering a partnership, we chose a powerful and flexible control for the age effect. We can imagine the risk of partnering associated to age as bell shaped: increasing since the entrance into the risk set at age 15, for reaching a maximum at a certain age after which it levels off and decreases at an accelerating rate. This is because with growing older there is an increasing number of potential mates getting ready for partnering and because the efficiency of successful completion of partner selection increases with time and the accumulation of mating experiences. However, after a certain age, the longer the time, the more likely are nonpartnered individuals to remain those less willing or able to partner. At the same time, the availability of attractive and suitable candidates in the marriage market will have shrunk accordingly, lowering the risk of union formation. We used a combination of two variables to control for this well-known nonmonotonic *age dependence* of the rate of entry into first marital and nonmarital partnerships (Bloom, 1982; Coale, 1971). Accordingly, the rate of entering first union was expected to increase with age up to a certain point and then decrease (Lillard, Brien & Waite, 1995). This approach assumes that women are at risk of entering first marriage or premarital cohabitation between the ages 15 and 39 and specifies the following two time-dependent covariates (Blossfeld & Huinink, 1991; Blossfeld & Rohwer, 1995a):

$\log(\text{current age}-15)$,

$\log(39-\text{current age})$.

These variables, introduced as time-dependent covariates in the rate equation, model the typical bell-shaped curve of the rates of entry into first union. This curve is symmetric around age 27 when the estimated coefficients have an equal magnitude, right skewed when the former exceeds the latter (union formation is clustered more around older ages), and left skewed in the reverse case (partnership entrance is clustered below the mean age).

Religiosity was measured through a dummy variable, which takes value '1' if the woman declared herself as being either 'very' or 'little' religious as against 'not' being religious. Controlling for religiosity aims at accounting for the decline in organised religion and rise in secularisation witnessed in many countries (Surkyn & Lesthaeghe, 2004), which might contribute to a rise in the adoption of cohabitation. Religion is generally found to be negatively associated with cohabitation and positively with marriage (Thornton et al., 1992). However, the estimates of this variable should be interpreted with caution because it was only measured at the time of the interview (see also Manting, 1996). A similar caution must be applied with regard to *region*, which in the case of Italy was also recorded at the time of the interview (the north is the reference category in this case).

We also used the variable place of *residence* at age 15, to control for the size of the urban centre: The reference category is *rural* or up to 10,000 inhabitants, *middle-size city* comprises between 10,000 and 100,000 inhabitants, and an urbanization above this size is defined as *large city*. These dummy variables are used to capture social control and the effect of urban contexts on the spread of cohabitation. Living in a more populated area affords more opportunity for alternative lifestyles and, possibly, less social control (Glick & Spanier, 1980), whereas having been brought up in a smaller or rural area may result in a lessened exposure to innovative behaviours and thus a more traditional lifestyle or a lower tolerance to alternative living arrangements.

To study continuous changes across birth *cohorts*, we introduced a set of yearly based dummy variables in the transition rate models. In the Swedish case, due to the sampling strategy adopted (Festy & Prioux, 2002), only four selected birth cohorts were available for comparison.

To measure the accumulation of women's qualifications in the school, vocational training (in the case of Germany), and university systems, we updated time-dependent dummy variables indicating *women's educational attainment level* at specific school durations (see Blossfeld & Huinink, 1991). Educational attainment levels were reconstructed along different educational careers on the basis of the average length taken to achieve each of the respective subsequent attainments. This strategy has been argued to produce valid, accurate, and comparable indicators (Selden, 1992). For each country, the recording of educational episodes has been coherently modelled on its corresponding national specific educational system. The upgrading of the attainment levels is triggered by the successful completion of the corresponding level, whereas the spells of education that were not successfully terminated by the respondent (abandonment or failure to attain a certain level) do not originate upgrading. When the month of completion of an educational episode was not recorded, the finishing date of the educational spell for that year was set at June. When the date at which a completed educational episode was not given, it was estimated and reconstructed backwards from the information about the level being reached[27]. For those individuals whose part, or all, of their educational history was missing, the career was retrospectively reconstructed from information on the highest level attained, or from the date at leaving the educational system, on the basis of the average number of years required to obtain the corresponding qualification (Blossfeld & Rohwer, 1995b).

In the FFS data sets, educational levels are recorded using the ISCED-97 code (OECD, 1999). To facilitate cross-country comparison, three educational attainment levels were distinguished in the model[28]: *compulsory education* (reference category, 8 to 10 years of schooling), *secondary education* (11 to 13 years) and *tertiary education* (14 to 18 years).

Enrolment in the educational system was controlled by the time-dependent dummy variable '*enrolled in education,*' which indicates whether or not a woman is still studying at a specific age. This variable was coded '1' while a woman was still enrolled in education, and it switched to '0' from the time she left the educational system.

Women's labour force participation was included with a time-dependent dummy variable indicating in each month whether she was *employed* (value '1') or not (being out of the labour force or unemployed) at a specific age. In the case of France, however, not all the employment career was recorded through the interview. Only information referred to the initial and last (at the time of the interview) episodes of women's labour career were available. For this reason, a different specification was chosen with the introduction of a control for the missing information. As a result, the reference category for this variable shifts from "not working" (either unemployed or inactive) to "never having worked" in the French case.

The introduction of a further indicator related to the working career permitted us to test for the effect of *accumulated employment experience* thorough the life course. This was done through the inclusion of a variable measuring the cumulated number of years of total employment in any job held before the current spell. This indicator does not reset at each beginning of a new employment episode and holds constant (but positive) for periods of unemployment or inactivity between successive jobs. Although it is expressed on a year basis in the model, it was measured and built at a monthly level. This indicator aimed to capture the opportunities women face in the labour market and their degree of investment in it as represented by the length of their attachment.

To model the time lags between the effect of a nonmiscarried *pregnancy* and the entrance into a first union, a series of time-dependent dummy variables was created. As described in the previous section, they were aimed at capturing the direct effect of a woman's fertility career on union formation. Reference categories for this set of dummy variables are those periods before a pregnancy took place (and then again from 6 months after a childbirth for subsequent pregnancies). These dummies are based on the entire fertility history of the women under analysis, before the entrance into a first union, and thus updated at any subsequent pregnancy[29].

With respect to interdependent careers, women can leave the parental home while single persons or to enter a partnership. This decision can be driven by a desire for independence or be linked to reasons pertaining to other interwoven life-course domains (such as pursuing a specific educational opportunity or entering a job). Those women who continue to live in the parental home may be more traditional because of a process of self-selection or else they may be more exposed to the norms and values of their parents. On the contrary, living alone affords more autonomy and freedom from parental views (Barbagli, Castiglioni & Dalla Zuanna, 2003; Dalla Zuanna, 2004; Goldscheider & Waite, 1986). However, Liefbroer (1991) argues that entering a partnership (including marriage) may also be a route to independence for those living in the parental home. This might be especially the case in more traditional societies, where living as a single person is not encouraged, particularly for women. The dummy variable '*Living independently*' was constructed as a time-varying indicator of women's residential autonomy from the parental home. It was assigned the value of '1' starting from the month *after* the exit took place and was meant to capture, on the one hand, the effect of greater independence and economic autonomy and, on the other hand, to be used as an indicator of having overcome possible housing difficulties. Because the transition out of the parental home and entrance into first partnership may often coincide in the same 'event,' to avoid bias in the estimates it changes value only *after* residential autonomy has taken place. In addition to this indicator, a variable controlling for the number of years (measured in months) from the acquisition of first residential independence was introduced in the models.

Table 5.2 reports some descriptive statistics for the dependent and independent variables used in the statistical models for the six countries. Statistics for time-varying variables are calculated at the time of entrance into first partnership or at time of interview (or age 39) when right censored. Relative proportions (percentages) are given for the frequency of each dummy variable (and set of dummy variables) inserted in the models. For metric variables, arithmetic mean and standard deviation (in brackets) are indicated instead of percentages.

Now we are proceeding to the testing of the model and in chapter 6 the results will be illustrated for the transitions out of the parental home, the entry into marriage, and the diffusion of cohabitation in each of the countries studied. We will discuss and compare the empirical evidence as against the effects expected on the basis of the set of hypotheses developed in the previous chapter.

Table 5.2 Descriptive Statistics for the Dependent and Independent Variables

		Sweden	France	West Germany	East Germany	Spain	Italy
Destination state	Censored (at interview)[a]	10.82	13.85	36.81	23.29	20.62	29.31
	Entered cohabitation[a]	82.13	60.03	35.84	33.97	9.40	6.62
	Married [a]	7.05	26.12	25.55	42.74	69.98	64.07
Time constant variables							
Birth cohort	1954	24.37	4.62	5.73	6.11	3.91	4.45
	1955	—	4.90	4.93	5.68	4.10	5.01
	1956	—	4.76	4.12	3.84	4.61	4.79
	1957	—	5.50	4.45	4.38	5.19	4.24
	1958	—	6.02	4.53	4.03	4.64	4.58
	1959	25.41	4.99	3.80	4.81	4.20	4.95
	1960	—	5.97	3.84	4.66	5.52	4.33
	1961	—	5.55	5.53	5.32	4.83	4.67
	1962	—	4.38	4.49	5.05	5.78	4.67
	1963	—	4.38	5.93	5.75	5.34	5.10
	1964	24.68	5.18	4.12	5.24	4.94	4.76
	1965	—	5.18	5.37	5.40	6.25	5.60
	1966	—	5.04	4.89	4.85	5.45	5.47
	1967	—	4.85	5.29	4.74	5.59	5.84
	1968	—	4.48	6.61	5.28	4.20	5.32
	1969	25.53	4.62	5.29	4.54	5.92	4.92
	1970	—	4.66	4.57	4.11	4.64	5.13
	1971	—	5.13	5.41	4.93	5.37	5.69
	1972	—	5.46	4.45	5.60	4.57	5.04
	1973	—	4.34	6.69	5.68	4.94	5.44

Normative contexts

	X	X	X	X	X	X
Region						
North	45.08					
Centre	18.58					
South	36.33					
Religiosity	91.22	81.39	18.79	55.31	16.60	14.02
Parental divorce	3.12	4.72	17.14	13.14		
Residence at 15 years						
Rural/small city	29.25	32.65	38.51	34.60	33.40	46.28
Middle-size city	42.39	31.15	38.90	33.12	20.38	36.97
Large city	26.72	35.39	20.51	30.88	46.22	16.48
Time varying variables						
Age						
Log (age-15)	4.65 (0.54)	4.55 (0.53)	4.31 (0.48)	4.45 (0.54)	4.29 (0.57)	4.19 (0.63)
Log (39-age)	5.17 (0.44)	5.24 (0.36)	5.35 (0.32)	5.27 (0.39)	5.34 (0.40)	5.36 (0.35)
Age in years[b]	24.24 (4.47)	23.38 (4.15)	21.42 (3.48)	22.52 (4.10)	21.52 (4.17)	21.08 (4.00)
Normative context						
Pregnancy						
Not pregnant	89.36	84.61	65.09	89.39	84.05	92.34
0 to 2 months	4.24	6.69	5.40	2.84	3.50	1.81
3 to 5 months	4.48	5.23	7.79	2.44	4.20	1.85
6 to 8 months	0.90	1.06	4.34	1.60	1.45	1.23
birth to 2 months after	0.43	0.44	2.78	0.28	0.70	0.46
3 to 5 months after	0.34	0.29	2.19	0.40	0.23	0.23
6 or more months after	0.25	1.68	12.41	3.04	5.88	2.08
Education						
Still enrolled						
In education	4.67	16.67	29.16	29.07	21.50	58.14
Educational level						
Primary	40.41	62.60	11.59	37.32	40.81	10.05
Secondary	49.81	24.42	80.82	57.83	36.15	52.45
Tertiary	8.63	11.77	7.05	3.88	23.04	29.73

(continued)

Table 5.2 Descriptive Statistics for the Dependent and Independent Variables *(continued)*

		Sweden	France	West Germany	East Germany	Spain	Italy
Housing	Living Independently	63.15	40.11	43.93	31.12	13.60	12.55
	Length Living Independ.	2.4 (3.6)	1.4 (3.2)	1.7 (3.3)	1.2 (2.9)	0.6 (2.2)	0.7 (2.6)
Labour markets							
Current status	Being employed	58.14	59.66	62.39	66.85	52.18	51.36
	(current is their 1st job)[b]	15.83	2.24	6.25	8.34	4.68	3.90
	(never worked yet)[b]	29.26	15.58	32.32	24.93	27.71	37.23
Years occupied	Labour experience	2.10 (2.96)	X	3.18 (3.86)	2.81 (3.31)	3.61 (3.83)	3.17 (3.90)
Diffusion covariates							
	Peer Group adoption	46.4 (24.7)	26.6 (19.4)	21.2 (13.3)	19.5 (11.0)	6.1 (4.1)	4.2 (2.8)
	Pre-Cohort adoption	X	34.1 (10.3)	30.5 (9.8)	24.9 (8.9)	5.8 (2.4)	4.4 (2.0)

Legend: statistics for time-varying variables are calculated at the time of entrance into first partnership, or at time of interview (or age 39) when right-censored;

[a] Summary statistics on the dependent variable: events by the time of interview or age 39, whichever occurs first.

[b] These variables are not inserted as independent variables in the model; related statistics are calculated and shown only to facilitate the comprehension and a comparison across countries.

6   Living Independently, Marrying, and the Diffusion of Cohabitation

In this chapter we present the results of a series of multivariate hazard rate models aimed at predicting young women's likelihood of exiting the parental home and that of forming a first partnership. In particular, we will be testing a diffusion model for adopting premarital cohabitation. The first part of the chapter discusses the transition out of the parental home (section 6.1) and its interrelationship with changes in the prevalence of marital and cohabiting unions across birth cohorts (6.2). In section 6.3 we focus more specifically on the description of the changes occurred across cohorts in union formation. To follow, we discuss the results of the explanatory models for the transition to residential independence (6.4.) and for entry into marriage (6.5). Sections 6.6 and 6.7 finally concentrate on the diffusion process of cohabitation and its driving mechanisms. The last section (6.8) provides a summary of the main findings about the diffusion of cohabitation.

In this chapter we show how the empirical results indicate that increasing rates of cohabiting unions are (also) driven by others' previous adoptions. We will find that the diffusion process seems to operate primarily through the vicarious experiences of peers. Each new birth cohort starts with selected groups of innovators with a specific interest in the adoption of cohabitation, whereby peers' examples appear to constitute an influential behavioural model for young women. This effect increases even further when, along with the accumulation of peer-group experiences, the diffusion spills over to broader parts of the entire birth cohort population. We will illustrate that after country-specific threshold points, peer-group influence becomes one of the most important driving forces for the individual adoption rate of cohabitation.

However, we will also show that the effect of peer groups' experiences on new adoptions decreases when cohabitation becomes the mainstream behaviour. When traditional social norms favouring marital unions lose ground in favour of an increasing social acceptance of cohabitation, it is rather the more general knowledge-awareness that seems to sustain the process within the entire population. We will also offer empirical evidence that, when cohabiting becomes increasingly more common over time and it is chosen by more broader groups of the population (which might not even have a specific interest in its adoption), the effect of an individual's background characteristics may become less influential than social influences in explaining further adoptions and differentials in its takeup.

6.1 LEAVING THE PARENTAL HOME OTHER THAN BY ENTERING A PARTNERSHIP?

As we discussed briefly in chapter 4, there are profound differences in the extent to which different countries facilitate young people's independence from their parental family. The degree of defamilisation varies across countries and is intertwined with the labour market systems, welfare provisions, and the gender division of labour. The Southern European countries do not offer specific support either to young people or to the employment of women, thus indirectly sustaining a high dependency for women on parental and/or marital support (Guerrero & Naldini, 1996; Orloff, 2002).

Young women's reduced autonomy from their parental families can have a dual effect on family formation patterns. On the one hand, the need for economic support hinders the process of residential independence for young women, making it conditional upon entrance into a partnership for which familial resources are more easily mobilised (Barbagli, Castiglioni & Dalla Zuanna, 2003). On the other hand, women's greater dependency on the spouse's income should lower the relative advantage of cohabiting over marrying. This is because women's generally greater investment in unpaid caregiving activities is better acknowledged and secured through an institutionalised marriage. Thus the advantages of greater flexibility offered by cohabitation can be indirectly offset by less defamilisation. These explanations may account for at least a part of the strong connection between leaving home and entrance into a partnership to be found in Italy and Spain (Barbagli, Castiglioni & Dalla Zuanna, 2003; Billari, Philipov & Baizán, 2001a; Corijn & Klijzing, 2001).

As we show in the following pages, the diffusion of cohabitation has helped to alter the relative proportions of women who leave the parental home and who enter a partnership, as well as the timing of these transitions. But increasing willingness to cohabit seems to have affected the transition to independent living to very different extents across countries.

6.2   RESIDENTIAL INDEPENDENCE BEFORE PARTNERING: CROSS-NATIONAL DIFFERENCES

When studying the transition out of the parental home, it is important to distinguish among destinations because different individuals' characteristics and institutional features may be associated with different modes of reaching residential independence (Cherlin, Scabini & Rossi, 1997; Corijn & Klizijng, 2001; Ermisch & Di Salvo, 1997; Iacovou, 1998, 2001; Ongaro,

2001). The analyses undertaken here thus distinguish, for each country, among three possible destinations: (1) women leaving as single, leaving with a partner for (2) direct entrance into cohabitation, or (3) into marriage (Table 6.1 summarizes the results of the corresponding pseudo-survival functions[1] for different birth cohorts).

Consistently with previous studies, age at leaving seems strongly associated with the proportions to each destination. In Italy and Spain, where young women tend to leave home later (see Figure 6.1), this event coincides most often with partnership entrance. In contrast, in those countries where exit occurs earlier, women usually leave the parental home when single, rather than to enter a partnership. A partial exception is the case of East Germany, where access to housing was strongly controlled by a central planning policy and thus subjected to institutional strict regulation of entitlement. This preliminary finding points up the importance of the interrelationship between the transition out of the parental home and into a first partnership. It suggests that part of the later, and increasingly delayed, home leaving in the southern countries could be explained by the frequent coincidence of residential independence and partnership (generally marriage) entrance (see also Barbagli, Castiglioni & Dalla Zuanna, 2003).

The comparatively late ages at which young people leave the parental home has strong roots in Italian history (Barbagli Castiglioni & Dalla Zuanna, 2003; De Sandre, 1988; Rossi, 1997). It is generally explained in terms of different cultural models and traditions (Dalla Zuanna, 2004; Rehrer, 1998) or of young people's uncertain economic conditions (Aassve, Billari & Ongaro, 2001; Becker, et al., 2002). In a review of the studies

Table 6.1 Changes in the Timing of the Transitions Across Birth Cohorts (1954–73)

Country	Leaving the parental home				Entering 1st partnership		
	overall	single	cohabitation	marriage	overall	cohabitation	marriage
Italy	*later*	const.	const.	*later*	*later*	const.	*later*
Spain	*later*	*later*	*earlier*	*later*	*later*	*earlier*	*later*
East Germany	*const.*	*earlier*	*earlier*	*later*	*later*	*earlier*	*later*
West Germany	*const.*	*earlier*	*(earlier-later)*	*later*	*later*	*(earlier-later)*	*later*
France	*const.*	const.	*earlier*	*later*	*const.*	*earlier*	*later*
Sweden	*const.*	*const.*	*const.*	*const.*	*const.*	*const.*	*later*

Pos. (+)

Neg. (-)

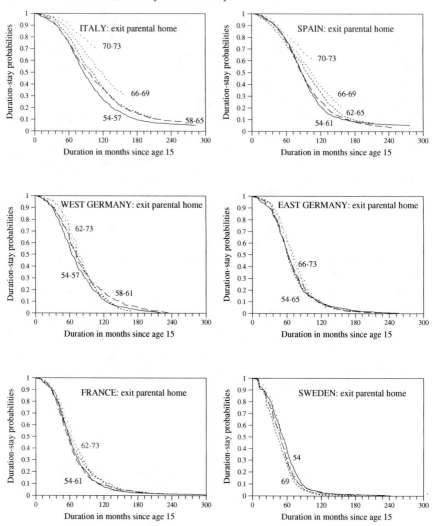

Figure 6.1 Survival functions for leaving the parental home.

on leaving the parental home, Jones (1995) distinguishes between the northern countries, where this transition tends to take place earlier but returns are more likely, and in southern countries, with a later pattern of exits, mainly in connection to marriage (Billari, Philipov & Baizán, 2001a) and returns are less likely to occur. Indeed, at least in France, situations of semiautonomy with repeated exits are found to be rather common (Villanueve-Gokalp, 2000). Also Goldscheider and Da Vanzo (1985; see also Goldsheider, Thornton & Young-DeMarco, 1993) found that the kind of 'semiautonomous' arrangements that favour an earlier exit in the north of Europe (student accommodations, shared apartments) are indeed more likely to lead to later returns. Early educational and labour market careers are then identified as the strategic factors in the stability of independent leaving in Sweden, especially for women (Nilsson & Strandh, 1999).

Iacovou (2001) also stresses the presence of different links between young people's and their families' economic resources and the timing of their reaching an independent living across countries. She finds that in those countries where home leaving occurs relatively early, young people are more likely to leave to a rented accommodation (particularly in the public sector) as singles rather than as part of a couple. The determinants of home leaving thus seem to vary according to the destination on leaving home and according to the chosen housing tenure. Indeed, it is easier for young people to rent because homeownership is more associated with the higher income typically reached at a later stage in the working career. In line with this, Laferrère and Bessière (2003) in a cross-sectional analysis of the French case found a positive effect of children's income on leaving the parental home, accompanied by a smaller nonlinear effect of parents' income (positive only for richer families) and a negative effect linked to the quality of the parental dwelling. Galland (1997, 2000) has suggested that since the late 1980s, the new generations of young French people tend to stay increasingly longer in the parental home because of a rising trend in youth unemployment, longer education, a delayed entry into marriage, a greater degree of comfort, and a higher standard of living enjoyed there. A similar argument is also proposed by other scholars accounting for young southern Europeans' late emancipation from the parental home (Dalla Zuanna, 2004; Mingione, 2001; Rossi, 1997), with particular stress on the poor economic opportunities for young people (Cordon, 1997; Ghidoni, 2002). However, as seen in Figure 6.1, the data used in this study do not show a significant delay in French women's exit from the parental home across subsequent cohorts, at least not with reference to the selection of birth cohorts studied here.

Among the countries under analysis, a delay across birth cohorts in exit from the parental home is displayed rather markedly only in the cases of Italian and Spanish young women (Figure 6.1), who are already distinctive for having the latest pattern of departure from the older birth cohorts onwards. As shown in Figure 6.1, by age 23 (the 96th month since age 15, set as the origin of the X-axis) around 50% of the women are still living with their parents in the southern countries, against a proportion of around or below 20% in all the other countries under analysis. For Italian and Spaniards, these figures then grew around a further 20% for the youngest cohorts considered in this study (1970–1973), witnessing how the vast majority of young women still co-reside with their parental families at 23 years of age.

Figure 6.2 presents the proportions of women in each country having exited the parental home by the time of interview, distinguishing between destination states[2].

Transition out of the parental home

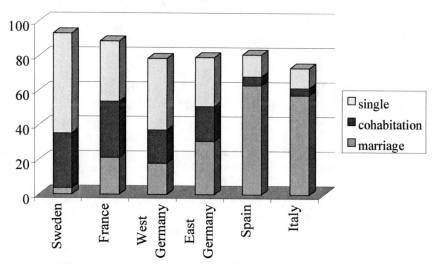

Figure 6.2 Destination states for the transition out of the parental home, selected sample.

Transition into partnership

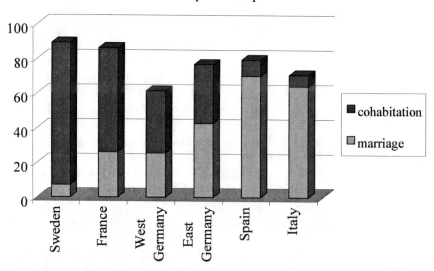

Figure 6.3 Destination states for the transition into first partnership, selected sample.

Similarly, Figure 6.3 reports the destination states of the selected cohorts of women upon entering their first partnership, whereby a proportion of the single women from the light-coloured part of the bars in Figure 6.2 have entered a union[3]. By comparing these two figures, we can see that there appears to be an association between a more widespread first transition to residential independence when single (lighter part of the bars in Figure 6.2) and a higher proportion of cohabiting unions at later entrance into first union (darker part of the bars in Figure 6.3). In other words, those who exit as single seem more likely to opt for cohabitation than those exiting by forming a partnership directly. Thus preliminary evidence suggests that the more young people reach residential independence as single, the more widespread will be the turn to cohabitation.

This first observation points to the importance of exploring further the effect of a period of residential independence on the likelihood of adopting cohabitation in the multivariate analyses. As suggested in chapter 4, in fact, living independently from the parental family ('*living independently*') affords more scope for the adoption of innovative behaviours (less control) and signals the enjoyment of greater economic autonomy.

6.3   EFFECT OF THE DIFFUSION OF COHABITATION ON EARLY FAMILY FORMATION PATTERNS: CHANGES ACROSS COHORTS

Before discussing in detail the results of the hazard rate models, it might be interesting to explore and illustrate the changes in timing of the transition to partnership across birth cohorts so as to get some more insights into the role played by cohabitation. Did cohabitation make up entirely for the progressive delay (and decrease) in marriage?

As described in chapter 2 and explored in the previous section, there are several distinctive features among the countries examined with regard to their prevalent family formation patterns. Southern European women are distinguished by a comparatively later departure from the parental home and its close connection with partnership formation (through marriage for the far greater majority; Bernardi & Nazio, 2005; Simó Noguera, Castro Martí & Bonmatí, 2005). In contrast, in France, Sweden, West Germany, and, to a smaller extent, East Germany, the time span between the acquisition of an autonomous residence and the formation of the first partnership is much longer (Blossfeld & Rohwer, 1995a; Hoem, 1995; Leridon & Toulemon, 1995).

However, with reference to a broader and more detailed set of birth cohorts than those considered in chapter 2, it appears that the time span between the two transitions does not remain constant in all countries across generations or, even in that case, its constancy may result from different compositional effects. Because cohabitation represents an emerging additional behavioural option, its rise can affect independently both changes in leaving the parental home and in the formation of first partnerships. In other words, the rise in nonmarital unions may even impact in contrasting ways on the timing in which the two transitions take place.

Indeed, a first partnership can be formed either when the transition to residential independence has already been achieved through the single state (as for a great number of youngsters in Sweden, France, West Germany, and East Germany) or when the young women are still living with their parental family (as in the case of most Spanish and Italian women). This difference must be taken into account because the choice to cohabit may assume different meanings for its adopters depending on whether or not it is linked to the acquisition of residential independence. This is especially relevant in an early phase of the diffusion process because living autonomously means individuals are subject to a lower social control from the family of origin while being somewhat economically independent and having already overcome possible housing difficulties.

At a descriptive level a clear example is the French case (see also Figure 2.2 in chapter 2), where the computation of survival functions by birth cohorts for the two transitions (Figure 6.1 and 6.4 top line) shows an overall stability of both curves, and thus of the gap between the two. This stability results from the absence of change in the timing of residential independence to the single state, combined with a progressively increased substitution of marriage with cohabitation among those who exited through a direct entrance into a union[4] (see middle and bottom lines of Figure 6.4; a result also found by Corijn, 2001b).

By contrast, in Sweden almost two thirds of the women in the selected sample have gained residential independence moving into the single state by the time of interview (followed mostly by entrance into cohabitation) and about a third by a direct entrance into a cohabiting union (see Figure 6.1). This pattern does not change across cohorts, resulting again in the stability of both curves through time (see Figures 6.1 and 6.4). However, cohabitation is largely predominant, whereas marriage for these birth cohorts is already a minority phenomenon and, as such, its relative decrease or postponement seems not to affect the overall pattern of home leaving across cohorts.

In East Germany, as in France, exiting as single (by the interview) was an option for around a third of the women in the sample. In this former communist country, contrary to Sweden, this figure is the result of a (relative) increased incidence through cohorts (see Table 6.1)[5]. Exit from the parental home appears not to be significantly postponed by the younger generations (Figure 6.1), but its modality has changed in a strongly diminished number of direct marriages and a relative increase in the proportion of both single people and cohabiters (Table 6.1). On the contrary, the transition to partnership overall is delayed, in that an increase in cohabiting unions only partially compensates for a sharp decrease in marriage. We thus observe an increase in the gap between the two survival curves due to the postponement of partnership formation combined with an overall stability in the timing of residential independence (see Table 6.1). This means an increasing number of young women are experiencing prolonged periods of their life course living independently as a single person.

Quite similar is the case of West Germany, where over half of the women have had experience of living independently as single by the time of interview. Across cohorts, more and more women exited the parental home as single, whereas an exit via direct marriage was increasingly delayed, with a resulting null net effect on the timing of this transition (Table 6.1).

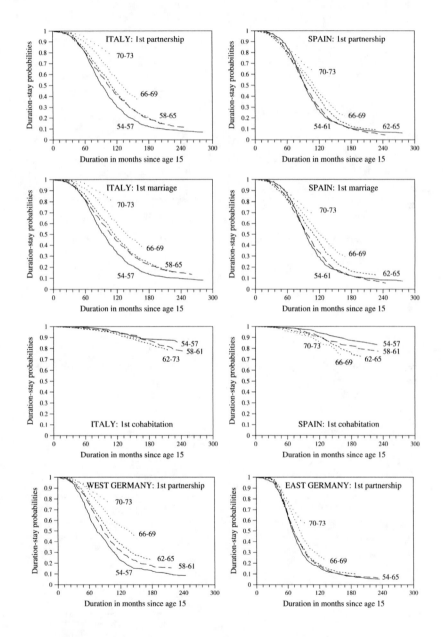

Figure 6.4 Survival and pseudo-survival functions for entrance into first partnership. (*continued over*)

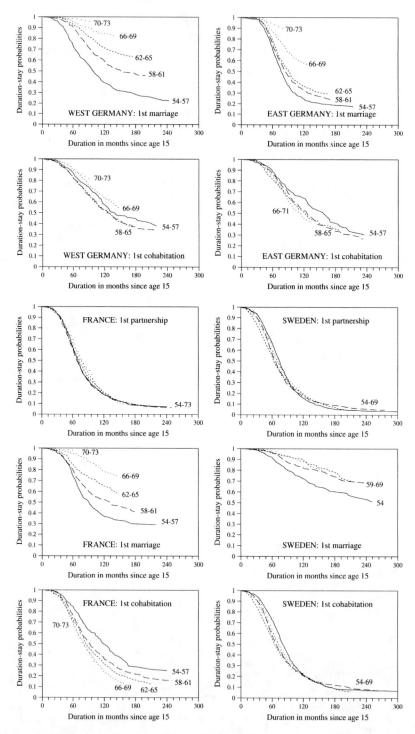

Figure 6.4 Survival and pseudo-survival functions for entrance into first partnership.

Entry into partnership was instead overall deferred by a greater delay in marriage (as compared to East Germany), which was not compensated by a proportional increase in cohabiting unions among the younger birth cohorts. Thus, as compared to East Germany, the already longer time span between the two transitions increased even more markedly.

With regard to residential independence, Italy and Spain again share a rather similar pattern of strong postponement of an already comparatively late exit, which mostly takes place through a direct entry into marriage (it is the case for around three quarters of the women in the sample). In other words, a strong postponement of marriage, coupled with only a small increase in cohabitation and a constant small proportion of women living alone, produces a parallel delay of both the transitions (Table 6.1). In the Italian case, however, the delay is even more pronounced due to the scarcer presence of women who exit as single or enter a consensual union.

Table 6.1 sums up the findings of the series of pseudo-survival functions already discussed. Reference to an earlier (or more frequent) and to a later (or less frequent) transition across birth cohorts may either mean an overall final higher level or an anticipation (versus postponement) of the pattern across birth cohorts (on this ambiguity, see also Bernardi, 2001b).

The positive effect of autonomous living before union formation on the likelihood of adopting cohabitation and the negative effect on entering into a marriage (with the exclusion of Italy and Spain) found in the multivariate analyses (Tables 6.3 and 6.4), are drawn below Table 6.1. The arrows synthesise the effects played by '*living independently*' (already achieved residential independence) onto the subsequent choice to enter a partnership, found in the hazard rate models. It is interesting to notice that the magnitude of this effect, with respect to cohabitation, is much greater in the southern countries (Table 6.4), where living autonomously as a single person it is much less frequent (a result further discussed in section 6.6). This finding is highly consistent both with the hypothesis of housing constraints in Italy and Spain (see Hypothesis (H) 12 in section 4.6) and with previous results (Iacovou, 2002), which pointed to the existence of a positive relation, across countries, between the age of leaving the parental home (and entry into partnership) and the proportion of homeowners.

6.4   TRANSITION OUT OF THE PARENTAL HOME.

Moving from a descriptive to an explanatory ground, we now discuss the most interesting results of event history analyses for the transition to residential independence (for the entire set of results, see Table 6.2). These analyses show that in all countries but Italy there is no effect of *school enrolment* in the transition to living independently as single. Thus being a student does not generally appear to be incompatible with the formation of an autonomous household when single. In Italy, however, the strong negative effect of enrolment in education points to a peculiar characteristic of the Italian context: Even after completing their studies, young women wait longer in the parental home. This may constitute a strategy to allow for the accumulation of resources (e.g., a stable entry in the labour market and some initial capital) needed to afford residential autonomy while enjoying economic security (see also Barbagli, Castiglioni & Dalla Zuanna, 2003). The reasons might lie in the comparatively longer time required to become established in the labour market (Bernardi, 2000; Bernardi & Nazio, 2005), coupled with the difficult housing market and with family responsibility in providing welfare to its members, given the absence of state support for young unemployed and job seekers (also discussed by Aassve et al., 2002; Becker et al., 2002; Dalla Zuanna, 2004). Another explanation for Italy may be that living as a single person is connected with geographical mobility adopted by students to gain access to university, especially for those living in small cities[6]. In the case of students and young employed adults, some authors have referred to this situation, in the Italian case, as a 'fuzzily' living with one's parents (Billari et al., 2001b). In Italy, Spain, and Sweden, in fact, the relatively bigger likelihood of exiting the parental home when single for those who live in small cities could point to a migration process on the grounds of study or work. The negative effect of school enrolment on the likelihood of leaving the parental household for entering a partnership, either by cohabiting or (even stronger effect) marrying, is everywhere in line with the expectations that being a student is an obstacle to family formation.

The impact of women's *educational attainment* is not linear, and its effect is event specific. The transition to the single state is the more favoured the higher the women's educational attainment in Italy, Spain, and France and to a smaller extent in Sweden. This also seems to be the case for cohabitation in West Germany. A tertiary education speeds up exit through cohabitation in East Germany and Spain. With the exception of East Germany, middle or high educational levels seem to discourage direct exit through marriage beyond that postponement due simply to the longer period spent in education.

It was argued that attachment to the labour market should enhance women's economic independence and thus have a positive effect on the transition to singlehood or cohabitation. The dimension of economic autonomy is captured by the cumulative number of years already worked (independently from the current employment status), the *employment experience*. The effect of the current working condition is represented instead by the variable *being employed*. As expected, *being employed* helps young women to leave when single or allows direct entry into cohabitation while it delays marriage in Sweden, without any effect of the length of previous experience in paid employment. The two southern countries have somewhat different profiles. In common they have a negative effect produced by having a job, which combines with a positive influence of working experience, as related

Table 6.2 Estimation of Covariate Effects on the Rate of Women's Leaving the Parental Home (Exponential model with time constant and time dependent covariates)

	Italy			Spain		
	Single	Cohabitation	Marriage	Single	Cohabitation	Marriage
Period 0-3	-9,10**	-9,31**	-20,91**	-14,88**	-19,89**	-24,24**
Period 3-6	-8,08*	-8,83*	-19,89**	-13,98**	-19,63**	-23,84**
Period 6-9	-8,27*	-8,81*	-19,34**	-13,56**	-19,06**	-23,46**
Period 9-12	-8,03*	-8,20*	-19,05**	-13,00**	-18,44**	-23,15**
Period 12 +	-8,23**	-8,28*	-19,14**	-12,01**	-18,37**	-23,40**
Log (Age-15)	-0,22*	-0,02	0,63**	-0,11	0,41	1,08**
Log (39-Age)	0,51	0,35	2,23**	1,58	1,81	2,64**
Enrolled in education	0,49**	-2,03**	-1,42**	0,01	-0,94**	-0,91**
(Ref. education: compulsory or below)	0	0	0	0	0	0
Education: secondary	0,97**	-0,36	-0,22**	0,37**	-0,03	-0,26**
Education: tertiary	2,08**	0,07	0,23	0,61**	0,66*	-0,13
Being employed	0,10	0,03	-0,27**	1,02**	-0,43*	-0,54**
Employment experience (years)	-0,02	0,08*	0,06**	-0,21**	0,04*	0,09**
Religiosity	-0,66**	-1,09**	0,33**	-0,78**	-0,71**	0,15*
Parental divorce	0,85**	0,69*	-0,04	1,28**	1,01**	-0,09
Pregnancy: -9 to birth to +6 months	0,21	2,92**	2,99**	0,89*	1,91**	2,99**
Residence: middle-size city	-0,23	-0,07	0,00	-0,69**	-0,13	0,07
Residence: large city	-0,82**	0,21	-0,02	-0,68**	0,14	0,03
(Ref. region: North)	0	0	0	—	—	—
Region: Centre	0,08	-0,68*	0,16*	—	—	—
Region: South and Islands	0,18	-0,27	0,16**	—	—	—

(continued)

Table 6.2 Estimation of Covariate Effects on the Rate of Women's Leaving the Parental Home (continued)

	Italy			Spain		
	Single	Cohabitation	Marriage	Single	Cohabitation	Marriage
(Ref. cohort: 1954)	0	0	0	0	0	0
Cohort 1955	-0,64	0,12	0,11	-0,17	-0,10	-0,05
Cohort 1956	-0,24	-1,02	-0,15	-0,14	0,59	0,23
Cohort 1957	-0,71	-0,24	0,14	-0,17	0,28	0,21
Cohort 1958	-0,12	0,13	-0,17	-0,67	0,80	0,30 *
Cohort 1959	-0,39	0,17	0,08	-0,47	0,08	0,27
Cohort 1960	-0,32	0,00	-0,38 **	-0,33	1,06	0,15
Cohort 1961	-0,02	0,20	-0,29 *	-0,26	0,41	-0,08
Cohort 1962	-0,06	0,70	-0,16	-0,11	1,18	0,00
Cohort 1963	-0,36	0,42	-0,17	-0,82*	0,92	0,06
Cohort 1964	-0,50	0,78	-0,16	-0,52	1,01	0,10
Cohort 1965	-0,88*	0,19	-0,38 **	-0,36	1,24	0,07
Cohort 1966	-0,14	0,19	-0,41 **	-0,61	1,35	-0,23
Cohort 1967	-0,43	0,22	-0,54 **	-0,55	1,28	-0,26
Cohort 1968	-0,62	0,81	-0,52 **	-0,66	0,95	-0,21
Cohort 1969	-0,32	0,79	-0,74 **	-0,18	1,49	-0,29
Cohort 1970	-0,29	0,01	-1,01 **	-0,76 *	0,67	-0,38 *
Cohort 1971	-0,35	0,44	-0,84 **	-1,48 **	1,28	-0,48 **
Cohort 1972	-0,55	0,13	-1,75 **	-0,63	1,33	-0,51 *
Cohort 1973	-0,51	0,95	-1,69 **	-1,14 *	1,81 *	-0,50 *
Events	374	136	1856	344	143	1725
Log-likelihood	(-15643,2) -14981,4	(-15643,2) -14972,4	(-15643,2) -14058,6	(-14287,1) -13591,7	(-14287,1) -13659,8	(-14287,1) -12648,1

	West Germany			East Germany		
	Single	Cohabitation	Marriage	Single	Cohabitation	Marriage
Period 0-3	-9,84 **	-23,31 **	-34,76 **	-6,35	-32,48 **	-27,05 **
Period 3-6	-7,95 *	-22,96 **	-34,10 **	-4,88	-31,76 **	-24,99 **
Period 6-9	-6,94 *	-22,68 **	-33,58 **	-4,34	-31,30 **	-24,77 **
Period 9-12	-6,73 *	-22,11 **	-33,17 **	-4,15	-30,91 **	-25,04 **
Period 12 +	-6,27 *	-22,05 **	-32,75 **	-4,09	-30,04 **	-25,15 **
Log(Age-15)	0,03	0,63 **	0,93 **	0,03	0,85 **	1,00 **
Log(39-Age)	0,45	2,65 *	4,65 **	-0,06	3,95 **	3,02 *
Enrolled in education	0,13	-0,60 **	-1,09 **	0,16	-0,36 **	-0,38 **
(Ref. education: compulsory or below)	0	0	0	0	0	0
Education: secondary	0,09	0,23 *	-0,17	-0,08	0,05	0,11
Education: tertiary	0,06	0,72 *	0,45	0,11	0,47*	0,12
Being employed	-0,14	0,51 **	0,00	-0,15	0,10	0,21
Employment experience (years)	-0,03	0,01	0,03	-0,01	0,02	-0,03
Religiosity	-0,26 **	-0,31 **	0,41 **	-0,21 *	-0,18	-0,15
Parental divorce	0,33 **	0,23	-0,26	0,42 **	0,41 **	-0,17
Pregnancy: -9 <birth> +6 months	0,38	1,61 **	2,67 **	0,21	1,50 **	1,88 **
(Ref. residence: rural/small city)	0	0	0	0	0	0
Residence: middle-size city	0,10	0,14	-0,01	0,11	-0,01	-0,06
Residence: large city	0,22 **	0,06	-0,31 *	0,16	-0,15	-0,21 *
(Ref. region: North)						
Region: Centre	—	—	—	—	—	—
Region: South and Islands	—	—	—	—	—	—

(continued)

Table 6.2 Estimation of Covariate Effects on the Rate of Women's Leaving the Parental Home (continued)

	West Germany			East Germany		
	Single	Cohabitation	Marriage	Single	Cohabitation	Marriage
(Ref. cohort: 1954)	0	0	0	0	0	0
Cohort 1955	-0,27	-0,25	-0,39 *	-0,21	0,79 *	0,00
Cohort 1956	0,01	-0,32	-0,49 *	-0,42	0,91 *	-0,04
Cohort 1957	0,08	-0,01	-0,19	-0,45	0,56	-0,24
Cohort 1958	0,07	0,32	-0,36	0,00	0,44	-0,33
Cohort 1959	-0,08	-0,11	-0,61 *	-0,38	0,71	-0,21
Cohort 1960	0,15	0,08	-0,35	0,15	0,62	-0,40 *
Cohort 1961	-0,08	0,06	-1,10 **	0,14	1,09 **	-0,33
Cohort 1962	0,12	0,63 *	-0,42	-0,12	1,08 **	-0,37 *
Cohort 1963	0,21	0,11	-0,94 **	-0,22	0,86*	-0,31
Cohort 1964	0,25	0,65 *	-1,19 **	-0,21	1,13 **	-0,33
Cohort 1965	0,17	0,09	-1,24 **	0,15	1,12 **	-0,45 *
Cohort 1966	0,36	-0,08	-1,36 **	-0,29	1,10 **	-0,63 **
Cohort 1967	0,22	-0,05	-1,10 **	-0,01	1,20 **	-0,89 **
Cohort 1968	0,34	0,24	-1,35 **	-0,08	1,56 **	-1,26 **
Cohort 1969	0,54 *	-0,06	-1,23 **	-0,14	1,58 **	-0,99 **
Cohort 1970	0,38	-0,16	-1,71 **	0,17	1,42 **	-1,15 **
Cohort 1971	0,78	0,32	-2,02 **	-0,25	1,59 **	-2,01 **
Cohort 1972	0,70	-0,25	-3,04 **	0,27	1,33 **	-2,17 **
Cohort 1973	1,01	-0,73	-2,42 **	0,65 **	1,22 **	-2,10 **
Events	1031	485	448	724	512	788
Log-likelihood	(-12742,9)	(-12742,9)	(-12742,9)	(-13044,4)	(-13044,4)	(-13044,4)
	-11949,4	-11939,7	-11669,2	-12164,5	-12048,3	-11814,7

	France			Sweden		
	Single	Cohabitation	Marriage	Single	Cohabitation	Marriage
Period 0-3	-12.42 **	-27.88 **	-17.14 **	-43.52 **	-33.26 **	-14.66
Period 3-6	-11.38 **	-27.00 **	-16.44 **	-42.41 **	-32.66 **	-13.83
Period 6-9	-11.31 **	-26.68 **	-16.41 **	-41.57 **	-32.49 **	-13.35
Period 9-12	-11.12 **	-26.48 **	-16.65 **	-41.38 **	-32.29 **	-13.23
Period 12 +	-11.08 **	-26.09 **	-17.30 **	-40.38 **	-32.40 **	-12.98
Log(Age-15)	0.11	0.63 **	0.51 **	0.59 **	0.62 **	0.46 *
Log(39-Age)	1.05	3.36 **	1.72	6.57 **	4.64 **	1.17
Enrolled in education	-0.20	-0.83 **	-1.65 **	-0.10	-0.42 **	-1.39 **
(Ref. education: compulsory or below)	0	0	0	0	0	0
Education: secondary	0.22 *	-0.07	-0.03	-0.10	0.01	-0.83 *
Education: tertiary	0.85 **	0.10	0.35	0.47 **	0.01	-0.73
Being employed	0.35 **	0.28 **	0.45 **	0.08	0.47 **	-1.59 **
Employment experience (years)	—	—	—	0.04	0.09 *	0.08
Pregnancy: -9 <birth> +6 months	0.51 *	1.33 **	2.46 **	0.02	2.22 **	2.50 **
Parental divorce	0.30 **	0.22 *	-0.68 **	0.55 **	0.35 **	-0.54
Religiosity	—	—	—	—	—	—
(Ref. residence: rural/small city)	0	0	0	0	0	0
Residence: middle-size city	0.08	-0.17	-0.34 *	-0.17 **	-0.03	0.12
Residence: large city	0.05	-0.01	-0.22 *	-0.53 **	-0.13	1.07 **
(Ref. region: North)	—	—	—	—	—	—
Region: Centre	—	—	—	—	—	—
Region: South and Islands	—	—	—	—	—	—
(Ref. cohort: 1954)	0	0	0	0	0	0

(continued)

Table 6.2 Estimation of Covariate Effects on the Rate of Women's Leaving the Parental Home (continued)

	France			Sweden		
	Single	Cohabitation	Marriage	Single	Cohabitation	Marriage
Cohort 1955	-0.14	-0.05	0.47 *	—	—	—
Cohort 1956	0.04	0.71 *	-0.04	—	—	—
Cohort 1957	0.02	0.77 *	0.54 *	—	—	—
Cohort 1958	0.05	0.43	0.15	—	—	—
Cohort 1959	0.19	1.13 **	0.35	0.14	0.26 **	-0.29
Cohort 1960	0.17	0.91 **	0.04	—	—	—
Cohort 1961	-0.30	1.21 **	-0.25	—	—	—
Cohort 1962	-0.09	1.22 **	-0.22	—	—	—
Cohort 1963	-0.32	1.39 **	0.00	—	—	—
Cohort 1964	-0.39	1.02 **	-0.31	0.01	0.14	0.02
Cohort 1965	-0.20	1.38 **	-0.53	—	—	—
Cohort 1966	-0.12	1.56 **	-1.10 **	—	—	—
Cohort 1967	-0.12	1.30 **	-1.06 **	—	—	—
Cohort 1968	-0.14	1.67 **	-0.66	—	—	—
Cohort 1969	-0.31	1.63 **	-1.08 **	-0.09	-0.07	0.02
Cohort 1970	-0.06	1.53 **	-1.89 **	—	—	—
Cohort 1971	-0.35	1.85 **	-3.22 **	—	—	—
Cohort 1972	-0.38	1.65 **	-1.83 **	—	—	—
Cohort 1973	0.11	2.00 **	-2.81 **	—	—	—
Events	749	697	453	1500	819	97
Log-likelihood	(-12138,0) -11544,6	(-12138,0) -11416,7	(-12138,0) -11197,6	(-13958,9) -13156,4	(-13958,9) -13096,3	(-13958,9) -13194,6

*: 95% significance   **: 99% significance level

to the direct entrance into marriage, both stronger in the Spanish case. This result suggests that an undeniable amount of savings is required to achieve residential independence, and that southern women have traditionally tended to practice a strong gender-role specialisation within marriage[7]. In both cases this effect shows a lesser impact on the transition to a cohabiting union. In Italy the accumulated working experience seems to favour cohabitation irrespective of the current working status. Whereas in Spain, although the amount of previous experience also has a statistically significant positive effect, the restraining effect of having a job impacts negatively, albeit with a lesser strength than on the transition to marriage.

In contrast, the effect of employment on exit when single is quite different for young women in Spain. Whereas in Italy there is no effect on its timing, in Spain having a job per se accelerates the transition to being single, at least in the initial stage of a career until some job experience is accumulated (5 years is the accumulated experience that would reverse the overall effect). Again, this result is consistent with the hypotheses that having reached some economic autonomy may change Spaniards' preference for a later exit as homeowners, whether it being as a single person or in a union. In West Germany being employed supports cohabitation, whereas in the dual-earning East Germany there is only a small influence on the transition to marriage. France is a particular case because the variable was constructed differently[8], and the positive effect registered on women's employment status across all transitions has to be interpreted as a greater likelihood of exiting for working women in comparison with those who have never worked. Here, economic independence translates into both a faster residential independence and a more rapid union formation.

The *cohort* trends observed in the empirical analyses also reflect what was presented in the descriptive part earlier. A postponement of marriage—although with different timing and strength—is to be observed everywhere but in Sweden, a country where marriage was already a minority phenomenon for the oldest cohort. Once individual characteristics are controlled for, the residual cohort trend points to the rise of exits due to cohabitation in the younger generations, especially in France, East Germany, and, to a much lesser extent, in Spain.

6.5   THE INCREASING POSTPONEMENT OF MARRIAGE

As detailed in chapter 5, in this and the following sections we synthesise the main statistically significant results of a piecewise constant exponential model with time-varying covariates in a competing risks framework. The two possible destination states comprise women's entry into first partnership through marriage (for detailed results, see Table 6.3) and the transition to cohabitation (here two models are reported, an equivalent model as for marriage and an improved one by insertion of the illustrated diffusion covariates; all results are

Table 6.3 Estimation of Covariate Effects on the Rate of Women's Entry into First Marriage (Piecewise Constant Exponential model with time constant and time dependent covariates)

	Model 1					
	Italy	Spain	West Germany	East Germany	France	Sweden
Period 0-3	-18,76 **	-23,02 **	-20,87 **	-35,21 **	-23,76 **	-11,07 *
Period 3-6	-17,80 **	-22,66 **	-20,11 **	-33,31 **	-23,04 **	-10,18 *
Period 6-9	-17,34 **	-22,27 **	-19,81 **	-33,07 **	-22,93 **	-9,66 *
Period 9-12	-17,12 **	-21,98 **	-19,72 **	-33,33 **	-22,94 **	-9,71 *
Period 12 +	-17,26 **	-22,14 **	-20,05 **	-33,33 **	-23,17 **	-9,28 *
Log(Age-15)	0,65 **	1,05 **	0,62 **	1,11 **	0,64 **	0,57 *
Log(39-Age)	1,86 **	2,44 **	2,34 **	4,47 **	2,87 **	0,57
Enrolled in education	-1,42 **	-0,81 **	-1,05 **	-0,36 **	-1,46 **	-0,85 **
(Ref. education: compulsory)	0	0	0	0	0	0
Education: secondary	-0,21 **	-0,24 **	-0,09	0,12	-0,06	-1,42 **
Education: tertiary	0,21	-0,22 *	0,28	0,24	0,41 **	-1,34 **
Being employed	-0,24 **	-0,54 **	0,06	0,14	(0,41) **	-0,81 **
Empl. experience (yrs.)	0,04 **	0,08 **	0,01	-0,02	—	-0,21 **
Religiosity	0,33 **	0,22 **	0,38 **	-0,11	—	—
(Ref. residence: rural/small)	0	0	0	0	0	0
Residence: middle-size city	0,01	0,10	-0,05	-0,04	-0,36 **	-0,35
Residence: large city	-0,03	0,10	-0,34 **	-0,11	-0,24 *	0,58 **
(Ref. region: North)	0	0	0	0	0	0
Region: Centre	0,13 *	—	—	—	—	—
Region: South and Islands	0,11 *	—	—	—	—	—
Length living indep. (yrs.)	-0,01	0,01	-0,04	-0,01	-0,13 **	0,05
Parental divorce	-0,01	-0,22	-0,32 *	-0,14	-0,50 **	-0,77 *
(Ref. pregnancy time before)	0	0	0	0	0	0
Preg.: up to 2 months since	2,84 **	2,93 **	2,77 **	1,57 **	2,16 **	1,66 **

Preg.: 3 to 5 months since	3,51 **	3,53 **	2,99 **	2,41 **	3,18 **	2,68 **
Preg.: 6 to 8 months since	2,51 **	2,44 **	2,89 **	1,78 **	1,83 **	1,16
Preg.: Birth - 2 months after	1,99 **	1,65 **	1,53 **	1,59 **	1,20 **	2,01 **
Preg.: 3-5 months after birth	2,05 **	1,54 **	1,66 **	1,61 **	-0,41	0,66
Preg.: 6-more m. after birth	1,06 *	0,15	0,58 *	0,68 **	-0,33	-1,00
(Ref. Cohort: 1954)	0	0	0	0	0	0
Cohort 1955	0,11	0,02	-0,23	-0,08	0,23	—
Cohort 1956	-0,14	0,19	-0,37 *	-0,08	-0,12	—
Cohort 1957	0,13	0,19	-0,19	-0,41 **	0,34	—
Cohort 1958	-0,15	0,28 *	-0,34	-0,34 *	0,02	—
Cohort 1959	-0,01	0,22	-0,65 **	-0,22	0,15	—
Cohort 1960	-0,31 *	0,09	-0,36	-0,51 **	-0,18	0,00
Cohort 1961	-0,33 *	0,04	-0,91 **	-0,39 *	-0,36	—
Cohort 1962	-0,17	0,00	-0,54 **	-0,51 **	-0,45	—
Cohort 1963	-0,24	0,05	-0,90 **	-0,43 **	-0,11	—
Cohort 1964	-0,22	0,11	-1,19 **	-0,54 **	-0,53 *	0,14
Cohort 1965	-0,39 **	0,06	-1,09 **	-0,57 **	-0,67 *	—
Cohort 1966	-0,46 **	-0,16	-1,47 **	-0,65 **	-1,28 **	—
Cohort 1968	-0,59 **	-0,18	-1,45 **	-1,37 **	-0,97 **	—
Cohort 1969	-0,76 **	-0,32 *	-1,44 **	-1,09 **	-1,17 **	—
Cohort 1970	-1,04 **	-0,38 *	-1,94 **	-1,26 **	-2,20 **	-0,09
Cohort 1971	-0,87 **	-0,45 **	-2,37 **	-2,03 **	-2,84 **	—
Cohort 1972	-1,73 **	-0,51 *	-2,53 **	-2,54 **	-2,17 **	—
Cohort 1973	-1,77 **	-0,49 *	-2,62 **	-2,48 **	-3,16 **	—
Events	2072	1914	638	1092	560	183
Log-likelihood	(-14626,0)	(-13566,3)	(-10321,4)	(-12461,5)	(-11438,4)	(-13317,3)
	-12916,0	-11801,0	-9418,0	-11082,7	-10419,4	-12696,3

*: 95% significance   **: 99% significance level

compiled in Table 6.4). As explained in chapter 5, all the models include controls for the nonmonotonic *age dependence* of the marriage rates in the data
(see Blossfeld & Huinink, 1991).

In chapter 4, two different kinds of effects of education on entry into partnership have been distinguished from a theoretical standpoint: educational
attainment level and enrolment in education. The 'new home economists' claim
that the decline of the family as a social institution is the result of women's rising earning power given their increasing investment in higher education and
improved career opportunities (Becker, 1981). This leads to the expectation
that there is a monotonically increasing negative effect of educational attainment level on entry into first marriage (H9). However, as Table 6.3 shows,
the influence of *educational attainment level* on entry into first marriage is
not as straightforward as this suggests. In none of the countries under study is
there a clear monotonically increasing negative pattern. Only the Spanish and
Italian cases might be considered as a partial confirmation of the economic
theory of the family. In both countries we find a delaying effect of secondary
education on entry into marriage consistent with previous findings from other
studies (Billari et al., 2002; Pinelli & De Rose, 1995). This indicates that the
'liberating effect' of women's educational attainment on entry into marriage is,
if at all, only working within more traditional family systems (also found by
Blossfeld, 1995).

The other key variable for entry into marriage is educational enrolment.
Because attaining an education makes it difficult to adopt long-term binding family roles (Blossfeld, 1995; Marini, 1984, 1985) and involves a high
degree of economic dependence, school enrolment should lead to an increasing
postponement of entry into marriage (H8). Table 6.3 shows that the variable
enrolled in education indeed has a strong negative effect in all the countries,
although it is much lower in East Germany. Finishing education seems thus
to be an important precondition for entry into marriage in these countries. In
addition, its comparatively much smaller effect in East Germany points to the
institutional setting that made it easier to combine the role of a student with
the formation of a family (see chapter 4).

The indicators *being employed* and *employment experience* are used as
proxy variables for women's growing (economic) independence. They are
particularly relevant in societies like Spain and Italy, where the traditional
view that men are still considered to be the main providers for the family
proves hard to change (Blossfeld & Drobnič, 2001)[9]. We expected a negative effect of women's labour force participation on entry into marriage in
these two countries, where the role of working wife still conflicts more with
traditional expectations and the load of domestic and care work associated
with it (H7). For countries characterised by a dual full-time earner family
model, such as East Germany, France, and Sweden, we expected that this
effect should disappear. The results for the variable *being employed* reported
in Table 6.3 support these expectations. There is a clear-cut negative effect
of women's labour force participation in Spain and Italy and no significant

effect of the employment status on women's rate of entry into marriage in East and West Germany. Quite surprisingly, in Sweden the marital commitment seems to be in conflict with an employment career. In our analyses, this result may depend on the limited number of events or point to a specific attraction of marriage for the (minority of) Swedish women who do not work. Unfortunately, no distinction could be made between unemployment and inactivity in the data, so that further research is needed for interpreting this result. Considering that the vast majority of Swedish women engage in continuous paid employment throughout their adult life course, and that only a minority opts for a direct entry into marriage, this result might also suggest that those women who postpone marriage on the ground of their employment commitment might be a highly selected group of women.

In Italy and Spain, the negative effect of having a job is counterbalanced by the effect of accumulated *employment experience*. It seems to be the case that for women who have a longer attachment to the labour market (at least 6 to 7 years) and whose economic autonomy is more established, the conflict between marriage and a working career becomes less severe (a similar result with respect to first motherhood has been found by González, 2002, in Italy, Spain, and West Germany). This is a relevant finding because it suggests that southern women who are in the labour market seem to wait until they have a relatively secure position before making the decision to enter a union. This effect may result from a more difficult and slow change to a dual-earning family model in these countries, in which women's paid employment strives to get acknowledged inside marriage. Working women who want to pursue a labour career seem required to make a substantial career investment and establish themselves in the labour market before they enter a union. Reciprocally, economically dependent women seem to have few incentives to postpone or avoid marriage (H10).

Alternatively, this effect may point to a more uncertain position of young women in the labour market and/or to a bigger amount of resources needed to reach residential autonomy and a stable economic independence. Again, in these analyses we could not distinguish the effect of unemployment from that of inactivity. Equally, it was not possible to control for the type of employment relationship (distinguishing dependent from temporary employment and self-employment), the earnings, the employment sector, working hours, or the degree of uncertainty in the employment prospects. Despite these limitations, this finding points to the distinctive pattern of family formation in the southern countries, where young working adults continue to live with their parental family until an exit via entrance into a union (generally a marriage) can take place (Alberdi, 1999; Barbagli, Castiglioni & Dalla Zunna, 2003; Billari, Philipov & Baizán, 2001a; Dalla Zuanna, 2004). The same is not true in Sweden, where all the indicators relating to women's resources, both educational and in terms of employment (status and experience), have a negative effect on entry into marriage. The coefficient for France cannot be directly compared or interpreted along the same lines. Here, 'being employed' signals the greater likelihood to engage in a union (it scores positive for both entry into marriage and cohabitation) for those women who have already accessed the labour market (as opposed to those who have not yet entered employment), and thus begun to acquire economic resources.

The models include a variable indicating whether or not a woman lives in her parental home, and one reporting the length of time since the acquisition of an autonomous residence. Having already acquired residential independence from the parental family was expected to have a negative effect on entry into marriage because it lowers the pressure of speeding up union entry as a way to acquire autonomy (H12). Furthermore, as an intermediate stage in the transition to adulthood, living autonomously as single can afford more time in the process of family formation. *Living independently* has indeed everywhere, but in Italy and Spain, a strong negative influence on the likelihood of women to marry. The effect on an achieved residential autonomy is further enhanced by its duration only in France.

With respect to the influence of *religiosity* on union formation, we expected a positive effect of being religious on women's entry into marriage in West Germany, Italy, and Spain, and we assumed that religiosity would play a negligible role in the atheist East Germany (H3). Again, the findings in Table 6.3 support these expectations.

We argued that having experienced a *parental divorce* is also an event that might induce marriage postponement. Its effect is strong and negative as expected (H5), being greater in Sweden, followed by France and West Germany. In Spain and East Germany, its effect is still negative but smaller and not statistically significant (surprisingly, given the high proportion of divorced parents witnessed in the German Democratic Republic as reported in Table 5.2), whereas in Italy it does not seem to have any remarkable influence on the choice to marry.

As discussed in chapter 4, the event of a *pregnancy* is often regarded as an important factor in young women's decision to marry (H4). Indeed, it seems to be one of the strongest predictors in the empirical analyses. As expected, its effect is greater everywhere before the birth of a child and strongest in the period between the third and fifth month since the beginning of the pregnancy (see also Blossfeld & Mills, 2001). Because women are mostly unaware of the pregnancy in the first month and the organisation of a wedding may take longer than a few weeks, the positive effect in the very first period cannot be directly interpreted as a reaction to the pregnancy. It may rather be that those women who already had plans to marry and to have children had already begun to relax their contraceptive measures shortly before the wedding was celebrated (Baizán et al., 2002, 2003). However, apart from the smaller positive effect found in the 2 months following conception, we believe a direct causal effect of a pregnancy onto the acceleration of entry into marriage may instead be attributed to the subsequent periods.

We do not find strong effects of *community size* on women's transition rate to marriage in Italy or Spain (Table 6.3), where marriage is still a ubiquitous phenomenon (H6). However, *regional* differences are confirmed in that marriage seems to take place slightly earlier for women living in the centre and south of these countries, a fact already observed in previous research. In West Germany and France, we observe that women who grew up in large urban areas marry significantly later (or less often) than women who grew up in rural environments or small towns. The explanation can be the lower degree of traditionalism and social control in large cities, the more heterogeneous marriage market, or the wider range of activities available to unmarried young people in larger metropolitan areas. In Sweden, on the contrary, having been brought up in a large urban centre increases the likelihood of marrying. This finding, though, is based on a rather selected group of women, and it may result from a saturation of the diffusion process of cohabitation (see the opposite effect for cohabitation in Table 6.4) or on the higher presence of immigrants in bigger cities.

Finally, a series of *cohort dummy variables* are included in the model, where the reference category is the oldest birth cohort of women born in 1954. Across birth cohorts, we find a monotonically increasing negative effect on entry into marriage in all countries but Sweden. This pattern across cohorts begins earlier in West Germany, followed by East Germany, France, and Italy, and finally by Spain (only for the youngest cohorts observed). Because women's educational enrolment and attainment levels as well as participation in the labour force and accumulated work experience are controlled for, these differences across cohorts cannot be explained in these terms. Instead, the increasing delay of entry into the first marriage across younger generations of women must be attributed to other sources of cohort-specific influences. As mentioned earlier, one possible explanation is the growing uncertainty generated by the economic systems among young adults in modern societies (Blossfeld et al., 2005). Based on these structural changes, it is increasingly difficult for each younger cohort of women to make long-term binding commitments early in their life course (see Aassve et al., 2002; Becker et al., 2002; Bernardi & Nazio, 2005; Kurz & Steinhage, 2001; Kurz, Steinhage, & Golsch, 2005; Mills et al., 2005). This argument leads us to the analysis of the diffusion of cohabitation.

6.6 THE DIFFUSION OF COHABITATION

In this section the results of the application of the proposed diffusion approach are discussed. This means an exploration of the impact of others' past behaviour on the individuals' choice to adopt cohabitation as a means of entering their first partnership. The effect of individual, time-varying characteristics is also included.

We have chosen to present our main results in the analysis of this transition in two separate statistical models (see Table 6.4). In model 1, we regress the event of entry into a cohabiting union on individuals' characteristics only, without controlling for their embeddedness in a time-specific social context. In model 2, we introduce the diffusion variables described: peer-group and precohort adoption. Thus Table 6.4 presents a competing risks model for women's rate of entry into cohabitation (model 1) that corresponds to the marriage model of Table 6.3, and an individual level diffusion model for women that explicitly incorporates theoretically important measures thought to drive the diffusion process (model 2). Both models include controls for *age dependence,* as in the model for marriage (see Blossfeld & Huinink, 1991).

With regard to *educational enrolment,* we hypothesised that still being a student not only has a negative effect on the decision to enter into marriage but also on the adoption of cohabitation (H8). However, because informal cohabitation is less binding and more flexible than marriage, we claimed that the effect should be generally smaller on the adoption of cohabitation (see also Wu, 2000). A comparison of the effects of this variable for entry into marriage and cohabitation shows that, in all countries, this effect is indeed smaller for cohabitation than for marriage. However, the differences in the magnitude of this effect across countries are remarkable. They range from two to three times lower in Sweden, France, and Germany. In contrast, in Italy and Spain, educational enrolment hinders both marriage and cohabitation (for which transition the effect is only slightly smaller). This result seems to reflect coherently the specific characteristics of the housing and labour markets and the strong dependencies of young people on economic support from the family in the case of both forms of union (Aassve et al., 2002). Staying longer in the parental home appears therefore to be the best solution for many young women in southern Europe, due to an extended participation in education, an increasing uncertainty in the labour market for young people, and a lack of welfare support for students, the unemployed, and first-job seekers (Bernardi, 2005; Naldini, 2003; Saraceno, 1994).

Table 6.4, once again, shows no clear pattern of *educational attainment level* having any bearing on the adoption of cohabitation. Thus the empirical results do not clearly support either the claim that educational resources made women less willing to enter any type of unions or the idea that more highly educated women have it easier (or find it more advantageous) to cohabit (H9). Further research, with better measurements of various educational attainment dimensions, is needed for evaluating further these competing dimensions of education.

Regarding the effect of *being employed,* we only find a significantly positive effect on the rate of adoption of cohabitation in Sweden (the effect in France is not strictly comparable). Working women do not only seem to postpone or avoid marriage in Sweden, but they also have a higher propensity to adopt cohabitation (H11). For both marriage and cohabitation, albeit

Table 6.4 Estimation of Covariate Effects on the Diffusion of Cohabitation among Women (Piecewise Constant Exponential model with time constant and time dependent covariates)

	Model 1						Model 2					
	Italy	Spain	West Germany	East Germany	France	Sweden	Italy	Spain	West Germany	East Germany	France	Sweden
Period 0-3	-11,42**	-23,55**	-25,93**	-25,32**	-27,21**	-17,18**	-13,25**	-28,34**	-31,68**	-26,60**	-33,04**	-20,00**
Period 3-6	-11,02**	-22,76**	-25,60**	-24,58**	-26,39**	-16,63**	-13,25**	-28,17**	-31,70**	-26,10**	-32,28**	-19,90**
Period 6-9	-10,80**	-22,28**	-25,41**	-24,38**	-26,07**	-16,64**	-13,50**	-28,15**	-31,66**	-25,94**	-32,08**	-19,79**
Period 9-12	-10,45**	-21,60**	-25,20**	-24,49**	-25,78**	-16,83**	-13,33**	-27,56**	-31,29**	-26,08**	-31,86**	-19,99**
Period 12 +	-10,35**	-21,22**	-25,38**	-24,19**	-25,24**	-16,89**	-13,30**	-27,09**	-31,40**	-25,71**	-31,21**	-20,14**
Log(Age-15)	-0,01	0,29	0,78**	0,78**	0,63**	0,47**	-0,32	0,00	0,50**	0,58**	0,49**	0,23**
Log(39-Age)	0,70	2,46**	3,08**	2,81**	3,33**	1,92**	0,95	3,38**	4,17**	3,18**	4,15**	2,40**
Enrolled in education	-1,37**	-0,68**	-0,41**	-0,22*	-0,73**	-0,34**	-1,24**	-0,65**	-0,36**	-0,17	-0,71**	-0,33**
(Ref. education: compulsory)	0	0	0	0	0	0	0	0	0	0	0	0
Education: secondary	-0,26	0,11	0,19*	0,03	0,07	-0,03	-0,30	0,09	0,20**	0,04	0,07	-0,02
Education: tertiary	0,24	0,36	0,22	0,31	0,24**	0,11	0,15	0,35	0,26	0,33	0,23*	0,10
Being employed	0,22	-0,40**	0,18	0,13	0,17*	0,27**	0,20	-0,43**	0,12	0,09	0,15*	0,21**
Empl. experience (yrs.)	0,08*	0,08*	0,02	0,03	—	0,04*	0,07*	0,07*	0,02	0,03	—	0,04*
Religiosity	-1,04**	-0,55**	-0,17*	-0,16	—	—	-1,00**	-0,56**	-0,16*	-0,16	—	—
(Ref. residence: rural/small)	0	0	0	0	0	0	0	0	0	0	0	0
Residence: middle-size city	-0,17	-0,04	0,11	0,01	-0,05	-0,09	-0,17	-0,03	0,11	0,02	-0,06	-0,09
Residence: large city	0,38*	0,16	-0,03	-0,06	-0,07	-0,21**	0,37*	0,17	-0,02	-0,03	-0,08	-0,20**
(Ref. region: North)	0	0	0	0	0	0	0	0	0	0	0	0
Region: Centre	-0,26	—	—	—	—	—	-0,27	—	—	—	—	—

(continued)

Table 6.4 Estimation of Covariate Effects on the Diffusion of Cohabitation among Women (continued)

	Model 1						Model 2					
	Italy	Spain	West Germany	East Germany	France	Sweden	Italy	Spain	West Germany	East Germany	France	Sweden
Region: South and Islands	-0,27*	—	—	—	—	—	-0,30*	—	—	—	—	—
Living independently	1,81**	2,16**	0,48**	0,35**	0,72**	0,21**	1,76**	2,11**	0,46**	0,33**	0,71**	0,18**
Length living indep. (yrs.)	-0,09*	-0,07*	-0,06**	-0,03	-0,06**	-0,01	-0,09*	-0,07*	-0,05**	-0,03	-0,06**	0,00
Parental divorce	0,54**	0,79**	0,31**	0,44**	0,28**	0,26**	0,48**	0,80**	0,33**	0,41**	0,30**	0,25**
(Ref. pregnancy time before)	0	0	0	0	0	0	0	0	0	0	0	0
Preg.: up to 2 months since	2,01**	1,66**	1,57**	1,44**	1,32**	1,64**	2,00**	1,65**	1,60**	1,45**	1,34**	1,65**
Preg.: 3 to 5 months since	2,73**	1,15	1,87**	1,41**	1,02**	1,80**	2,75**	1,17	1,89**	1,42**	1,04**	1,82**
Preg.: 6 to 8 months since	3,23**	1,62*	1,73**	1,78**	1,15**	1,91**	3,28**	1,62*	1,76**	1,79**	1,17**	1,92**
Preg.: Birth - 2 months after	3,09**	1,89**	0,32	1,42**	0,46	0,80*	2,96**	1,79*	0,28	1,39**	0,43	0,75*
Preg.: 3-5 months after birth	2,23*	1,42	1,15*	1,17**	-0,05	0,59	2,12*	1,37	1,15*	1,16**	-0,06	0,57
Preg.: 6-more m. after birth	1,74	-0,06	0,25	0,60**	-0,52**	-0,10	1,65	-0,15	0,25	0,59**	-0,53**	-0,11
(Ref. Cohort: 1954)	0	0	0	0	0	0						
Cohort 1955	0,09	-0,75	-0,19	0,35	0,15	—						
Cohort 1956	-0,60	0,39	0,14	0,36	0,40	—						
Cohort 1957	0,21	0,41	-0,06	0,27	0,50*	—						
Cohort 1958	-0,02	0,69	0,27	0,25	0,44*	—						
Cohort 1959	0,21	0,64	0,12	0,30	0,62**	—						
Cohort 1960	-0,13	0,69	0,23	0,29	0,60**	0,04						
Cohort 1961	0,27	0,47	0,26	0,56*	0,91**	—						

Cohort 1962	0,73	1,09*	0,41*	0,38	0,72**	—
Cohort 1963	0,45	0,89	0,08	0,12	0,89**	—
Cohort 1964	0,74	0,85	0,38	0,63**	0,69**	—
Cohort 1965	-0,06	1,09*	0,10	0,49*	0,99**	-0,05
Cohort 1966	0,23	1,20*	-0,06	0,45	1,08**	—
Cohort 1967	0,31	1,61**	-0,21	0,35	0,83**	—
Cohort 1968	0,72	1,11*	-0,01	0,82**	1,19**	—
Cohort 1969	0,69	1,29**	-0,41	0,82**	1,17**	—
Cohort 1970	-0,05	0,96	-0,61*	0,83**	1,13**	-0,02
Cohort 1971	0,07	1,21*	-0,09	0,73**	1,25**	—
Cohort 1972	0,00	1,07	-0,57	0,64*	1,08**	—
Cohort 1973	0,73	1,86**	-0,74*	0,55*	1,31**	—
Events	214	257	895	868	1287	2133
Log-likelihood	(-14626,0)	(-13566,3)	(-10321,4)	(-12461,5)	(-11438,4)	(-13317,3)
	-13882,9	-12781,5	-9820,5	-11427,1	-10644,8	-12599,3

Peer group adoption	1,23**	0,71**	0,20**	0,11*	0,04*	0,11**
(Peer group adoption)2 /100	-18,48**	-7,37**	-0,69**	-0,47*	-0,09*	-0,24**
(Peer group adoption)3 /1000	9,35**	2,69**	0,08**	0,07*	0,01*	0,02**
Pre-cohort adoption	0,67	0,72	-0,05	-0,04	0,20*	—
(Pre-cohort adoption)2 /100	-15,33	-13,06	0,30	0,34	-0,49	—
(Pre-cohort adoption)3 /1000	10,13	7,57	-0,05	-0,05	0,05	—
Events	214	257	895	868	1287	2133
Log-likelihood	(-14626,0)	(-13566,3)	(-10321,4)	(-12461,5)	(-11438,4)	(-13317,3)
	-13870,2	-12777,6	-9819,6	-11435,3	-10653,1	12584,7

*: 95% significance   **: 99% significance level

in opposite directions, these effects are strengthened by that of the 'length in employment.' This means that the stronger the women's attachment to the labour market, the lower their likelihood to enter a marriage and the higher to adopt cohabitation. Spain is the only country displaying a significant negative effect (a similar result was found by Simó Noguera, Castro Martín & Bonmatí, 2005). This result may capture the particularly strong difficulties faced by young Spanish women in the early stage of their working career (Polavieja, 2003), as discussed in chapter 4 with a description of unemployment rates and temporary contracts (H11). In Italy, however, being currently employed has no great effect on the adoption of cohabitation, in contrast to the negative effect found for the transition to marriage. This can be explained by the fact that cohabiting unions are still considered a 'modern' type of living arrangement in Italy, whereby traditional gendered expectations are not clear cut. Thus, in cohabiting unions, working women might expect to have more room for gender-role negotiation with their partners (H7). However, it is worth noticing that in both Spain and Italy the length of attachment to employment significantly induces an acceleration of both forms of unions. This result points to how, in the southern countries, the length of previous *employment experience* is likely to be a key factor in allowing young people to jump the hurdle of housing constraints and reach residential autonomy. As expected, there is no significant effect in socialist East Germany and in West Germany (H10).

The effect of *religiosity* on the adoption of cohabitation is negative and significant in three of the four countries for which this indicator was implemented and does reduce the adoption rate of cohabitation significantly, especially in catholic Italy and Spain (see Table 6.4). In atheist East Germany this effect is negative too, although it is not highly statistically significant (at a significance level of around 92%). It might therefore seem that religiosity, to some extent, is a good proxy variable for traditionalism, even in an atheist environment. As expected, the magnitude of the effect of religiosity is far greater in the southern countries (H3).

In contrast to the transition to marriage, having experienced parental *divorce* or separation has a similar positive and significant effect in all the countries analysed. This is in line with the hypothesis (H5) that having witnessed an unsuccessful marriage in the parental home could raise doubts about the institution of marriage and thus support the choice for an alternative, less binding form of union (see also Corijn, 2001b). A further explanation may also be that cohabitation tends to take place earlier among the daughters of divorced parents because they might be seeking a source of relative emotional stability but without incurring (yet) any marital commitment.

Given the degree of personal autonomy and signals of economic independence that having reached an autonomous residence implies (*living independently*), a positive effect was expected on entrance to a cohabiting union (H12) (Liefbroer, 1991). This is indeed the case in all the countries, with a particularly greater impact in Italy and Spain, where access to an afford-able, independent dwelling for young people is blocked by the structure of the housing market and the lack of welfare support (Barbagli, Castiglioni & Dalla Zuanna, 2003; Saraceno, 1994). In the southern countries, where cohabitation is not yet widespread and still stigmatised (Ermisch, 2005), and where housing constitutes a particularly big hurdle for youngsters, having succeeded in moving out from the parental home seems to be a crucial vari-able in favouring cohabitation. Its effect is between 3 and 10 times greater in the southern than in the other countries (depending on the country of com-parison). This means that the relative risk of entering cohabitation is almost 6 times greater in Italy and over 8 times greater in Spain (as calculated from model 2) for women having acquired residential independence with respect to women still living with their parents in the same country. We would sug-gest that such a strong effect hints at the difficulties faced by young Mediter-ranean people in affording an autonomous living other than by marrying, rather than to deep-rooted cultural differences. Cultural differences might be part of the explanation too, but it is difficult to imagine that they could account alone for the big magnitude of the cross-country differences in this effect. If, on the one hand, it is expected that living independently allows a greater autonomy and less social control (a greater 'readiness' to cohabit in a wider range of available behavioural option), on the other hand such an effect should result in a positive but smaller effect like in the other countries. Instead, Southern European women seem to be far more willing (or able) to take up a more flexible union arrangement than their other Europeans peers (whose relative risks range from 1.2 to 1.6 for autonomously living rather than co-residing with their parents) once the housing obstacle has been overcome. In this respect, it must be remembered that the southern countries are characterised by a remarkable (and increasing) delay in leav-ing the parental home, as shown in Figure 6.1. The remarkable difference in effects may also be attributed (at least in part) to the achievement of less normative control and less economic dependence from the parental family but also to a lessened need for their contribution to the provision of hous-ing[10]. This result thus supports the claim that the strong family ties and a high degree of reciprocal interdependencies in the southern family systems (Saraceno, 1994), by favouring a prolonged stay of young adults in the parental home, might indirectly have a negative impact on the diffusion of cohabitation (Barbagli, Castiglioni & Dalla Zuanna, 2003).

Beside this strong positive effect, a much smaller counterbalancing negative effect linked to the length of period of residential independence is found in all the countries with the exception of East Germany and Sweden. This indicates that the higher opportunity or convenience of cohabiting over marrying, which accompanies the achievement of residential autonomy, reduces over time. In other words, once residential independence has been established, there seems to be a small (although significant) reduction in the likelihood of entering a cohabiting union, which grows with the length of the independent living period. This reduction in the strength of the effect over time, once residential autonomy is controlled for, could also point to a selection into 'independent single living' of those women less willing or able to enter a partnership. This counteracting negative effect is true for entrance into cohabitation in four of the countries studied, although significant only in France for the transition to marriage. However, it is worth noticing that this effect is much smaller and it does not cancel out that of living autonomously per se, which would be counterbalanced only after 8 or 12 years in West Germany and France, respectively, and 20 or 30 years in Italy and Spain. Overall we register a positive effect of independent living onto the diffusion of cohabitation, paralleled by a negative effect in entering marriage instead. This hints at the lower social control offered by an autonomous living and to the weakening of the perception of marriage as a means to gain residential independence from parents.

Based on earlier research (e.g., Lesthaeghe & Neels, 2002), we expected to find ecological effects depending on the size of the city to have a bearing on the adoption of cohabitation as well (H6). Because bigger cities are less traditional with regard to family values, cohabitation was expected to diffuse faster among individuals brought up in bigger cities. Table 6.4 shows that only in the more traditional environment of Italy is there indeed a positive effect of a large city of *residence* that supports this hypothesis. This suggests that here large urban centres exert significantly less social control and offer a broader range of tolerable behaviour with regard to new forms of family formation, and thus tend to favour the spread of innovative practices, especially in the early stage of the diffusion process. The case of Sweden, where in large cities (i.e., Stockholm) entrance into cohabitation is postponed, points instead to the later stage the diffusion of cohabitation has reached there. In an environment where living independently is the norm and where, for most people, entering a union means entering cohabitation, being brought up in an urban area postpones somewhat the entry into a partnership.

Because regional differences are known to be very pronounced in Italy (Billari & Kohler, 2002), we introduced controls for *region* in the empirical analysis. The south of Italy was expected to be more traditional with regard to family values and norms of conduct (H6). We have already seen that women who live in the more traditional centre or south of the country tend to marry earlier than those living in the north (Table 6.3). The contrary is true in the case of cohabitation. The negative coefficients, as expected, point to a lower likelihood to enter cohabitation in the centre and south of the country with respect to the north, which reaches the chosen level of statistical significance for the south of Italy (Table 6.4; see also Billari & Kohler, 2002; Ongaro, 2001).

An ongoing *pregnancy* has a positive effect on the likelihood of entering a consensual union as previously seen in the transition to marriage, although its effect is everywhere lower than in the former case (H4). A second difference is that in France, Sweden, and West Germany, it precipitates the decision to cohabit only in the period before the birth, especially in the few months preceding the event. In East Germany, Spain, and Italy, it tends instead to spill over into the few months following the birth. Whereas the explanation in East Germany lies in the specific institutional arrangement that distinctly favoured 'single mothers,' for the southern countries the reason may be more linked to the traditional context and the visibility of the parental status. In the familialist Italy and Spain (Naldini, 2003), it may be the social norms that induce the parents of a newborn child to move in together "as if" they were married, had they not done so before the birth took place.

Surprisingly, with the exception of France, we do not get a clear-cut positive *cohort* trend for women's rate of entry into cohabitation in model 1 of Table 6.4, as documented in the description of *precohort adoption* in Figure 3.4. This suggests that the monotonic upward shifts of the curves of accumulative precohort adoption across cohorts to be seen in Figure 3.4 are, to a large extent, the result of a compositional effect. After controlling for cohort differences in educational participation and attainment levels as well as for women's participation in the labour force (and other important social background factors) in model 1, there is no clear autonomous *partial* cohort trend left. This suggests that the rising postponement of entry into marriage across cohorts was not simply compensated for by a monotonically increasing cohort trend in the adoption of cohabitation. A more detailed analysis of the mechanisms behind the diffusion process of cohabitation is therefore important.

6.7 MECHANISMS AT PLAY

A second model (model 2 in Table 6.4) replaces the cohort dummy variables of model 1 by two indicators linked to theoretically informed diffusion mechanisms. In statistical terms, this diffusion model is better than model 1 because it basically produces the same fit (in terms of the log likelihood[11]) for a more parsimonious model while all the described effects remain stable in substantive terms. Furthermore, when introducing the cohort dummy variables again into this second model (not shown), the overall fit of the models does not improve significantly in any of the countries[12]. This suggests that the indicators developed are a statistically efficient and theoretically meaningful substitution for the dynamic changes occurring across birth cohorts. The diffusion process can, in fact, account for the increasing practice of cohabitation across birth cohorts without attributing the change to a generic and unspecified historical or cultural change that increasingly affected the behaviour of successive generations of women. This is in itself an important result, which supports the existence of a meaningful mechanism linked to social influence in the process of diffusion of cohabitation (as we argued in chapter 2). It also means that individual characteristics are not sufficient to account for the changes in young women's propensity to cohabit (observed both over the life course and across birth cohorts), but that an element linked to the individuals' embeddedness in a changing social and cultural context is required. The proposed indicators seem not only to capture the diffusion process of cohabitation efficiently, but the empirical results also suggest that the model we propose is a meaningful explanation of changes in levels of cohabitation over time.

In chapter 3 we argued that the accumulated experiences of earlier generations with premarital cohabitation and the abstract dissemination of these experiences through the mass media might serve as an important mechanism in the transmission of cohabitation from one generation to the next. In particular, we expected that the accumulated proportion of prior cohabitation adopters from previous cohorts would have a positive effect on the conveyance of cohabitation on later birth cohorts. To capture these effects, we included the variable cumulative precohort adoption in the model (see Figure 3.4) for five of the countries. Specifically, as detailed in chapter 5, we used a third-degree polynomial in model 2 to capture possible nonlinear relationships between cumulative precohort adoption and the individual rate of adoption. However, only in France does the linear component of the three cumulative precohort adoption covariates have a high statistically significant effect. In France it is precohort adoption, rather than peer-group adoption, that is the prevailing force in driving the diffusion process. It thus seems that, after a certain threshold has been reached, it is not the direct examples of peers that fosters new adoptions but the general acceptance of the practice and more general communication, as reflected by the overall level of practice from previous cohorts. This suggests that the dissemination of knowledge-awareness about the experiences of previous cohorts through the mass media only has an important influence on the diffusion of cohabitation in an advanced stage of the process (H2). Better knowledge of the existence of cohabitation diffused through the mass media might be important, but such abstract 'theorisation' (Strang & Meyer, 1993) about the existence, functioning, and rationality of cohabitation alone is obviously not sufficient for the adoption of new living arrangements in practice at an early stage, when strongly held attitudes and traditional behaviour has to be modified. Unfortunately, it was not possible to compute this indicator for Sweden so as to further test this result in the case of the country furthest along the diffusion process. Results for Sweden cannot be directly compared because the effect of peer-group adoption is estimated in absence of the second diffusion indicator, precohort adoption. This remains an issue that needs to be better explored in future research.

In line with our hypothesis (H2), compared to the effect of cumulative precohort adoption, cumulative peer-group adoption (Figure 3.5) appears to be a much more important driving force for the diffusion of cohabitation in those countries that, because of a lower speed, are at an earlier stage of the process. As we expected, in the beginning, cohabitation is likely to attract a selective subgroup of the population, more ready or willing to overcome traditional social norms likely because of an higher interest in the potential advantages thought to be associated with the new practice. But the uncertainty linked to the functioning and consequences of cohabitation is greatest at the beginning of the diffusion process. Because social norms also have to be violated in the initial stage, adoption is likely to require stronger reinforcement influence to be undertaken. As we can see, the effect of the third-degree polynomial of cumulative peer-group adoption is rather strong on the individual's adoption rate of cohabitation in West and East Germany, Spain, and Italy. In the Swedish case, this indicator scores significant too, but it is not introduced together with the second mechanism described as is the case in the other countries and thus cannot be directly compared[13].

The effect pattern of the polynomial of cumulative peer-group adoption in Table 6.4, however, is hard to interpret because it describes a quite complex relationship between the individual rate of adoption and the cumulative proportion of peer-group adoption. A clearer picture of this relationship is therefore given in Figure 6.5. Here we plot the overall effect of the three terms of peer-group adoption on the hazard rate, against the observed cumulative percentage of peer-group adoption in each country.

Figure 6.5 shows that the examined countries tend to cluster together around their stage along the diffusion process. Similarities are indeed to be found in the diffusion process between Italy and Spain and between East and West Germany. Given their higher levels of practice with cohabitation, similarity is also expected between France, where precohort adoption proves

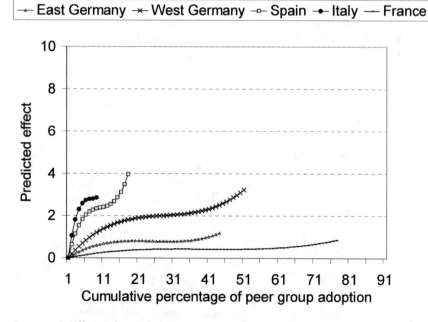

Figure 6.5 Effects of cumulative peer-group adoption.

a much stronger force, and Sweden, where this other indicator could instead not be tested. The relationship between the individual adoption rate and the cumulative *peer-group adoption* is generally S-shaped and monotonically increasing. The overall slope of the curves is greater in the southern countries, for reducing in West and East Germany, and even more so for France, as the diffusion process progresses.

We interpret the effect of peer-group adoption as the degree of social influence exercised by the experiences of cohabitation increasingly made by peer-group practitioners, along with the diffusion process. Each new cohort seems to start with selected groups of early innovators with a specific interest in the adoption of cohabitation. When cohabiting couples are still a minority within each birth cohort, peers' examples of practice with cohabitation seem to constitute an effective and influential behavioural model for young women. Then, with the accumulation of peer-group experiences, the diffusion spills over from these highly receptive specific groups to broader parts of the entire birth cohort population. At the level of about 15% (in Spain), 30% (in West Germany) to 40% (in East Germany) of cumulative peer-group adoption, the peer-group effect increases at an accelerating rate. After these threshold points, cumulative *peer-group adoption* clearly becomes one of the most important driving forces for the individual adoption rate of cohabitation, with the exception of Italy, France, and Sweden.

For the period under consideration, France and Sweden are the two countries in which the spread of cohabitation has already reached the entire population, and it is not confined to subgroups of women anymore. Even the older birth cohorts of women observed in this study have already adopted cohabitation up to 80% in Sweden and over 40% in France by age 30 (Figure 3.5). In these countries, already beyond their initial stage of diffusion, the further spread of cohabitation impacts on an already changing set of practices and social norms (Manting, 1996). Once the reservations and difficulties posed by a generally low level of practice are overcome, the adoption of cohabitation does not seem to require as much reinforcement influence from peer-group examples (H1). Indeed, in France and Sweden the effect of *peer-group adoption* is much flatter and is characterised by the lack of a hurdle, after which cohabitation starts to interest the entire population. Peer-group influence has a decreasing impact on a behaviour that has become mainstream behaviour. This suggests that the contagious influence of peer examples loses its centrality the more cohabitation becomes practised. In France, after the initial stage where general interest had to be gained and when the spread accelerates, it is instead the general awareness about cohabitation, captured by the cumulative rate of *precohort adoption*, that plays the greater role in further driving the diffusion process (Figure 6.7). The same could be thought for the Swedish case, where no increase is displayed in the impact of peer-group adoption (Figure 6.6). Unfortunately, due to the lack of data, it is not possible to test the influence of precohort adoption in Sweden, although this is the mechanism that is expected to exercise the strongest influence here. It follows that the relative influence of peer-group adoption cannot therefore be assessed.

East and West Germany share the same overall S-shaped diffusion pattern, which corresponds to an initial-central phase of the diffusion process, capturing it from its beginning to a seemingly advanced stage. Although there are similarities in the diffusion process, the spread of cohabitation in East Germany proceeds at a slower pace and the accelerating phase is triggered at a comparatively later point (see Figure 6.5). The influence exercised by peers' examples is comparatively lower in East Germany, despite the levels of practice within each birth cohorts that are generally lower than in West Germany (Figure 3.5). As we expected, in the former socialist East Germany there was obviously more resistance than in West Germany against the spread of cohabitation across the entire birth cohort population. This result is in line with the theoretical expectation. As mentioned in chapter 4, the German Democratic Republic was a political system that did not particularly favour social change. In capitalist West Germany on the other side, there has been a stronger orientation and support for social and economic change, as reflected in a greater effect of cumulative *peer-group adoption.*

We expected a particularly strong inertial force in the early process of the diffusion of cohabitation in Italy and Spain, too (H1). Compared to Continental and Nordic countries, these two have much more traditional family norms and organisation, which, coupled with a specific 'southern' model of

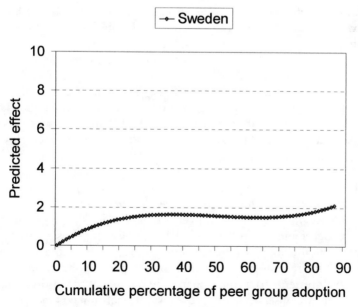

Figure 6.6 Effect of cumulative peer-group adoption, Sweden.

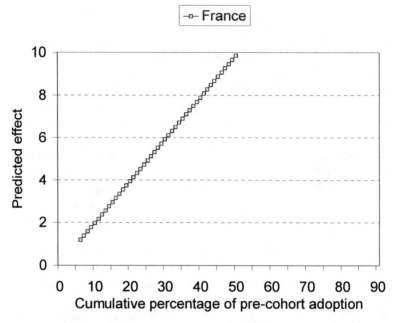

Figure 6.7 Effect of cumulative precohort adoption, France.

institutional setting (housing market, labour market for young people, con-figuration of welfare state measures, etc.), might hinder or even block the diffusion of cohabitation to broader groups within birth cohorts. We thus expected a particularly severe hurdle to get cohabitation off the ground or even a high probability for a failure of the diffusion process. Indeed, as can be seen in Figure 6.5, in Italy the diffusion process seems to remain at an ini-tial stage where it is still confined to select groups of women (not more than about 8% to 10% of a birth cohort). These groups of Italian women who have a higher individual propensity to adopt cohabitation might be charac-terised as follows: They are not religious, have left the educational system and are oriented towards employment (they have acquired some employment experience), are much more likely to have already gained independence from the parental home, live mainly in the north, and grew up in an urban con-text. They seem to be women who have a specific interest in breaking with traditional gender roles and family models. In Spain, somewhat differently, even though we observe a comparatively similar hurdle, the process seems to eventually trigger and get off the ground. Here, the contagious influence from peer behavioural examples remains very strong, pointing to a particularly high general interest in—or motivation for—a more flexible form of union but also to a greater inertia to the change on the side of the institutional set-tings. Overall, we observe that in those institutional contexts more resistant to change, the diffusion process proceed at a slower speed and mainly by influence of peer-group adoption, and where institutions are more prone to inclusive adjustment, it is precohort adoption that prevails.

6.8 SUMMARY

Our diffusion approach suggested that next to the claims made by cultural and economic explanations of demographic change, a focus on individuals' reciprocal influence is required to better understand the uneven rise in cohabiting unions across time and countries. This is also true, more in general, with regard to all those processes of social change involving the spread of new behavioural forms. The longitudinal analyses we have undertaken pointed out that changes in family formation since the mid-1960s were not only due to changed institutional circumstances, individuals' characteristics, or young women's inborn attitudes and values.

At first we have shown that, beside individuals' characteristics, increasing rates of cohabiting unions are also linked to the transitions out of the parental home and to the fertility history. Furthermore, we have seen that the emergence of cohabitation did not necessarily substitute or made up for the increasing postponement of legal marriage. But most importantly, although the individual level covariates worked the way we would have expected, reflecting country-specific institutional and cultural contexts (H2 to 12), we have shown the relevance of others' previously enacted behaviours. The key new contribution of this study is, in fact, the individual-level diffusion approach adopted. In this respect, we have found sound empirical evidence supporting our idea that individuals influence each others' behaviours (H1) and that this reciprocal influence at the micro level can be an engine for social change at the macro level.

Altogether, our results suggest that young people, especially in the initial phase of the diffusion process of cohabitation, tend to confirm their beliefs about its advantages and expected consequences through more direct experience (Strang, 1991). People are persuaded by concrete examples, which seem most convincing if they come from other individuals like themselves who have previously adopted ('structural equivalence'). Thus, as assumed by Bandura (1977), at the heart of the initial diffusion of cohabitation is the direct social modelling by potential adopters of their peers. When traditional social norms begin to loosen and an increasing social acceptance is gained, along with an increased practice of cohabitation, it is rather the more general knowledge-awareness that seems to sustain the process within the entire population. We have also offered empirical evidence that, when an innovative behaviour becomes increasingly more common over time (rising incidence), the effect of individual's background characteristics becomes less influential than social influences in explaining differentials in its takeup.

With this study we hope to have shown that a diffusion approach in the study of cohabitation, together with individual-level diffusion models, is an effective way to account for the combination of intercohort and intracohort processes of change. We revealed the concomitant relevance of both individuals' characteristics and social determinants in gaining a deeper understanding of the recent changes in partnership formation. The diffusion analyses have shown that an individual-level diffusion approach can offer an efficient account of the changes in the takeup rate of an innovative practice, offering new insights in the social determinants of the cross-country differences in the practice and spread of cohabitation. It does so without neglecting individuals' heterogeneity and changing individuals' characteristics along the life course. This approach can provide a substitution for the general notion of 'being grown up in different historical periods' (birth cohort effects) with a theoretically grounded mechanism that links the diffusion of cohabitation to social influences while taking into account both the (changing) individual characteristics and social determinants in union formation. It thus represent a meaningful account for a less clearly specified 'cohort effect' (Hobcraft, Menken, & Preston, 1982). With regard to the study of social change more in general, we believe having shown that our diffusion approach goes beyond a pure 'culturalist' or 'materialist' views focussing exclusively on individuals' moral values or on social structures constraining people's agency. Our dynamic analyses offered empirical evidence that added a focus on how behavioural change can also be linked to individuals' reciprocal influence. In the final chapter we discuss some more in depth about the meaning of these results and the relevance of a diffusion approach.

7 Conclusions

This book has focussed on an emerging form of family living, premarital cohabitation, which has recently become increasingly common in many modern societies (Kiernan, 1999). These types of unions consist of opposite-sex individuals in a couple who choose to live together in the same premises instead of (or prior to) entering a legal marriage. We described its incidence, trends, and patterns from a diffusion perspective. We also explained its process by describing how it begins and changes across time and birth cohorts. We illustrated that there are, however, also marked differences in the pace and extent of the spread of cohabitation among the European countries (Prinz, 1995).

We have argued that the recent rise in premarital cohabitation (and decline in marriage rates) constitutes one of the most remarkable changes in Europe in the last decades. It is a social and normative change that might have long-term consequences, not only on the organisation of family living, but also on intergenerational and interhousehold relationships and transfers, on fertility rates, welfare provisions, and (upon disruption) on the risk of poverty for children and single-headed households. An objective of this study was the exploration of how, for explaining the rapid increase in cohabiting unions beyond its mere accounting, we need to pay more attention to individuals' reciprocal influence. A key idea in this explanation is that cohabiting is the outcome of an individual-level decision-making process, whereby individuals are influenced by their knowledge about others' previous adoption. We have argued that young women have good reasons to extract valuable information from others' previous experiences with cohabitation because they constitute valuable vicarious trials and provide information about its functioning, consequences, and social acceptance. The higher the number of people who choose to cohabit, the higher will be the perceived social acceptance of cohabitation and the easier to do it for the subsequent individuals. Diffusion theory was thus connected with an empirical application to help understand social stability and change in partnership behaviours.

Using representative longitudinal data and individual-level diffusion models, we have analysed the diffusion of cohabitation among young women in six countries. They were selected for being characterised by different family

traditions and institutional contexts: social-democratic Sweden, conservative-corporatist West Germany and France, former socialist East Germany,
and familistic Italy and Spain. We were interested in the question of what
drives the diffusion process in these countries and what forces might lead
to a divergence or convergence in trends over time. Because the choice to
cohabit is an alternative to living single or marrying, we have also examined
the transitions to residential independence (leaving the parental home) and
the entry into marriage.

We have found a progressive postponement of marriage across birth
cohorts; which was not necessarily compensated by cohabitation. We have
also provided some empirical evidence for the 'contagiousness' of cohabitation (whereby peer groups seemed more influential than the experiences
made by older cohorts). We have suggested that after a certain threshold is
reached, the diffusion process becomes self-reinforcing, and we have shown
nation-specific developments of the process. We have stressed the importance of the interdependence between careers, where an easier residential
autonomy would favour family formation, especially in the southern countries. In this concluding chapter we review these major findings in more
detail, discuss their implication for individuals and society, and offer some
suggestions for policy making.

7.1   CENTRAL FINDINGS:
THE THEORETICAL FRAMEWORK

Chapters 2 and 3 provided many ideas about the fruitful use of a diffusion
approach to supplement the understanding of rising cohabitation levels.
Making use of social diffusion theory, we argued that—beside individuals'
specific advantage in alternative and more flexible union arrangements than
marriage—social influence is an endogenous mechanism driving the increasing levels of practice of cohabitation. A fundamental assumption underlying
social diffusion approaches is that the adoption of innovative practices is primarily a learning process. Social influence was said to enhance the perception of a relative advantage entailed in cohabiting rather than marrying in
two distinct ways: by informing the potential adopters of its rationale (social
learning) and through (the lowering of) social pressure. However, our intent
in the theoretical discussion of social influence was not to present and directly
break down these abstract concepts into a measurable and directly testable
construct. As argued, such an idea would have been a senseless task because
those factors are extremely difficult to measure. In fact, they exercise influence
on individuals' behaviours without being consciously perceived, and their size
and strength are subject to change over individuals' life course[1]. According
to diffusion theory, an increasing level of cohabiters in the social system was
expected to have a positive effect on women's likelihood to adopt it themselves, regardless of which influence is specifically at work.

We believe comparative static analyses cannot easily reveal causal processes. Even less so if we are interested in capturing processes of social and cultural change. It is thus important to embed the macro-sociological diffusion argument about rising trends in cohabiting unions and changes in partnership formation in a micro-sociological dynamic framework. The event history framework adopted here was then to provide a link between theoretical and methodological means of investigation of the diffusion process, wherein diffusion theory helped us bridging the macro and micro divide. These theoretical ideas were connected with empirical applications through individual-level diffusion models, which were tested in different institutional contexts to offer new insights on the changes in cohabitation levels across time and countries.

We aimed at disentangling the various dimensions of the process at the level of individuals' life courses. As described in chapter 2, in diffusion theory the individual's rate of adoption of cohabitation is conceived as a function of prior adoptions from other individuals in the social system. The overall shape and speed of the macro-level diffusion process of cohabitation is thought to be a result of the influences exercised by both individual-level risks factors and by the social context (namely, age and cohort-specific measures of the level of cohabitation practice in a society) in which individuals frame their actions. In this framework, cohabitation is conceived as an innovative behavioural option for entering a partnership when it emerges within a national context. Its degree of 'novelty,' and the uncertainty that goes with it, thus varies for different birth cohorts of individuals and along with their growing older. As the result of our focus on the specificity and complexity of the time-related characteristics of the process, we made a distinction between two mechanisms potentially fostering new adoptions. In chapter 3 we described, beside the effect of institutional features, two mechanisms through which social influence could be driving the diffusion process: 'knowledge-awareness' about experiences of previous cohorts (measured as the general level of *precohort adoption*), and 'direct social modelling' of peers (measured as the cumulative proportion of *peer-group adoption*).

According to the first mechanism, in the process of diffusion every new birth cohort experiences an increasing proportion of 'cohabiters' among previous birth cohorts, and thus a bigger incidence of the phenomenon. Later birth cohorts will then experience cohabitation as less deviant (or stigmatised) and more socially accepted right from the beginning. Mass media channels will increasingly disseminate knowledge-awareness on the growing popularity of nonmarital cohabitation among older birth cohorts, inform about its functioning, and enhance its social acceptability (through 'theorization'; see Strang & Meyer, 1993). This mechanism was expected to have a comparatively small effect at the beginning of the process when behavioural norms had to be violated and there was a high degree of uncertainty, which required strong influences.

With the second mechanism, attitudes towards cohabitation are confirmed through direct experiences made by *similar* others, who constitute concrete examples and reference models ('vicarious trials'; see Bernardi, 2003; Kohler, 2001; and Strang, 1991). It does not necessarily operate through direct interpersonal contacts but rather relates to the perception of the behaviour 'proper' to the occupants of an individual's position (Cialdini, 1984; Strang, 1991). This mechanism is related to a persuasive influence where peer behaviours are taken as a reference model because of individuals' *'structural equivalence'* (Burt, 1987). This mechanism was expected to exercise a bigger effect on the spread of cohabitation, especially in the early phase of the process, given the presence of conflicting standards or behavioural models (Bandura, 1977), and social stigma to be eroded.

It must be remembered that the aim of this book was not to argue for the importance of mechanisms linked to social influence against traditional explanatory factors. On the contrary, it was suggested that traditional 'structural' models are complementary, and necessary, to properly test hypotheses about diffusion processes (Palloni, 2001; Reed, Briere, & Casterline, 1999; Strang, 1991; Strang & Tuma, 1993). Indeed, this study has explicitly recognised that there can be more mechanisms affecting women's decision process in choosing to adopt cohabitation. By using a diffusion approach, we have also stressed the relevance of not neglecting women's embeddedness in the social world because of the important effect exercised through social influence by others' adoptions.

7.2   CENTRAL FINDINGS:
THE DIFFUSION OF COHABITATION

A first description of the diffusion process across generations showed that in France, East Germany, and West Germany, each successive birth cohort experienced not only an impressive rise in the proportions of cumulative *precohort adoption* but also a steep increase in the cumulative proportions of *peer-group adoption* at each age. This suggests there has been an increasing social acceptance of cohabitation for each younger birth cohort, especially in Germany and France, to the extent that cohabitation has become a normal form of partnership in the process of family formation. Among the youngest birth cohorts, more than 85% of women in Sweden and 75% in France, about 50% in West Germany, and 40% in East Germany have adopted cohabitation before they (possibly) started a first marriage. In contrast, in Italy even among the youngest birth cohorts not more than about 10% of women, and in Spain only 16%, have adopted cohabitation instead of (or before eventually) entering into first marriage.

The core finding of this study is that *cohabitation is indeed 'contagious' and that the shape of this influence varies across countries reflecting their institutional contexts and their stage along the diffusion process.* A first substantive important result is thus about the appropriateness and relevance of a diffusion approach in the study of cohabitation's emergence and spread. In fact, the findings from the empirical test of the diffusion model strongly support the hypothesis of cohabitation 'contagiousness' through others' enacted behaviours. The results have also shown the importance of institutional-specific effects on the shape of these influences, and thus on the hindering or favouring of the diffusion process.

The diffusion analysis has stressed that it is not only individuals' characteristics at play in young women's decisions to cohabit, and it has offered an empirical test of two different mechanisms potentially affecting the diffusion process. What does this result mean exactly in terms of expected consequences for the individuals and societies? The model predicts that increasing levels of cohabitation are, at least partially, produced through an endogenously (self-)driven process led by social influence. This means that, especially in the long run, individuals' specific advantages entailed in cohabitation can become quite secondary in motivating its adoption once attitudes and values (social approval) have changed to the point where these unions are fully institutionalised and become the norm. Through the influence exercised on the ground of previous adopters' experiences, the effects of initial changes in 'structural' conditions are amplified beyond their original magnitude. This way, even small or temporary changes in individuals' characteristics or attributes associated to a higher advantage in cohabiting can explain (later) bigger changes at the aggregate societal level. The diffusion process, after a certain spread is being reached, will enhance the advantage entailed in cohabiting also for those individuals whose characteristics did not necessary make for a high preference for cohabitation, and this hasn't changed. In other words, cohabiting may become 'the norm' even for those who have not a specific advantage in its adoption. This is to say that after the process gets established, specific factors that might make cohabitation attractive to particular kinds of individuals lose their relevance. Beyond a certain threshold, cohabitation will become an increasingly accepted and appealing behavioural option to everyone, regardless of their characteristics (Rogoff Ramsey, 1994).

In the theoretical section we have argued that social acceptance of cohabitation is a function of the prevalence of the practice among earlier adopters. This means that next to the behavioural change, a change in social norms will follow because normative standards, as well as the judgement of appropriateness and efficiency of cohabiting, are associated with the prevalence of its practice. Thus, depending on the responsiveness of the institutional context, the higher the rate of cohabiting unions, the faster the change in social norms. Then, along with the diffusion process, the moral costs of an initially 'socially unaccepted' behaviour are increasingly reduced and its adoption further sustained. This can lead to long-run social changes that make previously stigmatised behaviour not only accepted but even desirable. Indeed, as changes in the family values and attitudes are produced by social change in the society, a trend of decreasing marriage and increasing cohabitation may well be sustained by a formal and legal convergence of the two forms of unions. More specifically, the model presented in this study suggests that an initial increasing advantage in a more flexible family arrangement can result in gradual changes in how cohabitation is perceived and the meaning attached to it (Manting, 1996). This in turn can lead to gradually increasing levels of cohabiting couples among those who still have a bigger advantage in less-binding commitment, but as well as among those who might not have a specifically high interest or need. Furthermore, after a certain time, cultural changes (in terms of how cohabitation is viewed) may progress to a point past which exogenous factors and individuals characteristics cannot prevent the rise in the levels of cohabitation.

7.3   CHANGING MODES OF PARTNERSHIP FORMATION: MARRIAGE POSTPONEMENT

First, *there has been a clear postponement of entry into marriage in all countries across cohorts.* As the indicators of educational enrolment capture, this is partly the case because young women stay longer in school and therefore are simply 'ready' for marriage later (Blossfeld, 1995; Oppenheimer, 1988). Further important factors in the decay of marriage are declining religiosity and growing urbanisation, both of which weaken the importance of marriage as a social norm for many people. Finally, and beyond all these factors, there is an autonomous cohort trend of increasing postponement of entry into marriage for all countries but Sweden. To a large extent this postponement is connected with increasing uncertainties of the youth labour markets and employment relationships in the process of globalisation (Mills et al., 2005). In many countries, the growing tendency among young adults to opt for informal cohabitation instead of marriage might therefore be a rational answer to these new challenges. Indeed, premarital cohabitation permits the postponement of long-term binding commitments while providing an alternative form of family living and a way of avoiding sexual promiscuity and/or singlehood. It also offers other benefits of the single state, such as fewer legal responsibilities, while retaining advantages like the pooling of resources and the economies of scale provided by living together (Oppenheimer, 1988).

Has cohabitation generally offset the decline in marriage across birth cohorts? The answer must be qualified because cohabitation represents a possible destination state in both the transition to residential independence (together with living single of marrying) and entry into a union (as alternative to marriage). This is because an increasing propensity to cohabit across birth cohorts has affected the timing of both these events.

With reference to the transition to *residential independence*, we have shown that cohabitation contributes to reduce (or avoid) the postponement of this transition across birth cohorts, especially in France and East

Germany. In West Germany instead, it was more an increasing transition to the single state that compensated for delayed (or forgone) exit through marriage. Thus, from our analyses, the postponement of the exit from the parental home would appear to be less dramatic than it has been suggested in the social policy debate, at least when considering both institutionalised and informal unions. In the southern countries, in the period observed, cohabitation was still too little practised to compensate significantly for an increasing delay in marriage.

In the transition to *first partnership*, in Sweden and France the late entry into marriage seems again to have been effectively compensated by an earlier, and more frequent, entrance into cohabitation. Instead, in the remaining countries an earlier (or more frequent) entry into cohabitation did not seem to entirely compensate for the progressive delay in marriage timing. Quite contrasting was the case of the southern countries. Here an already later, and further delaying acquisition of residential independence, went hand in hand with a parallel postponement of entrance into partnership across birth cohorts. This means that, in Italy and Spain, where leaving the parental home is still mostly on the ground to marry and cohabitation proved much slower to diffuse, we see a progressive delay of young women's transition to adulthood.

7.4 CHANGING MODES OF PARTNERSHIP FORMATION: THE DIFFUSION OF COHABITATION

We have also shown that the growing age gap that has been produced by an increased postponement of entry into marriage has not been automatically filled by cohabitation. Young people can choose between various alternatives: They might stay longer in the parental home, live in a single household, or cohabit. The degree to which cohabitation is perceived as being more advantageous than its alternatives is strongly determined by the cultural and institutional settings.

Indeed, the analyses show that cohabitation is not an attractive choice in Italy or Spain. First, young Italians and Spaniards have great difficulties in getting somewhere to live. The rental market, which is squeezed by specific rental laws and distorted by an (unprotected) 'informal' housing market, is rather expensive and public housing is extremely scarce. Thus the best choice for young people would often be either staying with their parents or buying a house. But buying a house not only requires a huge financial investment, it is also a long-term binding decision. For this reason marital and cohabitation decisions would implicitly have very similar consequences for the life course of young Italians and Spaniards. Secondly, the Mediterranean welfare state provides only a weak protection against the increasing labour market risks of the young generations (Jurado Guerrero, 1995), in which the cohesive Mediterranean family is the relevant locus of social aid and parents are responsible for their children and vice versa (Barbagli, Castiglioni, & Dalla Zuanna 2003; Bettio & Villa, 1998; González et al., 2000; Naldini, 2003, Orloff, 2002; Saraceno, 1997). In other words, increasing youth unemployment and uncertainties of employment relationships (Bernardi & Nazio, 2005; Simó Noguera et al., 2005), together with the peculiarities of the housing market and the traditional familialism, make the extended stay of young people in the parental home more attractive than cohabitation or living as a single person. Italy and Spain thus share a cultural and institutional setting that does not provide fertile ground to the diffusion of living arrangements as an alternative to marriage.

As the longitudinal analyses have shown, cohabitation in Italy and Spain is therefore confined to small, highly selective groups of women who have a good reason to break with traditional gender roles and family models. As a rule, these women are not religious, have left the educational system and have already gained some years of working experience, have reached residential independence, and, in the case of Italy, live mainly in the north and grew up in an urban context. Particularly in Italy, the diffusion of cohabitation to broader groups of the population appears to be blocked, at least until the early 1990s, time we could cover in this analysis. Social forerunners who are practising cohabitation consist of very specific groups of people whose experiences obviously cannot serve as appropriate models for their peers in other groups, so that the mechanism of the 'strengths-of-weak-ties' (Granovetter, 1973) seems not to work in the Italian diffusion process. Although Spain shares most of the characteristics of the Italian environment, the results show that the process of diffusion of cohabitation seems to have recently passed a threshold that could allow for an increasing spread of this alternative living arrangement in the near future.

In East Germany, the relatively low average age at marriage was the result of a comparatively high level of individual life-course predictability in the socialist society and a consequence of a specific housing allocation policy. In the historical period between the mid-1970s and 1989, there was a strong incentive to adopt cohabitation for young women, even when they were still in school. After the breakdown of the socialist society in 1989, a historical period that could not be covered very well with these data, the institutional framework of West Germany was introduced in East Germany, and economic uncertainty and rising unemployment have increased dramatically. It is well known that these changes resulted in rapidly declining nuptiality and fertility rates and increased the rate of cohabitation and extramarital births in East Germany.

In West Germany, the housing market has been accessible for young people for many decades. It has been easy to rent a flat and the prices are—with the exception of some few expensive cities—generally affordable. In cross-national comparative terms, the proportion of homeowners is also relatively low in West Germany at 45% (Kurz & Blossfeld, 2004). If young people don't work, they are normally supported by the conservative welfare state or by their parents. Thus, given increasing unemployment and growing employment uncertainty, cohabitation or living as a single person are attractive options compared to staying with parents in West Germany.

Somewhat different is the case of France, a country well beyond the initial stage of the diffusion process of cohabitation. Here cohabitation diffused more rapidly, and the biggest effect in the dissemination of the practice has been found in the precohort adoption measure. In France, a bunch of experiences has accumulated and the practice has gained an increasing tolerance and consensus along with its spread. For young French women, the welfare system, together with a controlled and highly subsidised housing market, make cohabitation and living single very attractive and rather affordable alternatives to marrying or living with parents.

7.5   THE DIFFUSION PROCESS: MECHANISMS AT PLAY

A further important result of this study is that, surprisingly, with the exception of France, when we discount for the effect of a prolonged education and employment attachment, no increase in cohabitation is found across birth cohorts. In fact, we could see that in model 1 there was no autonomous partial cohort trend left on women's rate of entry into cohabitation, after controlling for cohort differences in educational participation and attainment levels as well as for women's labour force participation. At a first glance, this result makes it seem like no diffusion process would occur across cohorts as the measures of precohort and peer-group adoptions suggested. Instead, apart from the trend towards secularisation and increasing divorce rates, none of the (significant) effects in the analyses can point to the influences responsible for the rising levels in cohabiting unions observed in Figures 3.3 and 3.4. However, the results of model 2 show that the diffusion process strongly affects the likelihood of cohabiting, which is mainly driven by peer-group influences in its early stage (insights for intergenerational mechanisms are only found at a later stage of the process). It is also important to notice that reintroducing controls for birth cohorts, together with the *diffusion* covariates, does not produce any further improvement of the models. This means that the measures of previous adoptions (diffusion covariates) effectively capture an influential mechanism linked to social influence. It also means that the lack of a cohort pattern observed in model 1 was probably the result of two counteracting effects: the first of a progressive postponement of partnership across cohorts, and the second of a diffusion process that makes it increasingly attractive and easier to cohabit over time.

More specifically, the diffusion analysis shows that the dissemination of abstract knowledge based on the cohabitation experiences of earlier generations does not seem to have any substantial influence on the diffusion of cohabitation in the population in an early phase of the process. Thus, at the beginning of the diffusion process, the increase in cohabitation does not imply a mechanism that links the experiences across generations but seems rather to be driven mainly by direct social modelling of peers. Concrete experiences of the same age group clearly constitute a sort of useful vicarious trial for potential adopters. The diffusion process begins with groups of innovators who have a specific interest or motivation to cohabit and who are particularly sensitive to reinforcement influences, and it then spills over the entire population of potential adopters when it accelerates after having reached a country-specific threshold. The strength of the influence from peers decreases along with the stage of the diffusion: highest in the southern countries, medium in Germany, and lowest in France and Sweden (the latter is not strictly comparable due to the lack of controls for precohort influence). In a later stage of the diffusion process, the adoption of cohabitation seems rather influenced by an acquired abstract knowledge. Altogether, the strength and shape of the effects played by the mechanisms linked to diffusion reflect the country-specific stage along the diffusion process. The effects found are highly consistent with a progressive development of each nation out of their own institutional roots. At the beginning of the process of change, the different initial conditions define and delimit individuals' agency. We also saw that in the institutional settings less compatible with cohabitation, the diffusion process is much slower and peer examples have stronger effects. After a certain threshold has been reached, however, a new trajectory of institutional development will be triggered and its consolidation is then difficult to reverse. We saw that in those countries where institutional settings were more favourable to cohabitation instead, the process seemed less confined to specific subgroups and peers' models had a relatively smaller effect. The faster the process in turning cohabitation into an accepted alternative to marriage and the more institutions seconded this change, the lower the effect of direct social modelling.

7.6   THE INTERDEPENDENCE BETWEEN THE UNION AND FERTILITY CAREERS

We have stressed how the timing of entrance and type of union people chose are strongly bound up with finishing education, the kind of tenure they can afford, and whether they plan or expect children. Indeed, the experience of an event on a parallel career (such as completing education, gaining residential autonomy from the parental home, or experiencing a pregnancy) can significantly affect the likelihood to marry or to adopt cohabitation. However, these effects are quite different for the entrance into cohabitation or a marriage. Specifically, the estimates of the transition rate to first marriage or to the adoption of cohabitation have shown both a significant time-dependent effect of the discovery of a pregnancy on women's entry into a union. This consists as one of the strongest predictors and is in line with the expectations that women may want to accelerate partnership formation not to have an out-of-wedlock (or out-of-union) birth to comply with social norms and expectations, as well as to offer their child a more secure family environment. But whereas in the case of marriage this influence is stronger and generally more concentrated in the period before the birth, in the case of cohabitation the effect is lower and tends to spill over after the birth has taken place (see also similar findings for the United States by Brien, Lillard, & Waite, 1999, and for Britain by Steele et al., 2005).

7.7 A STEPPING-STONE INTO ADULTHOOD: RESIDENTIAL INDEPENDENCE

Corijn (2001a) underlines how the route to residential independence develops in a context of both socioeconomic and sociocultural opportunities and constraints: Residential autonomy requires financial resources to access privacy and autonomy. For young women, the financial means to independence can come from different sources (or from their combination): the parental families, the welfare state, or their own paid work. The amount and the origin of the resources necessary to undertake this transition are highly dependent on the national institutional contexts and on the characteristics of the housing markets, as we described in chapter 4 (see also Aassve et al., 2002, Klijzing & Corijn, 2002).

Consistently with the findings of previous research, our results have shown that the transition out of the parental household is a key issue for women in the southern countries when the aim is to allow for an earlier family formation. Indeed, in Italy and Spain, in contrast to other European countries, the transition out of the parental home is still strongly connected with partnership formation (and very often with house purchase). This, in turn, is impaired by a slow diffusion of cohabitation and by institutional and cultural settings that resist adjusting to its spread. The results of the multivariate analysis have shown that living single, thus having already overcome housing obstacles and having reached some degree of economic autonomy, has everywhere a significant positive effect on entry into cohabitation. But they have also pointed at this effect being far much stronger in Italy and Spain[2]. Moreover, in these two countries (together with France) it is where pursuing higher studies proves to be particularly conflicting with union formation[3]. It follows that state measures directed to lower students' dependence on their families would lower the particularly strong incompatibility with residential independence and partnership formation in these countries. Additionally, in line with these findings, it seems that—especially in Italy and Spain—a more accessible housing market, coupled with a system of unemployment benefits and/or support for first-job seekers, could dampen the postponement of both transitions (to residential independence and to first partnership) and eventually make them more independent from one another, as it is for the other countries.

7.8 IMPLICATIONS OF RESEARCH

A last important result of this study was the development and empirical test of an explanatory model that allows for different mechanisms to affect individuals' decision-making process.

Building on previous analyses of the determinants of the timing of entry into cohabitation, this study goes beyond them in several respects. First, we presented a theoretical framework and individual-level diffusion models through which effects of important social influences can be interpreted. In particular, we allowed the incorporation of individuals' heterogeneity together with the identification of several dimensions of social and structural changes in the study of the diffusion process of cohabitation. Second, the individual-level diffusion analysis undertaken takes into account the complex time-related structure of the process with a changing population of potential adopters while including a wide range of other influences[4]. Finally, this research presents the results of highly comparable studies for six different institutional contexts, on the basis of a continuous succession of birth cohorts, over the same historical period. Over three recent decades, this study covers a range of variations in important characteristics such as tempo, pace, and level of the diffusion of cohabitation, political, economic, and welfare systems as well as family traditions.

In the light of these new insights, the following paragraphs are devoted to a discussion of the possible future consequences attached to growing rates of cohabiting unions. For organisational purpose, we cluster the following arguments around three domains: implications for individuals, for the society, and for policy making.

Among the implications of rising levels of cohabitation *for individuals*, we need to mention a further delaying effect on marriage timing (Oppenheimer, 1988; Wu, 2000), a potentially more equitable division of household labour (see, among others, Domingo i Valls, 1997; Huinink, 1995; MacAllister, 1990; Shelton & John, 1993), and a possible increase in union instability connected to the higher risk of disruption of cohabiting unions (the greater is the share of cohabiting unions and the earlier they tend to take place in the life course). The latter may be caused by several factors: The first is a process of self-selection into cohabitation of those individuals whose partnerships originally have an higher risk of disruption (Boyle, 2006; Lillard, Brien, & Waite, 1995, Steele, Kallis, & Heather, 2006). This may happen especially at the beginning of the diffusion process. In fact, until a certain point of the diffusion process when cohabiting becomes a common choice, its adoption requires stronger motivations to overcome doubts, constraints, and/or social pressure because young women are engaging in a behaviour (cohabiting) that has not traditionally been socially accepted. It follows that this form of union tends to be selected preferentially by those who can see a specific relative advantage in cohabiting rather than marrying. It is probably a more attractive option to those who held a less traditional attitude towards marriage and the family (Axinn & Thornton, 1992; Wu, 2000), to those who are—or feel—not ready for long-binding commitments or do not feel secure enough about their relationship ('marriage trial'), to "poorer" marriage candidates, or else to those who reject the marital institution and the roles and responsibilities attached to it[5]. A second reason lies in the higher risk of mismatch between partners (Oppenheimer, 1988), especially if the partners are relatively young and their future perspectives and desires are not yet well understood or if their labour careers are not yet established, which may require a greater effort to combine them with one another in the long run. The third reason for the higher risk of disruption generally displayed by cohabiting unions is that of the lower legal barriers and financial costs to exit the union. Cohabiting supposedly (although not always) requires and implies a lower investment and degree of commitment than that of a traditional marriage right from the beginning. The rising proportion of cohabiting union may contribute to a more equitable distribution of household (unpaid) labour between partners, however, because its lower exit costs may make for a better breakdown position in intra-household negotiations (Breen & Cooke, 2005; Sen, 1990). For all these reasons, it would be important to focus on the consequences of union disruption, especially on the weaker partner (generally the woman) and on the children. We come back to this issue on the discussion about the consequences for policy making.

There are then a series of implications of higher proportions of cohabiters *for society*. A first consequence is an ambiguous effect on the general level of fertility. Are (absolute) reductions or (relative) increases on total fertility to be expected? Marital unions are still widely recognised as the best setting to give birth and bring up children because of their relatively long duration and for the legal protections they offer to both spouses and their children. Consistent with this view, the long-term decline in fertility experienced in Europe in recent decades is primarily attributed to the postponement of marriage and a decline in marital fertility, especially on higher order parities. However, as cohabitation increases and becomes more institutionalised, it is reasonable to expect an increase in cohabiting fertility (examples of this trend can be the recent reverse trend in fertility in the Nordic countries and the high rate of extramarital births in France), which may eventually offset part of this decline. Wu (2000) notices also that because cohabiting fertility tends to be lower than its marital counterpart, increasing levels of cohabiting unions may result in a further reduction in fertility levels. Against this argument, it must be remembered that cohabitation might not only be an alternative to marriage in partnering but to increasing difficulties to afford marriage and singlehood in the transition out of the parental home. In this respect, if marriage is to be postponed and living independently as single is not an appealing or affordable alternative, cohabiting may represent a further option associated with a higher risk of conception than singlehood (especially if coupled with residence in the parental home). Furthermore, because cohabiting unions tend to take place earlier in the life course than marriage, they provide the locus for a more regular sexual activity, and we saw that an ongoing pregnancy accelerates the entry into a union, especially a marriage (on 'shotgun' weddings, see Blossfeld et al., 1999; Blossfeld & Mills, 2001; Mills, 2000). Therefore, in a scenario where the only feasible alternative to an increasingly difficult marriage is to live single or to prolong the stay in the parental family, a rise in cohabiting unions may nevertheless positively influence fertility. However, the more cohabiting unions become widespread and child rearing in them is accepted, the more is nonmarital fertility going to grow. Thus the effect of cohabitation on future developments of overall fertility is extremely difficult to predict. They may be altogether more dependent on other social and institutional changes that could offer economic security and incentives to parenthood and, more important, for both women and men, to ease the combination of the role of parents with paid employment (Nazio & MacInnes, 2007).

A second implication of the emergence of cohabiting unions as a widespread phenomenon in society is the (possible) decline of the marital institution and its undermining the definition of the '*family.*' On the one side, given the higher risk of dissolution of marriages preceded by cohabitation, a higher rate of cohabiting unions could be viewed as a threat to the notion of permanence that marriage embeds (Rindfuss & Van den Heuvel, 1990; Cherlin, 2004). On the other side, with an increasingly accessible alternative to marriage, this latter may be no longer perceived as a necessary event in the life course and may be postponed or forgone; which would weaken the marital institution. The latter is of tremendous importance for policy making, for what concerns the definition of a societal unit to which are attached legal responsibilities and entitlements. Several societal organisations and institutions are confronted with the 'family' as their unit of reference, and the definition of what makes a family (whether it is the marital or another form of contract, sharing of a residence for a given amount of time, or the presence of children) can be crucial for different purposes (see also Rogoff Ramsey, 1994; Kiernana, 2004a). A few examples would be tax benefits, public housing provision, health insurance, pensions rights, as well as for the rules of entitlement to other social security (means-tested) benefits and services[6]. Among other aspects of public concern, the state of 'single-parenthood' is particularly affected by the definition of 'family unit'[7]. As this study has shown, the nature of family living is undergoing a profound, and partly self-driven, changing process. Insofar as the diffusion process changes the meaning of cohabitation and marriage, the traditional definition of the 'family' unit must confront the emergence and rise in cohabiting couples and should thus be open to recognise and comprise nonmarital cohabitation.

Finally, following the acknowledgement of this development towards a plurality of family forms and to the need to adapt legal regulations accordingly, we would like to mention some of the implications of this research *for policy making*. We refer here to those policy issues that mainly regard the rights and responsibilities of cohabiters and former cohabiters: couples' registration, property rights, partner support, occupation rights in the family home, provisions on death (pension rights, inheritance, and intestacy), private contracts (cohabitation agreements), social security benefits, and finally the responsibilities for the custody, education, and maintenance of children. As seen in chapter 4, legal reforms have developed along quite different routes and towards varying solutions. Some countries have reacted promptly to the social change and changed the normative to narrow the gap between the two partnership forms (with Sweden having almost completely removed the distinctions), whereas others (especially the southern countries) have strongly resisted changing them. However, everywhere (including Sweden) married couples still have more rights and enjoy more protection that those cohabiting. But if there is to be a self-driving mechanisms favouring an increasing acceptance (and practice) of cohabiting unions together with their becoming widespread as this analysis suggests, a progressive reduction in the legal distinction between marriage and cohabitation would make sense. A legal convergence would help recognise the important function of social reproduction that both types of union undertake. Indeed, in both these living arrangements there is some sort of pooling of resources, there is reciprocal emotional and financial support, and there is a family environment for the raising of children (Oppenheimer, 1988; Prinz, 1995; Waite, et al., 2000; Wu, 2000). Together with a widening of the definition of the 'family' to comprise family-living arrangements other than marriage, it must be acknowledged how the family remains a central institution for social reproduction and is still the main provider for its members' well-being. Therefore, in the face of growing individuals' willingness and ability to enter family living, which does not necessarily imply engaging or maintaining high commitment in long-term relationships, some consequences of increasing family instability should attract policy interest. Higher family instability, in fact, might affect former partners' and children's well-being and raise the risk of falling into poverty or experiencing other adverse outcomes for some of the former union members.

In this direction, and given the previously mentioned higher risk of disruption of cohabiting unions, we would suggest some policy recommendations aimed at extending the marital protections to the weaker spouse (and children) upon partnership breakdown. Imposing some sorts of rights and obligations of marriage to cohabiters would ensure more economic security to the family members, especially to the children. Moreover, given a still pervasive gender-role specialisation of labour, such an extension of guarantees would also offer some recognition to the burden of unpaid reproductive work undertaken (mainly by women) within the family units, regardless of their being marital or cohabiting unions. In fact, for the many reasons briefly touched on in chapter 4, it is generally (although not always) women who happen to take in charge of the bigger part of the load of unpaid work within the family, thus constraining their possibilities and returns in the paid labour market. Granting some kind of protection after the (possible) dissolution would avoid the risk that cohabitation makes the already weaker spouse's position even weaker while partially compensating for the investment made in the reproduction of the family at the price of economic and career sacrifices. However, in equating cohabitation to marriage, it is also important to give an option-out to such a regulation for those who consciously and autonomously do not want to marry for the very reason of avoiding the responsibilities that this involves (Glendon, 1989; Wu, 2000). This alternative option is intended to preserve individuals' agency and right to choose, and it could well take the form of privately defined contracts ('cohabitation agreements'). The mere imposition[8] of some sort of (self-)regulation would force people to explicitly make a choice and hence to think and discuss the functions, expectations, and responsibilities in their relationship. Beside providing a legal status to cohabiting unions, it would also offer recognition of this family form, which could turn useful in the definition of entitlement to welfare provision, thus avoiding the risk of distortions among recipients. An equation of legal status and entitlements might also enhance the feeling of security enjoyed in the relationship and hence foster cohabiting fertility by making cohabitation a safer setting for raising children.

Referring back more directly to the results of the analysis, we have also shown the importance of institutional contexts on the pace of the diffusion process. In this respect, cross-national comparative research has offered a unique insight into the effects of normative and institutional dimensions and their dynamic interplay. The findings support the view that all those policies directed towards the promotion of young people's independence from the family (defamilisation) are of especially great importance for promoting earlier family formation. On the basis of the results obtained, we suggest that housing and employment policies are of crucial importance for young women's family formation, especially in the southern countries. Institutional support to students living arrangements and/or directed to promote young people residential independence through an affordable housing market, coupled with a system of unemployment benefits and/or support for first-job seekers, could be among the crucial measures to contrast a further delay in family formation, especially so in Italy and Spain.

7.9   CONCLUDING REMARKS

The main purpose of this book was to study recent changes in partnership formation, focusing on the uneven rise in cohabitation across countries. We were interested in the question of what drives the diffusion of cohabitation and which elements are responsible for its convergence or divergence across countries. Using data from different European countries, we described women's timing of adoption of cohabitation across successive birth cohorts. We then dynamically analysed, by means of hazard rate models, the determinants of entry into cohabitation and marriage, and we deepened the study of the adoption of cohabitation with individual-level diffusion models. There are several results of substantive importance in this volume.

First, by focussing on the time frame of the diffusion process of cohabitation, we provided an innovative description of the rising levels of cohabitation over time within birth cohorts and among earlier generations. These descriptions have shown how the diffusion process of cohabitation spreads at different rates and reached rather different levels across countries. Second, we found evidence of 'social contagion' and observed that the diffusion process is mainly driven by peer-group examples in its early stage, whereas precohort adoption influences are only determinant after a certain spread has been reached. Third, we have found that the diffusion of cohabitation does not necessarily make up for the progressive postponement of marriage across birth cohorts, which (together with the lower fertility observed in cohabiting unions) may further contribute to childbirth postponement. Fourth, we observed that educational expansion delays family formation (more so marriage than cohabitation) as a result of a prolonged schooling period rather than due to increasing attainment levels being reached. Despite a longer educational enrolment brought about by educational expansion that translates in delayed partnership formation, pregnancy does accelerates either form of union. We also found the expected effects of increasing secularisation trends and parental divorce on entry into marital and cohabiting unions. Finally, we saw how residential independence from the parental household might be a crucial element in the diffusion of cohabitation, especially in the Southern European countries.

To conclude, despite the limitations of any multivariate analysis of this breadth and the difficulties entailed in applying a diffusion approach to such complex phenomena, the diffusion approach proposed here provides a sound theoretical explanation that builds on rational action theory and links the uneven rise in cohabitation across countries to individual-level decision making, within changing normative and institutional contexts. It does so, accounting for the complex time structure of this dynamic process, in a way that is plausible and consistent with empirical facts while being supported by the findings of severe empirical testing. The results of the diffusion analysis prove robust to different specifications and point to the existence of social multipliers in the diffusion process of cohabitation.

Although the effects of peer-group and precohort adoption do not prove conclusively that the mechanism behind the increasing levels of cohabitation is diffusion via social influence operated through 'direct social modelling' and 'knowledge-awareness' of the emerging practice, they are clearly consistent with such an interpretation. Our individual-level diffusion analysis provides empirical evidence that others' experience with cohabitation can efficiently and meaningfully account for the historical change in the practice with cohabitation (birth cohort patterns) and its different levels across countries. This interpretation is also coherent with that of a progressive 'ideational change' (Bumpass, 1990; Lesthaeghe, 1995; Lesthaeghe & Surkyn, 1988; Surkyn & Lesthaeghe, 2004; Van de Kaa, 1987) and allows for the changing meaning of cohabitation (and marriage) along with the diffusion process. The diffusion model proposed also allows for a possible failure of the diffusion process, as the Italian case seems to indicate. Both southern countries analysed share a slow diffusion pace and a steep effect of 'peer-group adoption' on the likelihood to cohabit. However, in Italy, peers' influence seemed still confined within selective groups of the population. By contrast, the Spanish case looks in a stage where more rapidly increasing levels of cohabitation are to be expected among the broader population.

Still, there may be alternative explanations for the rise in cohabiting unions over time. One alternative interpretation could be that (unmeasured) increasing uncertainty in young people's labour careers would increase women's advantage in choosing cohabitation over marriage[9]. As we discussed in chapter 4, it may also be that increasing women's labour force participation urges for a new gender-role negotiation, which is easier to reach in living arrangements less charged with traditional expectations, such as cohabitation. As a consequence, it should be expected that in those countries where young people suffer higher employment uncertainty and/or where women more rapidly increased their investment in educational credentials and a working career, cohabiting union should have risen faster to higher levels. However, if these alternative accounts for change were true, one would expect that in the Southern European countries, like Italy and Spain, where temporary contracts and youth unemployment are highest and where women's activity rates rose the most, cohabitation would be highest and diffusion faster, and the opposite for France and Sweden. We have shown, however, that this was not the case. We observed marriage being increasingly postponed across birth cohorts to a similar extent across countries, whereas cohabitation rising only much slower in the south of Europe than in the other countries over the same 30-year time span. Our diffusion approach, instead, has offered a statistically efficient and theoretically meaningful account of the different changes occurred over time and across birth cohorts in a wide range of institutional contexts. The results obtained proved very coherent with earlier findings from previous analyses ('structural explanations'), to which they added a deeper insight on the mechanisms related to others' behaviours ('diffusion explanation'). Therefore, in waiting for some alternative interpretation that proves to be at least as plausible and powerful as the diffusion explanation for which dynamic comparative empirical evidence is provided here, we are inclined to provisionally accept the diffusion account. Furthermore, we believe the diffusion framework outlined here can be a useful analytical tool to be more generally applied to a wider range of societal change processes of interest to the social sciences.

Notes

NOTES TO CHAPTER 1

1. This definition thus does not include Living Apart Together (LAT) arrangements, nor does it include living communities, but it may include those cases were either partner retain his or her legal residence but in practice they live together.
2. Some demographers and economists, however, strongly oppose the idea of a "delayed" diffusion in the southern countries and speak about a specific "southern model" of family formation strategies. See, for Italy, Bettio and Villa (1998); Billari, Castiglioni, Martin, Michelin & Ongaro (2002); Castiglioni and Dalla Zuanna (1994); Dalla Zuanna (2004).
3. See Schneider (1988), Aronson (1999), and, in the field of historical studies of the family, Stone (1977).
4. A more thorough discussion of these points is given in chapter 2.
5. *Cohort* is defined as a group of individuals sharing a common characteristic or experience at the same time (e.g., a 'school leavers cohort' is the group of individuals who have terminated education on the same year, and a 'birth cohort' are those born on the same year, or interval of years).
6. For an interesting example of an empirical application about partnership behaviours, see Mills (2000).
7. Only heterosexual couples were retained in the study on the ground that the possibility to marry legally for same-sex couples was not available in the period covered by the analyses. Thus cohabitation for same-sex couples did not constitute a *choice* option because marriage was (and in some countries still is) not viable. For the empirical analyses, a definition was derived from the FFSs questionnaires' question wording about partnership experiences. Are considered as cohabiting those "partners with whom respondents have had an intimate relationship and with whom they have lived for sometime in the same household" without being married (Festy & Prioux, 2002).
8. East Germany is treated here as a country because of having been a separate and very different institutional context from West Germany, across almost all the period covered by the analysis (up to 1992).
9. By 'welfare regime' is meant the cluster of several countries on the basis of their commonalties in institutionalised patterns in welfare state provisions, which establish systematic relations between the state and social structures of conflict, domination, and accommodation (Esping-Andersen, 1990).
10. The United Kingdom is missing because Britain did not participate in the FFS enterprise, and no equivalent data could be found at the time of the study (see Ermish & Francesconi, 2000).
11. See Blossfeld and Rohwer (1995b) and Bernardi (1999) for the opposite effect of entry into marriage on work careers, Goldsheider and Waite (1986),

Blossfeld and Huinink (1991), Bernardi and Nazio (2005), and Kurz, Steinhage and Golsch (2005) on sex differences on entry into marriage.

12. Parallel careers are those capturing events along different realms of the life course. For example, does an event in the fertility career (e.g., pregnancy) affect the rate of occurrence of an event in the partnership career (e.g., marriage)? Does achieving residential autonomy impact the type and timing of partnership formation?

13. All variables employed in the statistical models are derived from the answers to equivalent questions in each survey and have been coded the same way for each country.

14. For a discussion of individual-level-based diffusion models, see Strang (1991) and Strang and Tuma (1993).

15. For a discussion on different temporal calendars, see Mills (2000, pp. 47–60).

NOTES TO CHAPTER 2

1. In chapter 4 a more detailed discussion of institutional factors is offered, and in chapter 5 a discussion of the effects of interrelated life-course events on parallel careers.

2. For an empirical analysis of the interrelations between transitions, see Baizán et al. (2003) and Martín-García and Baizán (2006) for Spain, and Baizán, Aassve, and Billari (2002) for West Germany and Sweden.

3. In the case of Greece a different birth cohort was selected, given the non-availability of the same birth cohort for this second set of figures (data from Standard Country Report).

4. By transition is meant a qualitative change in a state, for example the change from childless to parent (or pregnant), from student to out of the educational system, from unemployed to working (or vice versa), from living with one's own parents to achieving residential independence, and so on.

5. For a more in-depth discussion of the models, see chapter 5, and for the results, chapter 6.

6. We refer here to the role that cohabitation may play in lowering the age at entrance into first partnership, given that its more flexible nature requires less investment in resources and commitment than a formal marriage. We suggest that a progressive increase in the proportion of cohabiting unions would alter the overall profile of the curves in Figure 2.1.

7. Relative proportion of cohabiters in successive age groups, which should capture age dependency.

8. A measure of inequality in a population based on the Lorenz curve, a cumulative frequency curve that compares the distribution of a specific variable with the uniform distribution that represents equality. It produces a sort of 'relative mean difference,' that is, the mean of the differences between each possible pair of units of observation.

9. Rational action theory refers to "any theoretical approach that seeks to explain social phenomena as the outcome of individual action that is construed as rational, given individuals' goals and conditions of action, and is in this way made intelligible (*verständlich*)" Goldthorpe (1996, p. 109).

10. See chapter 5 for a more in-depth discussion and illustrations of this issue.

11. See, among others, Billari et al. (2002), Kiernan (2001), Villeneuve-Gokalp (1991), Kravdal (1999), Mills (2000), Blossfeld and Mills (2001), Blossfeld et al. (1999), Thornton (1991), Leridon and Villeneuve-Gokalp (1989), and Wu (2000).

12. By individual level is meant an explanatory model that builds on mechanisms and indicators with reference to individuals' characteristics and circumstances.

13. See chapter 4 for a country-specific discussion and hypotheses about the role of institutional factors in the choice to cohabit or marry.

14. Chapter 4 offers a more detailed discussion of the specific institutional features that might make for the relative convenience to cohabit over marrying across the different institutional contexts.

15. A longitudinal approach takes into account the time dimension of the processes and studies the occurrence of events over time, along the life course of individuals, and across successive birth cohorts.

16. A partial exception is Ermich's work (2005), although an empirical test is missing.

17. See, among others, Åberg (2001) on divorce; Phillips (1974) on suicide; Kahan (1997) on criminal behaviour; Hedström (1994), Hedström, Sandell and Stern, (2000), McAdam and Rucht (1993), Strang and Soule (1998), and Soule (1997) on social movements; Myers (1997) and (2000) on rioting; Pitcher, Hamblin, and Miller (1978) on collective violence; Cready, Fosset and Kiecolt (1997) on marriage; Kohler (1997) and (2001) on fertility and contraception, Greve (1995) on organisations' strategies.

18. For interactions, not only direct "face-to-face" interactions are understood here, but also indirect models stemming from structural equivalents (Burt, 1987) or other role equivalents (Erickson, 1988). Channels for the exercise of social influence and the diffusion of information in the course of these interactions include not only individuals but also the mass media and any other potential source of information: printed press, Internet, as any other actor, also when not belonging to the individual network and despite their influence not being consciously perceived.

19. In line with Boudon's (1985) suggestion, this approach aims to explain the diffusion process of cohabitation by specifying all the terms of the relation between actors and their time-varying contexts of action. The analytical model he proposes can be resumed into the equation $Mi = MmSM'$. In this equation a social phenomenon (M) is seen as a function of individual's actions (m) dependent on the actor's situation (S), which in turn is influenced by macro social factors (M'). In this frame, we specifically aim at dynamically addressing all the terms of this relation by exploring the contextually linked (micro-level) mechanisms, which produce the (macro phenomena) diffusion of cohabitation within different institutional settings.

20. And what Manski (1993a, 1993b, 2000) terms respectively 'correlated effects' and 'exogenous (contextual) effects.' *Correlated effects* occur when "agents in the same group tend to behave similarly because they have similar individual characteristics or face similar environments" (Manski, 2000, p. 127, and Manski, 1993b, p. 533). This specie of effect is termed *environmental effect* by Hedström (Hedström & Åberg, 2002). *Contextual effects* (later termed *contextual interactions*) are to be found when "the propensity of an individual to behave in some way varies with the exogenous characteristics of the group" (Manski, 2000, p. 127, and Manski, 1993b, p. 532). This is when the propensity to adopt cohabitation tends to vary with, say, the socioeconomic composition of the group (i.e., for effect of a general increase in educational attainment or in female labour force participation). This determinant is termed *selection effect* in Hedström typology.

21. 'Endogenous interactions' in Manski's terminology, 'social-interaction effects' and 'diffusion explanation,' respectively, in Hedström and Palloni's analyses.

22. For an overview of these changes in family law, see Glendon (1989), Ditch, Barnes, Bradshaw, Commaile, and Eardley (1996), Millar and Warman (1996), and Gauthier (1996).
23. The 'principle of social proof' (Cialdini, 1984, pp. 114–166) is described as the tendency of individuals to "view a behaviour as more correct in a given situation to the degree that we see others performing it" (Cialdini, 1984, p. 116).
24. This incremental chain of changes is produced by possible direct modifications in (1) individuals' beliefs about cohabitation (through learning about the availability and functioning of cohabitation); (2) individuals' perception of rewards or sanctions associated to specific behaviour or attitudes (observation of cohabitation as an increasingly 'proper' or more beneficial option); or (3) by indirect changes in the structural conditions of individuals produced in response to an increased level of adoption (like, for example, an adaptation of laws). See also Hedström's distinction among (1) *belief* (social learning); (2) *desire* (social pressure); and (3) *opportunity* (structural conditions) based interactions (Hedström & Åberg, 2002).
25. A large body of literature and sociopsychological experiments have analysed this phenomenon. Already in the early 1940s, Newcomb (1943) found that pressure from others (i.e., peers in a university college) could produce value changes by conformance to others' opinions and expectations with the intention of gaining their acceptance and approval. In the same period, Sherif (1936) argued that social groups and cultures, more than only encouraging conformity, provide information and an interpretative framework. He stressed that, in absence of clear structures of the physical environment that point to what is 'real,' 'valuable,' or 'proper,' individuals may accept realities and definitions provided by others. Asch (1952) further tested this hypothesis, demonstrating that this does not only apply when information is lacking, but that it is true even in a clear decisional context: people still tended to go along with the crowd. His experiments showed that individuals often adjust their judgements to conform to a group, even to the point of ignoring clear evidence to be wrong by doing so.
26. Hedström's translation of the proverb "A Roma fai come i Romani" (Hedström, 1998, p. 314).
27. My translation of the proverb "Allà donde fueras haz lo que vieras."
28. My translation of the proverb "Dónde va Vicente ahí va la gente."
29. Zarife Soylucicek's translation of the popular saying "Üzüm üzüme baka baka kararır."
30. Deutsch and Gerard (1955) were pioneers in making this analytical distinction between what they termed 'normative' and 'informational' social influence in producing conformity to prevailing types of behaviour. Manski (1993b) kept this distinction within 'endogenous social effects' (later termed 'endogenous interactions'), as those for which "the propensity of an individual to behave in some ways varies with the prevalence of that behaviour in some reference group containing the individual" (Manski, 1993b, p. 531). He acknowledges this twofold dimension of social influence by distinguishing within them between *expectations interactions* and *preference interactions* generated by observational learning (Manski, 2000). 'Expectations interactions' occur when individuals form expectations about future outcomes of uncertain courses of action by drawing upon observation of the actions previously chosen and outcomes experienced by others (Manski, 2000, p. 130). It is a process in which individuals extract valuable information from observing others' actions under similar circumstances. This natural tendency has also been termed 'social learning,' where influence is based on information and

evaluations stemming from experiences made by others in the social system
(Aronson, 1999; Montgomery & Casterline, 1996). 'Preference interactions'
occur when individuals' preference ordering over the alternatives [of marrying or cohabiting] depends on the choices made by other individuals in the
social system for their link to perceived moral values (Manski, 2000, p. 130).
It refers to the enforcement of social norms through an influence linked to
behavioural expectations of social members and the perception of behaviour
acceptability. Since it is produced by individuals' ability to impose positive or
negative sanctions to their expectations about others' behaviour, networks of
strong ties are seen to be more influential in this case (Coleman, 1990). The
stress of this aspect of social influence is on the decreasing moral costs and the
lowering degree of social pressure along with the spread of cohabitation. It
points to how cohabitation is easier as the stigma associated with the practice
falls together with its rising adoption and prevalence.
31. Also termed 'informational social influence' (Deutsch & Gerard, 1955).
32. For instance, by progressively enlarging the size of a group of people mod-
    elling a type of behaviour, it has been possible to increase dramatically the
    number of individuals who followed a given example (Milgram, Bickman &
    Berkowitz, 1969).
33. The earliest formal scientific account of this influence was that of Sherif's
    experiment (Sherif, 1936). His research on the formation of social norms indi-
    cated that, when an objective rule of conduct is absent, individuals are most
    likely to behave according to the group consensus (Sherif, 1936; Sherif &
    Sherif, 1964).
34. Also termed 'normative social influence' (Deutsch & Gerard, 1955).
35. For example, in line with this argument Rosina and Fraboni (2004) claim
    that Italian later and slower diffusion of cohabitation is to be attributed to
    youngsters' convenience not to oppose their parents' hostile view on cohabit-
    ing before (or instead of) marrying, given their strong material and emotional
    dependence on them (see also Di Giulio & Rosina, 2007).
36. Even a legally sanctioned behaviour may be subjectively perceived as 'legiti-
    mate' to the degree that is seen being largely undertaken. A clear example is
    the relation between the willingness to cheat on taxes and the perception of the
    pervasiveness of such behaviour (Slemrod, 1992). A number of other empiri-
    cal studies have revealed a strong association between individuals' choices
    and the perception of others' behaviour and attitudes towards social or legal
    norms with respect to those same decisions (Grasmick & Green, 1980; Kahan,
    1997).
37. A feature that makes it difficult to establish its direct effect on enacted behav-
    iour, even if it was by collecting (prospective) network data on individuals'
    perceptions about others' attitudes and behaviours. Individuals' emotional
    reactions, such as a sense of inadequacy, guilt, embarrassment, or anxiety, can
    already induce individuals to comply to others' expectations as regards appro-
    priate behaviour, even when external punishment or rewards are not necessar-
    ily expected to follow (Homans, 1961; Moscovici & Personnaz, 1980).
38. Whereby a person observes others cohabiting, forms an idea of the perfor-
    mance and results of this observed behaviour, and uses that idea to guide his
    or her future decision about adoption (Bandura, 1977).
39. Recent research on fertility decisions documents the significance of both
    mechanisms of social learning and social pressure in the effects played by
    social influence (Bernardi, 2003; Kohler, 2001; Kohler, Behrman and Watkins,
    2001).
40. As Palloni (2001) points out, an incorrect specification of reference networks
    may not only result in biased and inconsistent estimation, but it may also be

endogenous to the process being studied in that membership of a specific network may be originated by—and thus follow—the choice to adopt cohabitation. In his words: "Finally, a more troublesome feature of a diffusion process is that its own progress may affect the likelihood of reducing, eliminating, or inventing new social networks. Maintaining social networks that are not responsive to the new behavior may force adventurous individuals to seek new social attachments among those better prepared to embrace the new behavior. [. . .] what matters is that such endogenous change will produce the appearance that networks do have an influence on choice of behavior when actually they have none" (Palloni, 2001, p. 101).

41. What is also termed 'feedback effect.'

NOTES TO CHAPTER 3

1. As was been illustrated in chapter 2, great variability has emerged in the terms used to describe the two main rationales of social influence, which have been generally detected across studies and disciplines (see also Casterline, 2001; Manski, 2000), beside the role played by institutional factors. For the purpose of this study we have grouped them into influences related to 'social pressure' and 'social learning.'

2. See also Casterline (2001), Palloni (1999, 2001), Reed et al. (1999), Durlauf and Walker (2001).

3. We refer the interested reader to chapter 5 for a more detailed discussion of how these theoretical considerations determine the statistical techniques chosen for the analysis.

4. Exceptions to this tendency in the fields of sociology and demography are the recent studies from Hedström and Åberg (2002), Strang (1990, 1991), Hedström (1994), and Kohler (1997, 2001).

5. Not only due to the unavailability of suitable data, but also because the social influences of interest here are hardly consciously perceived, distinguished and reflected on by the individuals onto which they display their effects. It is thus extremely difficult to capture them other than in an experimental setting.

6. In the frame of a study on fertility control, Palloni (2001) refers to an additional aspect, that of the length and degree of 'persistence' in the adoption of a reversible innovation (e.g., innovative contraceptive methods.) The duration of cohabiting unions is not in the scope of this study, however, which focuses on the innovative content of cohabiting captured through getting to its first adoption ever by each woman, and not on the length of these experiences or on their subsequent repetitions.

7. We have previously referred to this aspect as to the 'willingness' to adopt cohabitation, drawing on Lesthaeghe and Vanderhoeft (1998) and Coale's (1973) analyses.

8. Burt (1987) distinguishes instead among early (belonging to the first third of the population studied), late (the last fourth), and median (others) adopters.

9. What in chapter 2 were termed 'correlated' or 'environmental' effects.

10. In a longitudinal perspective, it is termed 'risk set' the group of subjects or actors exposed to the risk of occurrence of a certain event of interest during a defined observation time. In this analysis, all the women yet to enter their first partnership from age 15 to age 39 belong to the risk set of potential adopters of cohabitation.

11. In correspondence to a determined historical time, relative to each women's cohort of birth.

12. Identified as 'heterophilous contacts' by Rogers (1985) as those individuals who do not share a similar background knowledge and understanding of the world (Lazarsfeld & Merton, 1964), as opposed to homophilus when, for example, belonging to similar educational or occupational backgrounds. The more the actors communicate, the higher their degree of similarity is thought to become (Rogers, 1985).

13. As opposed to "strongly tied" individuals, who see each other frequently over long periods of time and are in a close and intimate relationship (e.g., family members and close friends), weakly tied actors see one another infrequently and their relationships are casual rather than intimate (e.g., acquaintances, distant friends, colleagues, and the like) (Granovetter, 1973).

14. Bandura (1977) distinguishes three modes of behavioural reinforcement, of which *vicarious reinforcement* is the one referred to others' behaviour. Otherwise, in direct *external reinforcement*, people regulate their behaviour on the basis of consequences they experience directly. The force of this mechanism is limited, however, to the period of enforcement of a reward (or a positive outcome) to that behaviour. Finally, *self-administered reinforcement* is the mechanism through which people regulate their behaviour on the basis of the consequences that they create for themselves.

15. Among others, see Sherif (1936), Homans (1950, 1961), Festinger, Schackter & Back (1950), Festinger (1954), Katz and Lazarsfeld (1955), Cialdini (1984, 1993), Cialdini and Trost (1998), Bernardi (2003), Strang and Meyer (1993), Palloni (2001), Reed, Briere & Casterline (1999), and Kohler (1997).

16. Having selected the same birth cohorts and having followed them along the same age span also means having captured the same historical period in each of the country studied: a period of almost three decades, beginning in the late 1960s and up to the early 1990s.

NOTES TO CHAPTER 4

1. East Germany is treated here as a "country" because of its having been a separate and very different institutional context from West Germany, across almost all the period covered by the analysis (up to 1992 for Germany).

2. See, among others, Blossfeld (1995), Klijzing and Corijn (2002), Marini (1985), Blossfeld and Nuthmann (1989), Huinink (1995, 2000), Corijn and Klijzing (2001), and Blossfeld et al. (2005).

3. This until 1999 since when, with the introduction of Civil Solidarity Pact law (Pacs), cohabiting couples are treated as partners for social security purposes and after 3 years their income is taxed as if they were married.

4. We refer here to a (self-defined) feeling of being religious, which goes beyond the belonging to any specific religion or confession. In the countries studied, the dominant religion is the Christian, present with different proportions of its specific confessions. There are also minorities of Jewish, Muslim, and Buddhist, however, as well as members of specific sects (Scientology, Geova).

5. Marriage is subject to a higher normative pressure against separation, there are higher costs for terminating it (due to the need of a legal procedure that requires a varying length time period before dissolution can take place), and it entitles the economically weakest part to several compensations in case of dissolution. This legal dimension is what distinguishes marriage as a long-term binding commitment and what could help couples better to comply with social norms and expectations.

6. Baizán et al. (2003) also argue that conversely, individuals more prone to have a child may accelerate the entry into a union, considering it as part of

their family-building strategy. The authors thus claim that the time order of the events may not always (though often) reflect a causal relationship. They see the strong interrelation (in time and intentions of the individuals) between entrance in a union and parenthood as being affected by individual's value orientation and family plans. They therefore choose a statistical model specifically apt to control for these unmeasured shared factors thought to influence both processes simultaneously.

7. See, among others, Saraceno (1987b), Ross and Mirowsky (1996), Wan, Jaccard and Ramey (1996), Reinhard and Horwitz (1995), Yeandle (1996, 1999), Beccalli (1986), and Marin Muñoz (2003).

8. See Korpi (2000) for a thorough discussion and a more complete typology.

9. This is thus not properly a longitudinal measure but only a proxy of women's employment in relation to age. These figures are not retrospectively collected and are based on different birth cohorts of women sampled the same year.

10. Note that in the Italian case, what is categorised here as 'high part-time' for the purpose of comparison is mainly due to the proportion of employment in the public sector, which is regulated and normatively considered as full-time employment in Italy.

11. In a cross-sectional analysis of data from the Labour Force Survey, the two authors found that the share of part-time work accounts for a significant part of occupational sex segregation in each country. Part-time jobs seem to offer indeed relatively disadvantaged occupational conditions with respect to full-time occupations, although with great cross-national variations. Part-time work is however not, per se, the principal reason for segregation, but by dropping this type of jobs from the analysis the level of occupational segregation decreases in the majority of countries under study. This happens because in each labour market, part-time jobs are more concentrated in the female-dominated segments, as seen in Table 4.1.

12. Public day-care facilities achieved an almost complete coverage, and were aimed and tailored at serving the needs of working mothers. The day-care system included all day care for children of all ages, flexible opening hours, and provision of meals at lunchtime. Additionally, youth organisations were charged with providing care for school-age children during term's holidays. Conversely, to favour women's full and continuous participation in the labour market, the tax and transfer systems pressured paid employment by not granting maintenance claims in case of divorce (Kreyenfeld, 2000, quoting Berghahn & Fritzsche, 1991, Frerich & Frey, 1996, Frerich, 1996). Yet the East German government actively opposed the spread of part-time employment, forcing women to work full time (Kreyenfeld, 2000).

13. Among others, Saraceno (1997, 2003a, 2003b), Apter and Garnsey (1994), Orloff (1996, 2002), Daly (1994, 1996, 2000a), O'Connor (1993, 1996), Lorber and Farrell (1991), Yeandle (1996), González, Jurado & Naldini (2000), and MacInnes (2006).

14. Pension entitlements are especially affected by interrupted work careers and periods of low income (see Hansen & Larsen, 1993; Hernes, 1987; Palme, 1990; Quadagno, 1988; Sainsbury, 1994; and Sheiwe, 1994, for Germany).

15. "It is as markets become universal and hegemonic that the welfare of individuals comes to depend entirely on the cash nexus. Stripping society of the institutional layers that guaranteed social reproduction outside the labor contract meant that people were commodified. In turn, the introduction of modern social rights implies a loosening of pure commodity status. De-commodification occurs when a service is rendered as a matter of right, and when a person can maintain a livelihood without reliance on the market" (Esping-Andersen, 1990, pp. 21–22). Or, more synthetically, de-commodification indicates "the degree

to which the individual's typical life situation is freed from dependence on the labor market." (Esping-Andersen and Korpi, 1987, p. 40).

16. See section 4.2 for a discussion on the laws framing partners' obligations and individuals' entitlements attached to cohabiting unions.

17. Although these data strongly underestimate the possible impact of fix-term contracts because these measures especially apply to new labour market entrants, thus to young people, whereas the presented figures refer to all people employed. Unfortunately, comparable data on temporary contracts are still scarce. However, in Germany for example, the Microcensus of 1991 reported an incidence of fixed-term contracts of 7.5% among all employees, whereas in the age group 30 and below this figure rises to 21% (Kurz et al., 2005; Statistisches Bundesamt, 2001).

18. The figures presented here are not strictly comparable because they reflect differences in national definitions of 'social' rental dwellings. In Italy and France data refer to dwellings owned or administrated by the government, with lowered rents or with some other criteria towards social insertion; in West Germany, they refer to regulated rented dwellings that receive some form of financing and are administrated by both public and nonprofit private entities; in Sweden, they are instead rented dwellings by public or private collective nonprofit entities that directly receive public aid to residential access; and in Spain, public or private owned dwellings, with no clause on nonprofit character but under the condition of rents below the limit defined by the "Plan de la Vivienda." All considered, the Spanish definition is among the broadest, which may mean an upward bias of the estimate and thus an even bigger real difference with other European countries (Consejo Económico y Social, 2002, pp. 66–68). The official statistics for East Germany estimates 1% of social housing in the early 1990s, a figure clearly noncomparable to those provided by the other countries.

19. For an overview of fiscal measures in favour of home ownership in Europe, see European Central Bank, 2003, pp. 35–38.

20. Owner-occupied houses are still one of the most defiscalised goods in the Spanish tax-system: They enjoy no taxation on imputed rent, allowances on IRPF, together with deductions for purchase and a favourable fiscal treatment of savings destined at home ownership (for an in-depth treatment, see Banco de España, 2002, p. 56).

21. With the 'Ley de Protección de Vivienda' (1939) and the 'Ley de Arrendamientos Urbanos' (1946).

22. The Equo Canone Act, while establishing a four-year lease and continued rent controls, enabled landlords to sell out at the time of renewals. This resulted in over 900,000 evictions of former tenants, which constituted a dramatic social problem (Ball, 2003; Bernardi & Poggio, 2004).

23. In addition to distortions in eligibility criteria (to meet the needs of individuals evicted as a consequence of the Equo Canone Act); absence of policies to control for real prices in this sector and lack of an effective control for the fulfilment of requirements to access; as well as undergoing privatisation since its origin.

24. Beside tax incentives, contractual saving schemes (Plan d'épargne-logement) have been a traditional way to access home ownership; banks also provided other sources of state-regulated mortgage finance, with a mortgage rate below the market level (or even to 0% for low-income households) for some types of private loans (Ball, 2003, p. 50).

25. The most common is APL (Aide Personalisée au Logement), used to promote home ownership by covering part of the mortgage costs; ALF (Allocation de Logement à caractère Familial) is paid instead to young couples without

children or household with children for renting, restoring, or purchasing of a dwelling; and ALS (Allocation de Logement à caractère Social) is paid to single individuals, mainly students, who are not entitled to receive APL.

26. The indexation clause of rental contracts is linked to housing costs rather than to consumer price inflation and/or various freely negotiated adjustment clauses.

27. The legally determined system of rent setting in both private and public sectors requires negotiations at the local level between tenants' organisation, MHCs (Municipal Housing Companies, to whom predominantly belong social dwellings) and private landlords' organisations. In the course of negotiations, private rents are compared to social ones and the overall cost of MHCs sets the average rent level. Aimed at avoiding that MHCs make profit out of the housing stock, negotiations set rents to be largely historic cost based and to mainly reflect both quality differences and the age composition of the social housing stock.

28. This form of home ownership implies that cooperative nonprofit associations take out a mortgage for most part of the cost and own the estate or apartment buildings while the remaining part is covered through self-financed (or personal mortgage) contributions. Tenants acquire the right to occupancy of a particular dwelling and are then charged a negotiated monthly amount to cover the costs of the collective mortgage and of maintenance and repairs.

29. In Sweden, given the strict regulation applied to private renting, dwellings owned by the public sector (half or more of the rented dwellings) are sometimes rented subject to conditions similar to those in the private one. Moreover, anybody can apply to live in a social rented dwelling because there are no means-tested criteria.

30. These companies are organised within the Gesamtverband der Wohnungswirtschaft (GdW), an influential organisation representing bodies owning around 7 million flats.

31. In fact, a characteristic of the German system is that social dwellings pertain to the social rental sector only for as long as they receive subsidies (Ball, 2003).

32. Similar values are found, for the year 1997, by Bernardi and Poggio (2004).

33. Until the mid-1990s, mortgage conditions in Italy were among the worst within Europe, and credit was rationed by limiting the loan to a maximum of 50% of the property value (Chiuri & Jappelli, 2000).

NOTES TO CHAPTER 5

1. For the purpose of this analysis, we refer to the distinct socialist institutional context of the former German Democratic Republic as a 'country.'

2. More specifically, 'left truncation' arises when individuals are observed only some *known* time after the natural time origin of the phenomenon under study (in the example we were interested in the likelihood to cohabit since age 15).

3. Are defined 'left censored' those spells that are already in progress when an observation period begins, but we have no information on their starting time.

4. Processes are termed 'censored' when they cannot be observed until their completion (or from their beginning) because they are still in progress (or already in progress) at the end (/beginning) of the observation window. In other terms, an episode is said to be censored if the information about the

duration of the time interval before the occurrence of the event is incomplete (Yamaguchi, 1991, pp. 3–9).

5. An individual's history is said to be censored on the left side when the initial part of it is not being observed (so the length of a spell in a certain state of interest is not knows), whereas it is said to be right censored when the observation ends before the event of interest has happened yet (in our case, when women have not yet entered a partnership by the time of interview). See Blossfeld and Rohwer (1995b) and Allison (1984) for a discussion of the ability of event history techniques to handle right censorship.

6. With event history analysis it is meant a set of techniques that deal with the patterns and correlates of the occurrence of events over time (e.g., entry into cohabitation). Event history addresses not only the type of events taking place (*what* happens), but also its timing (*when* it happens). Together with other dynamic analysis methods, such as panel or time series, it shares the capability of better analysing the processes leading to an observed sociological phenomena because it focuses on the producing of the phenomena over time rather on its statistical distribution at a given point in time.

7. We refer to the sort of 'endogenous feedback effects' described in chapter 3.

8. We have already argued that the effect of social influence goes generally unperceived and that measures of networks' structure and characteristics may suffer the risk of selectivity over time: "[A] more troublesome feature of a diffusion process is that its own progress may affect the likelihood of reducing, eliminating, or inventing new social networks" (Palloni, 2001, p. 101).

9. The problem of 'unmeasured heterogeneity,' far from being specific to diffusion models, is a common problem of duration models in general (Allison, 1984; Duncan & Kalton, 1987; Yamaguchi, 1991). Because some of the characteristics that comprise the risk profile are unmeasured, analysts are unable to include in their models all the factors linked to women's individual propensity to adopt cohabitation over time. As a result, those women who have a greater resistance to cohabit may have a longer survival in the risk set of potential adopters. A comparatively longer survival also means their increasing relative proportion over time: "[A]s individuals who are more resistant to adopting become a larger fraction of the pool of non-adopters, the overall risk of adoption will tend to decrease. But this is not a reflection of a risk profile of adoption that decreases over time. Rather, it is an artefact of the changing composition of the pool of non-adopters as the process progresses over time" (Palloni, 2001, p. 72).

10. In which all women are simultaneously exposed to the risk of making either of the transitions (to marry or cohabit) in the decision to enter a union, until they eventually opt for one or the other.

11. Individuals may fail to recall precisely all events in their lives, typically the more so the further back in time the event took place, the more frequent its taking place, the shorter its duration, and the older the respondent. However, panel surveys are not exempted from recall bias, although they suffer from it to a lesser extend due to the shorter duration between successive interviews. Panel data, in contrast, would be far more expensive to collect and would suffer from the additional drawback of being subject to attrition over time (respondents not willing or available to participate to subsequent waves), especially so over the long time span covered by these analyses.

12. When information on the month of the event taking place was missing, month was set to June.

13. Common starting and ending times were defined (on the basis of the Century Month Coding), as well as common origin and destination states, for each of the career. A common coding for the variables was chosen when possible,

and correction for spells and inconsistencies, within and across careers, was undertaken in an analogous way.

14. The time interval that a unit of analysis spends in a specific state, preceding the event occurrence, is defined as an episode or duration. Whereas episodes are records defining the characteristics of the individual's state between two events (e.g., from married to divorced or from single to cohabiting), spells are partitions of an original episode in subunits created for updating time-varying variables (Blossfeld & Rohwer, 1995b).

15. Comparable data for the United Kingdom have not been collected, whereas those for the Netherlands and Greece were not yet available at the time of these analyses.

16. A complete record of the job histories is missing for France, where only information about the first and last job was collected.

17. In this study we are specifically interested in peer-group adopters in contrast to individuals from previous birth cohorts.

18. See also later studies from Brüderl and Dikmann (1995), Diekmann and Engelhardt (1999), Braun and Hengelhardt (2002), although they directly model the rate of adoption in the entire social system.

19. Adding a quadratic and a cubic term to a simple linear specification allowed us to explore rather flexibly more complex functional forms.

20. As discussed earlier in the chapter, this is a relevant assumption being relaxed because unobserved differences in the propensity to cohabit may affect parameter estimates: The more 'resistant' to the adoption of cohabitation would otherwise tend to stay longer in the risk set (Dechter, 2001).

21. Piecewise constant exponential models are a more flexible generalisation of the basic rate exponential model. In these models, the time axis is split into periods (we have chosen here five partitions: 0–3, 3–6, 6–9, 9–12, or more than 12 years *after* the 15 years of age that begins the exposure to risk), and it is assumed that the transition rates are constant in each period but are allowed to vary across periods (the baseline hazard is given by period-specific constants). In the specification adopted here we assumed that the baseline hazard rate could vary between periods, but the estimated effect of the covariates was the same (proportional) in each period.

22. Regression is the statistical operation by which the distribution of values of a variable of interest (dependent variable) is estimated as the resultant of the combination of the effects of a set of covariates (independent variables), plus a residual (unexplained) component.

23. Parametric specifications such as constant exponential hazard rate models were also estimated, and each of the diffusion covariates was tested separately too. Results revealed neither statistical improvement in the goodness of fit of the models nor substantial changes in either the effects of individuals' characteristics or in the diffusion covariates.

24. For example, Lillard and colleagues explored why individuals more prone to cohabit were also more likely to divorce once married. They did it by means of correlating the residuals across the two processes of entry into cohabitation and marital dissolution: "Insofar as cohabitation before marriage is endogenous in the process that causes disruption, cohabitation is correlated with the error term for the disruption equation" (Lillard et al., 1995, p. 453). In explaining the higher dissolution rates for marriages preceded by cohabitation, they found that individuals with particular (unobserved) traits that made them more at risk of short-lived marriage (such as a weaker commitment to the marital institution or more uncertainty about the goodness of the match with the partner) self-selected themselves into premarital cohabiting unions in

the first place. They probably chose to cohabit rather than marry *because* a marriage would have had a higher risk of failure. Once this unobserved heterogeneity was taken into account in the statistical model, the difference in the risk of dissolution between direct marriages and those preceded by cohabitation disappeared.

25. However, it is worth noticing that even the estimates obtained by simultaneously modelling a set of interrelated equations for the processes of entrance into cohabitation or marriage and that of a pregnancy seem to point in the same direction than those obtained in the model chosen here (Baizán et al., 2002, 2003). Previous results offer some confidence in the lack of a significant difference in the estimates obtained with simultaneously modelling the two processes by different equations.

26. In the case of France, given the absence of a complete record of women's employment career, the variable controlling for labour force participation has been constructed somewhat differently, and it reports the status of being employed against having never worked. It follows that the coefficient for this variable cannot be directly compared with those for the other countries in the tables.

27. This was done on the basis of the standard time taken to complete the corresponding degree (OECD, 1999).

28. In a preliminary model, seven levels were distinguished in the German case: *compulsory education* (up to lower secondary school qualification without vocational training; reference category, 9 years); *HMB* (lower secondary school qualification with vocational training, 11 years); *MOB* (Realschule, intermediate school qualification without vocational training, 10 years); *MMB* (intermediate school qualification with vocational training, 12 years); *ABI* (Abitur, upper secondary school qualification, 13 years); *FHS* (Fachhochschule, Ingenieurschule, Höhere Fachschule, professional college qualification, 17 years); and *UNI* (university degree, 19 years). This specification was then reduced to improve the overall comparability across countries (for detailed results on this former classification, see Nazio & Blossfeld, 2003).

29. Second pregnancies before forming the first co-residential partnership were not rare events, especially in the cases of East Germany and Sweden. This fact is interpreted as related to the specific institutional contexts, which allowed or favoured nonmarital childbirth.

NOTES TO CHAPTER 6

1. Survival functions show the relative proportion of women who are still at risk of experiencing the event of interest over time (thus have 'survived' up to each time point). So, for example, in the graph for Italy in Figure 6.1, a value of 0.5 (on the Y-axis) in combination with 80 (months since age 15, on the X-axis) to be seen for the birth cohort born in 1954 to 1957 indicates that 50% of the young women of that cohort are still living with their parents, having 'survived' the event leaving the parental home. In the same figure we see that for a younger birth cohort, for example that born from 1966 to 1969, at the same age (21 years = 15 years + 80 months) the curve shows that approximately 70% of young women have survived (30% only has thus already left the parental home). Pseudo-survival functions are computed on a transition to *multiple* destination states, like in the case of competing destinations: for example, cohabiting or marrying or leaving as single. This means that all women are simultaneously exposed to the risk of experiencing any of the (competing) events, although each woman will concretely experience

only one of the possible destination states. Statistically, this produces that the corresponding survival functions are in a multiplicative relation to each other instead of additive (Rohwer & Pötter, 1998).

2. Note that different overall proportions in exits are not only dependent on the relative timing at exit but also on the age at interview. In Germany and Sweden, where the surveys fieldwork took place a few years earlier, having selected a common sample of birth cohorts resulted in an average younger age.

3. Note that in the case of West Germany, the bar in Figure 6.3 is comparatively shorter due to the higher proportion of young women living single for a longer time before entering a partnership in this country.

4. This substitution process between marriage and cohabitation is further reinforced in the transition to a first partnership, as discussed later with reference to the results of the hazard rate models in Tables 6.3 and 6.4. We show that having experienced a period in the single state before entering the first partnership (a case that makes up over a third of the women in France) displays a strong positive effect on the likelihood of engaging in cohabitation and, in four of the countries, a negative effect on that of marrying.

5. This increase in exits as single across cohorts in East Germany, however, will not hold in the multivariate analysis where individual-level factors are controlled for (Table 6.2). Remembering that these pseudo-survival functions by birth cohorts are in a multiplicative relations to each other, this result points to a (relative) anticipation of the transition to the single state across birth cohorts as being the outcome of an absolute postponement of marriage combined with an anticipation of exits through cohabitation.

6. Given the high degree of decentralisation of the university system in Italy, this affects a small minority of university students, around 4% as estimated by Billari and others (Billari, Philipov & Baizán, 2001a).

7. Saraceno reports that a not negligible number of young women still nowadays leaves or has left the labour market because of difficulties in reconciling paid employment with household responsibilities, also at the time of marriage, even before children are born (Saraceno, 2003).

8. See chapter 5 for details.

9. New insights from ISSP data only very recently begin to point to a change in attitudes towards women's employment taking place from the mid-1990s, a period not well covered in these analyses (MacInnes, 2006).

10. For the lack of measures on psychological traits, attitudes, and aspirations, in these analyses we cannot distinguish between a "selection" effect (some unmeasured personality traits, like a higher desire of autonomy, make especially Southern women more willing to *both* leave the parental household earlier as single and prefer a less binding union like cohabitation) from a "cultural" (independent dwelling affords more autonomy from societal and parental views) or a "resource" effect (it signals an higher achieved economic independence, especially from the need to obtain family contribution to housing).

11. In the process of model selection, significance test was performed by comparing the log likelihood ratios of nested models, where $Chi^2 = -2[ln$ (log-likelihood Model 1—log-likelihood Model 2)].

12. Changes in the log-likelihood determined by the reinsertion of the 19 birth cohort dummies in model 2 do nowhere show a significant improvement of the models, ranging between 0.2 (in Sweden) and 18.6 (in East Germany).

13. When only 'peer-group adoption' is tested in the French case, its effect scores somewhat higher. It can thus be expected that the introduction of both polynomials could lead to a lowering, or disappearing, of the peer-group effect in

favour of precohort adoption in Sweden too. Unfortunately, this expectation cannot be tested with the available data.

NOTES TO CHAPTER 7

1. Palloni (2001) also notices that even a network approach to diffusion, when it does not provide repeated measures over the life course of individuals, is not optimal for testing hypotheses about diffusion processes because networks are subject to a selection by individuals over time.
2. Having exited the parental home increases the probability for young women to cohabit of around 20% in Sweden, almost 40% in East Germany and 60% in West Germany, 100% in France (doubles it) while more than 480% to 720% (around five to seven times higher) in Italy and Spain, respectively. These effects decrease only slightly with the length of the period after independence has taken place. Even after 2 years from achieving residential autonomy, the change in risk of cohabiting keeps constant in Sweden and East Germany while it remains over 40% in West Germany, 80% in France, 380% and 620% in Italy and Spain, respectively. Percentage change in the hazard rate calculated as $(e^{(ß)}-1)*100$ from the coefficients of *living independently* in model 2 of Table 6.4.
3. Finishing one's education increases the probability to cohabit of more than 2.5 times in Italy while it doubles it in Spain and France (from the coefficients of *enrolled in education* in model 2 of Table 6.4).
4. Using longitudinal data from different European countries we have first described the changes across birth cohorts in women's exit from the parental home and entry into partnership. We have then modelled as time-varying processes over the life course women's changing characteristics and situations (Blossfeld, Hamerle & Mayer, 1989). Namely, their growing older, their educational enrolment and attainment levels, their working careers and job investments, as well as possible events happening on interrelated careers (exit from the parental home and pregnancies). Then, the effects of these factors have been estimated on the rate of exit from the parental home and on the entry into a first union, through marriage or cohabitation. In a second step, the prevalence of (ever) first experiences with cohabiting unions in the social system was measured by the two indicators described (*peer-group* and *precohort adoptions*), and introduced into the statistical models, to serve as a predictor of women's behaviour. In other words, we have then also modelled the age and cohort-specific measures of others' experiences of cohabitation, expressions of social influence, as factors affecting women's likelihood of cohabiting.
5. This, however, might not necessarily be the case in those countries where short periods of cohabitation are tolerated 'shortcuts' to marriage into which are soon after being converted.
6. See also Saraceno (2003a) for criteria of access to a scarce provision of childcare in Italy, and the example of East German housing policies for 'lone mothers' discussed in chapter 4, or else the "Ehegattensplitting" financial incentive, which does not (yet) apply to nonmarried couples (Steiner & Wrohlich, 2004).
7. For an interesting discussion and examination of this issue in the United States, see Bumpass and Raley (1995) and Bumpass and Sweet (1995).
8. Against the recognition of entitlements to social security benefits and some of the protections associated to marital unions.
9. A factor that we could not explore thoroughly with these data.

References

Aassve, A., Billari, F. C., Mazzuco, S., & Ongaro, F. (2002). Leaving home: A comparative analysis of ECHP data. *Journal of European Social Policy, 12*(4), 259–275.

Aassve, A., Billari, F. C., & Ongaro, F. (2001). The impact of income and unemployment status on leaving home: Evidence from the Italian ECHP sample. *Labour: Review of Labour Economics and Industrial Relations, 15*(3), 501–529.

Åberg, Y. (2000). Individual social action and the macro level dynamics: A formal theoretical model. *Acta Sociologica, 43*, 193–205.

Åberg, Y. (2001). Is divorce contagious? The marital status of coworkers and the risk of divorce. *Working Papers on Social Mechanisms*, No. 8, University of Stockholm.

Adler, M. A. (1997). Social change and decline in marriage and fertility in Eastern Germany. *Journal of Marriage and the Family, 59*(1), 37–49.

Akerlof, G. A. (1980). A theory of social custom, of which unemployment may be one consequence. *Quarterly Journal of Economics, 94*, 749–775.

Ajzen, I. (1988). *Attitudes, personality, and behavior*. Milton-Keynes, England: Open University Press.

Ajzen, I. (1991). The theory of planned behavior. *Organizational Behavior and Human Decision Processes, 50*, 179–211.

Akerlof, G. A., Yellen, J. L., & Katz, M. L. (1996). An analysis of out-of-wedlock childbearing in the United States. *Quarterly Journal of Economics, 61*, 277–317.

Alberdi, I. (1993). La familia, propriedad y aspectos jurídicos. In G. Medina, L. Gil Calvo, & E. Gil Calvo (Eds.), *Estrategia familiares* (pp. 271–298). Madrid: Alianza Editorial.

Alberdi, I. (1999). *La nueva familia española*. Madrid: Taurus.

Allison, P. D. (1984). *Event history analysis. Regression for longitudinal event data*. Sage University Paper series on Quantitative Applications in the Social Sciences, 07–046. Beverly Hills, CA: Sage.

Altieri G. (1992). I redditi da lavoro delle donne: Lontano dalla parità. *Polis, 6*(1), 65–80.

Apter, T., & Garnsey, E. (1994). Enacting inequality. Structure, agency and gender. *Women's Study International Forum, 17*(1), 19–31.

Arber, S., & Ginn, J. (1995). The mirage of gender equality: Occupational success in the labour market and within marriage. *The British Journal of Sociology, 46*(1), 21–43.

Arnalaug, L. (1990). Coping with care: Mothers in a welfare state. In C. Ungerson (Ed.), *Gender and caring: Work and welfare in Britain and Scandinavia* (pp. 133–159). Toronto: Wheatsheaf.

Aronson, E. (1999). *The social animal* (8th ed.). New York: Worth Publishers.

Asch, S. E. (1952). *Social psychology.* Englewood Cliffs, NJ: Prentice-Hall.
Asch, S. E. (1951). Effects of group pressure upon the modification and distortion of judgement. In M. H. Guetzkow (Ed.), *Groups, leadership and men* (pp. 177–190). Pittsburgh: Carnegie.
Audirac, P-A. (1986). Cohabitation: A million unmarried couples. *Economie et Statistique, 185*, 13–33.
Axinn, W. G., & Thornton, A. (1992). The relationship between cohabitation and divorce: Selectivity or causal influence? *Demography, 29*, 357–374.
Axinn, W. G., & Thornton. A. (2000). The transformation of the meaning of marriage. In L. Waite et al. (Eds.), *Ties that bind: Perspectives on marriage and cohabitation* (pp. 147–169). New York: Aldine de Gruyter.
Baizán, P. (2001). Transition to adulthood in Spain. In M. Corijn & E. Klijzing (Eds.), *Transitions to adulthood in Europe* (pp. 279–312). Dordrecht: Kluwer Academic.
Baizán, P., Aassve, A., & Billari, F. C. (2002). Institutional arrangements and life course outcomes: The interrelations between cohabitation, marriage and first birth in Germany and Sweden. *MPIDR Working Paper* 26. Rostock: Max Planck Institute for Demographic Research.
Baizán, P., Aassve, A., & Billari, F. C. (2003). Cohabitation, marriage, and first birth: The interrelationship of family formation events in Spain. *European Journal of Population, 19*, 147–169.
Balchin, P. (1996). *Housing policy in Europe.* London: Routledge.
Ball, M. (Ed.). (2003). European Housing Review, research report for RICS: The Royal Institution of Chartered Surveyors. Available at http://www.rics.org.uk/resources/research/ehr_2003/page_1/page_1.htm Banco de España. (2002, September). El Mercado de la Vivienda en España. *Boletín Económico.*
Bandura, A. (1971). Vicarious and self-reinforcement processes. In R. Glaser (Ed.), *The nature of reinforcement.* New York: Academic Press.
Bandura, A. (1977). *Social learning theory.* Englewood Cliffs, NJ: Prentice-Hall.
Bandura, A. (1986). *Social foundations of thought and action: A social cognitive theory.* Englewood Cliffs, NJ: Prentice-Hall.
Bandura, A., Blanchard, E. B., & Ritter, B. (1969). The relative efficacy of desensitization and modeling approaches for inducing behavioral, affective, and attitudinal changes. *Journal of Personality and Social Psychology, 13*, 173–199.
Bandura, A., & McDonald, F. J. (1963). The influence of social reinforcement and the behavior of models in shaping children's moral judgements. *Journal of Abnormal and Social Psychology, 67*, 274–281.
Bandura, A., Ross, D., & Ross, S. A. (1963). Vicarious reinforcement and imitative learning. *Journal of Abnormal and Social Psychology, 67*, 601–607.
Barbagli, M. (1989). *Sotto lo stesso tetto.* Bologna: Il Mulino.
Barbagli, M. (1990). *Provando e riprovando. Matrimoinio, famiglia e divorzio in Italia e in altri paesi occidentali.* Bologna: Il Mulino.
Barbagli, M., Castiglioni, M., & Dalla Zuanna, G. (2003). *Fare famiglia in Italia. Un secolo di cambiamenti.* Bologna: Il Mulino.
Barlow, A., Duncan, S., Evans, G., & Park, A. (2001). Just a piece of paper? Marriage and cohabitation in Britain. In *British Social Attitudes 18th Report. Public Policy, Social Ties*, 2001–2002 edition, NCSR/Sage.
Baxter, J. (2005). To marry or not to marry: Marital status and the household division of labour. *Journal of Family Issues.* 26(3): 300-321
Beccalli, B. (1986). Storia delle donne e il caso sears. Nota introuttva. *Rivista di Storia Contemporanea, 4*, 497–500.
Becker, G. S. (1973). A theory of marriage: Part I. *Journal of Political Economy, 81*, 813–846.
Becker, G. S. (1981). *A treatise on the family.* Cambridge, MA: Harvard University Press.

Becker, P., & Moen, P. (1999). Scaling back: Dual-earner couples' work-family strategies. *Journal of Marriage and the Family,* 61, 995–1007.

Becker, S. O., Bentolila, S., Fernandes, A., & Ichino, A. (2002, September). Job insecurity and children's emancipation: The Italian puzzle. paper presented at the ESSLE CEPR-IZA meeting, Ammersee.

Berghahn, S., & Fritzsche, A. (1991). *Frauenrecht in Ost-un Westdeutschland. Bilanz-Ausblick.* Berlin: BasisDruck Verlag.

Bergmann, L. (1986). *The economic emergence of women.* New York: Basic Books.

Bernardi, F. (1999). *Donne fra famiglia e carriera.* Milano: Franco Angeli.

Bernardi, F. (2000). Globalisation and social inequality: Changing patterns of early careers in Italy. *GLOBALIFE Working Paper Series* No. 7, Faculty of Sociology, Bielefeld: University of Bielefeld.

Bernardi, F. (2001a). The employment behavior of married women in Italy. In H.-P. Blossfeld & S. Drobnič (Eds.), *Careers of couples in contemporary society.* Oxford: Oxford University Press.

Bernardi, F. (2001b). Is it a timing or a probability effect? *Quality & Quantity,* 35(3):231–252.

Bernardi, L. (2003). Channels of social influence on reproduction. *MPIDR Working Paper* 19. Rostock: Max Planck Institute for Demographic Research.

Bernardi, F. (2005). Public policies and low fertility: Rationales for public intervention and a diagnosis for the Spanish case. *Journal of European Social Policy,* 15(2):123–138.

Bernardi, F., & Nazio, T. (2005). Globalization and the transition to adulthood in Italy. In H.-P. Blossfeld et al. (Eds.), *Globalization, uncertainty and youth in society* (pp. 349–374). London: Routledge.

Bernardi, F., & Poggio, T. (2004). Home ownership and social inequality in Italy. In K. Kurz & H.-P. Blossfeld (Eds.), *Homeownership and social inequality in comparative perspective* (pp. 187–232). Stanford: Stanford University Press.

Bettio, F. (1988). *The sexual division of labour. The Italian case.* Oxford: Clarendon Press.

Bettio, F., & Villa, P. (1998). A Mediterranean perspective on the breakdown of the relationship between participation and fertility. *Cambridge Journal of Economics,* 22(2), 137–171.

Bianco, M. L. (1993). Percorsi della segregazione femminile. Meccanismi sociali e ragioni degli attori. *Polis,* 7(2):277–300.

Billari, F., Castiglioni, M., Martin, T. C., Michelin, F., & Ongaro, F. (2002). Household and union formation in a Mediterranean Fashion: Italy and Spain. In E. Klijzing and M. Corijn (Eds.), *Dynamics of fertility and partnership in Europe: Insights and lessons from comparative research* (Vol. II, pp. 17–41). Geneva/New York: United Nations.

Billari, F., & Kohler, H.-P. (2002). The impact of union formation dynamics on first births in West Germany and Italy: Are there signs of convergence? In E. Klijzing and M. Corijn (Eds.), *Dynamics of fertility and partnership in Europe: Insights and lessons from comparative research* (Vol. II, pp. 43–58). Geneva/New York: United Nations.

Billari, F., & Ongaro, F. (1999). Lasciare la famiglia di origine: Quando e perché? In P. De Sandre, A. Pinnelli, & A. Santini (Eds.), *Nuzialità e fecondità in transformazione: Percosi e fattori del cambiamento* (pp. 327–346). Bologna: Il Mulino.

Billari, F., Philipov, D., & Baizán, P. (2001a). Leaving home in Europe: The experience of cohorts born around 1960. *International Journal of Population Geography,* 7(5):339–356.

Billari, F., Rosina, A., Ranaldi, R., & Romano, C. (2001b, November 8–9). *Young adults fuzzily living with their parents: A multilevel analysis of the Italian case.*

Paper presented at the workshop La Bassa Fecondità in Italia tra Costrizioni Economiche e Cambio di Valori, Florence.

Bloom, D. E. (1982). What's happening to the age at first birth in the United States? A study of recent cohorts. *Demography*, *19*(3): 351–370.

Blossfeld, H.-P. (1990). Changing educational careers in the Federal Republic of Germany. *Sociology of Education*, *63*, 165–177.

Blossfeld, H.-P. (Ed.). (1995). *The new role of women. Family formation in modern societies.* London: Westview Press.

Blossfeld, H.-P. (1996). "Macro-sociology, Rational Choice Theory and Time. A Theoretical Perspective on the Empirical Analysis of Social Process." *European Sociological Review.* 12(2):181-206

Blossfeld, H.-P. (1999, October 25–27). *Causal inference based on observational studies. An application example of the opportunities and limitations of event history data.* Paper presented at the workshop Longitudinal Research in Social Science: A Canadian Focus, London, Ontario, Canada.

Blossfeld, H.-P. (2000). Bildung, arbeit und soziale ungleichheit im globalisierungsprozess. Einige theoretische überlegungen zu offenen forschungsfragen. In T. Kurtz (Ed.), *Aspekte des berufs in der moderne (pp. 239–263).* Opladen: Leske Budrich.

Blossfeld, H.-P. (2003). Globalization, social inequality and the role of country-specific institutions. Open research questions in a learning society. In Pedro Conceição, Manuel V. Heitor, & Bengt-Åke Lundvall (Eds.), *Innovation, competence building and social cohesion in Europe. Towards a learning society* (pp. 303–324). Cheltenham: Edward Edgar.

Blossfeld, H.-P, & Drobnič, S. (Eds.). (2001). *Careers of couples in contemporary society. From male breadwinner to dual-earner families.* Oxford: Oxford University Press.

Blossfeld, H.-P., & Hakim, C. (1997). *Between equalisation and marginalization: Women working part-time in Europe and the United States of America.* New York: Oxford University Press.

Blossfeld, H.-P., Hamerle, A., & Mayer, K. U. (1989). *Event history analysis.* Hillsdale, NJ: Erlbaum.

Blossfeld, H.-P., & Huinink, J. (1991). Human capital investments or norms of role transition? How women's schooling and career affects the process of family formation. *American Journal of Sociology*, *97*(1), 143–168.

Blossfeld, H.-P., Klijzing, E., Pohl, D., & Rohwer, G. (1999). Why do cohabiting couples marry? An example of a causal event history approach to interdependent systems. *Quality and Quantity*, *33*, 229–242.

Blossfeld, H.-P., Manting, D., & Rohwer, G. (1993). Patterns of change in the Federal Republic of Germany and the Netherlands: Some consequences for the solidarity between generations. In H. A. Becker & P. L. J. Hermkens (Eds.), *Solidarity of generations. Demographic, economic and social change, and its consequences* (pp. 175–196). Amsterdam: Thesis.

Blossfeld, H.-P., & Mills, M. (2001). A causal approach to interrelated family events: A cross-national comparison of cohabitation, nonmarital conception, and marriage [Special issue]. *Canadian Studies in Population*, *28*(2): 409–437.

Blossfeld, H.-P., Mills, M., Klijzing, E., & Kurz, K. (Eds.). (2005). *Globalization, uncertainty and youth in society.* London: Routledge.

Blossfeld, H.-P., & Nuthmann, R. (1989). Strukturelle veränderungen der jungendphase zwischen 1925 und 1984 als kohortenprozess. *Zeitschrift für Pädagogik*, *35*, 845–867.

Blossfeld, H.-P., & Rohwer, G. (1995a). West Germany. In: H-P Blossfeld (Ed.), *The New role of women. Family formation in modern societies* (pp. 56–76). Boulder, CO: Westview.

Blossfeld, H.-P., & Rohwer, G. (1995b). *Techniques of event history modelling. New approaches to causal analysis.* Hillsdale, NJ: Erlbaum.

Blossfeld, H.-P., & Rohwer, G. (1997). Causal inference, time and observation plans in the social sciences. *Quality & Quantity, 31,* 361–384.

Blossfeld, H.-P., & Timm, A. (Eds.). (2003). *Who marries whom? Educational systems as marriage markets in modern societies.* Dordrecht: Kluwer.

Bongaarts, J., & Watkins, S. C. (1996). Social interactions and contemporary fertility transitions. *Population and Development Review, 22*(4), 639–682.

Borchorst, A. (1993). Working lives and family lives in Western Europe. In S. Carlsen & J. E. Larsen (Eds.), *The equality dilemma* (pp. 167–180). Copenhagen: Danish Equal Status Council.

Borchorst, A. (1994a). The Scandinavian welfare states. Patriarchal, gender neutral or women friendly? *International Journal of Contemporary Sociology, 31,* 1–23.

Borchorst, A. (1994b). Welfare state regimes, women's interests and the EC. In D. Sainsbury (Ed.), *Gendering welfare states* (pp. 26–44). London: Sage.

Borchorst, A., & Siim, B. (1987). Women and the advanced welfare state. A new kind of patriarchal power? In A. S. Sasson (Ed.), *Women and the state. The shifting boundaries of public and private* (pp. 128–157). London: Hutchinson.

Boudon, R. (1981). *The logic of social action.* London: Routledge.

Boudon, R. (1985). *Il posto del disordine.* Bologna: Il Mulino. (Original work published 1984 as *Le place du désordre. Critique des théories du changement sociale,* Paris: Presses Universitaires de France)

Boudon, R. (1998a). Social mechanisms without black boxes. In P. Hedström & R. Swedberg (Eds.), *Social Mechanisms* (pp. 172–203). Cambridge: Cambridge University Press.

Boudon, R. (1998b). Limitations of rational choice theory. *American Journal of Sociology, 104*(3), 817–828.

Boudon, R. (2003). Beyond rational choice theory. *Annual Review of Sociology, 29,* 1–22.

Boyle, P. J. (2006). Does cohabitation prior to marriage raise the risk of marital dissolution and does this effect vary geographically? *MPIDR Working Paper* 2006–051. Rostock: Max Planck Institute for Demographic Research.

Braun, N., & Hengelhardt, H. (2002). Diffusion processes and event history analysis, *MPIDR Working Paper* 7. Rostock: Max Planck Institute for Demographic Research.

Breen, R., & Cooke, L. P. (2005). The persistence of the gendered division of domestic labour. *European Sociological Review, 21*(1), 43–57.

Brien, M. J., Lillard, L. A., & Waite, L. J. (1999). Interrelated family-building bahaviors: Cohabitation, marriage and nonmarital conception, *Demography, 36*(4), 535–551.

Brüderl, J., & Dikmann, A. (1995). The log-logistic rate model: Two generalisations with an application to demographic data. *Sociological Methods & Research, 24,* 158–186.

Bumpass, L. L. (1990). What's happening to the family? Interactions between demographic and institutional changes. *Demography, 27*(4), 483–498.

Bumpass, L. L., & Raley, R. K. (1995). Redefining Single-Parent Families: Cohabitation and changing family reality. *Demography, 32,* 97–109.

Bumpass, L, L., & Sweet, J. A. (1995). The changing character of stepfamilies: Implications of cohabitation and nonmarital childbearing, *Demography, 32,* 425–436.

Bumpass, L. L., Sweet, J. A., & Cherlin, A. (1991). The role of cohabitation in declining rates of marriage. *Journal of Marriage and the Family, 53*(4), 913–927.

Burt, R. S. (1987). Social contagion and innovation: Cohesion versus structural equivalence. *American Journal of Sociology, 92,* 1287–1335.

Bygren, M., Duvander, A-Z, & Hultin, M. (2005). Elements of uncertainty in life courses: Transitions to adulthood in Sweden. In H.-P. Blossfeld et al. (Eds.), *Globalization, uncertainty and youth in society* (pp. 135–158). London: Routledge.

Cabré Pla, A., & Módenes Cabrerizo, J. A. (2004). Home ownership and social inequality in Spain. In K. Kurz & H.-P. Blossfeld (Eds.), *Homeownership and social inequality in comparative perspective* (pp. 233–254). Stanford: Stanford University Press.

Caldwell, J. C. (1976). "Towards a restatement of demographic transition theory." *Population and Development Review*. 2(3/4):321-66.

Carter, A. T. (2001). Social processes and fertility change: Anthropological perspectives. In John B. Casterline (Ed.), *Diffusion processes and fertility transition: Selected perspectives* (pp. 138–178). Washington, DC: National Academy Press.

Casterline, J. B. (Ed.). (2001). *Diffusion processes and fertility transition: Selected perspectives*. Washington, DC: National Academy Press.

Castiglioni, M., & Dalla Zuanna, G. (1994). Innovation and tradition: Reproductive and marital behaviour in Italy in the 1970s and 1980s. *European Journal of Population*, 10(2), 107–141.

Castiglioni, M., & Dalla Zuanna, G. (1997). Matrimonio tardivo senza convivenza. La formazione delle unioni in Italia negli anni '80. In P. Giorgi & S. Strozza (Eds.), *Studi di popolazione: Temi di ricerca nuova*. Dipartimento di Scienze Demografiche, Università di Roma La Sapienza.

Chaffe, S. (1982). Mass media and interpersonal channels: Competitive, convergent, or complementary? In G. Gumpert & R. Cathcart (Eds.), *Inter/Media: Interpersonal communication in a media world*. New York: Oxford University Press.

Charles, M. (1992). Cross-national variation in occupational sex segregation. *American Sociological Review*, 57, 483–502.

Charles, M. (2003). Deciphering sex-segregation. *Acta Sociologica*, 46(4), 267–287.

Cherlin, A. (2000). Toward a new home economics. In L. J. Waite et al. (Eds.), *Ties That Bind. Perspectives on Marriage and Cohabitation* (pp. 126–144). New York: Aldine de Gruyter.

Cherlin, A. (2004). The deinstitutionalization of American marriage, *Journal of Marriage and the Family*, 66, 848–861.

Cherlin, A., Scabini, E., & Rossi, G. (1997). Delayed home leaving in Europe and the United States. *Journal of Family Issues*, 18, 572–576.

Chiuri, M. C., & Jappelli, T. (2000). Financial markets imperfections and home ownership: A comparative study. *Working Paper* No. 44, Centro Studi in Economia e Finanza, Dipartimento di Scienze Economiche, Università degli Studi di Salerno.

Cialdini, R. B. (1984). *Influence. The psychology of persuasion*. New York: Quill/William Morrow.

Cialdini, R. B. (1993). *Influence: Science and practice*. New York: HarperCollins.

Cialdini, R. B., & Goldstein, N. J. (2004). Social influence: Compliance and conformity. *Annual Review of Psychology*, 55, 591–621.

Cialdini, R. B., Kallgren, C. A., & Reno, R. R. (1991). A focus theory of normative conduct: A theoretical refinement and re-evaluation of the role of norms in human behaviour. *Advances in Experimental Social Psychology*, 21, 201–234.

Cialdini, R. B., Reno, R. R., & Kallgren, C. A. (1990). A focus theory of normative conduct: Recycling the concept of norms to reduce littering in public places. *Journal of Personality and Social Psychology*, 58, 1015–1026.

Cialdini, R. B., & Trost, M. R. (1998). Social influence: Social norms, conformity and compliance. In D. T. Gilbert, S. T. Fiske, & L. Gardiner(Eds.), *The handbook of psychology* (pp. 151–192). New York and Oxford: Oxford University Press.

Clarkberg, M. (1999). The price of partnering: The role of economic well-being in young adults' first union experiences. *Social Forces, 77*(3), 945–968.

Clarkberg, M., Stolzenberg, R., & Waite, L. (1995). Attitudes, values, and entrance into cohabitational versus marital unions. *Social Forces, 74*(2): 609–632.

Clausen, J. S. (1991). Adolescent competence and the shaping of the life course. *American Journal of Sociology, 96*(4), 805–842.

Cleland, J. (1985). Marital fertility decline in developing countries: Theories and the evidence. In J. Cleland & J. Hobcraft (Eds.), *Reproductive change in developing countries* (pp. 223–254). Oxford: Oxford University Press.

Cleland, J. (2001). Potatoes and pills: An overview of innovation-diffusion contributions to explanations of fertility decline. In John B. Casterline (Ed.), *Diffusion processes and fertility transition: Selected perspectives* (pp. 39–65). Washington, DC: National Academy Press.

Cleland, J., & Wilson, C. (1987). Demand theories of the fertility transition: An iconoclastic view. *Population Studies, 41*(1), 5–30.

Coale, A. J. (1971). Age patterns of marriage. *Population Studies, 25*, 193–214.

Coale, A. J. (1973). The demographic transition reconsidered. *IUSSP—Proceeding of the International Population Conference* (Vol. 1, pp. 53–72). Liège: USSP.

Coale, A. J., & Watkins, S. C. (1986). *The decline of fertility in Europe.* Princeton: Princeton University Press.

Coleman, J. S. (1986). Social theory, social research, and a theory of action. *American Journal of Sociology, 91*(6), 1309–1335.

Coleman, J. S. (1990). *Foundations of social theory.* Cambridge, MA: Harvard University Press.

Coleman, J. S., Katz, E., & Menzel, H. (1967). *Medical innovation.* New York: Bobbs-Merrill.

Conlisk, J. (1980). Costly optimizers versus cheap imitators. *Journal of Economic Behaviour and Organization, 1*, 275–293.

Consejo Económico y Social. (2002). *La emancipación de los jóvenes y la situación de la vivienda en España.* Informe 3/2002. Madrid: CES.

Cordon, J. A. F. (1997). Youth residential independence and autonomy: A comparative study. *Journal of Family Issues, 18*(6), 576–607.

Corijn, M. (2001a). Transition to adulthood: Sociodemographic factors. In M. Corijn & E. Klijzing (Eds.), *Transitions to adulthood in Europe* (pp. 1–25). Dordrecht: Kluwer.

Corijn, M. (2001b). Transition to adulthood in France. In M. Corijn & E. Klijzing (Eds.), *Transitions to adulthood in Europe* (pp. 131–151). Dordrecht: Kluwer.

Corijn, M., & Klijzing, E. (Eds.). (2001). *Transitions to adulthood in Europe.* Dordrecht: Kluwer.

Cousins, C. (1994). A comparison of the labour market positions on the women in Spain and the UK with reference to the 'flexible' labour debate. *Work, Employment and Society, 8*(1), 45–67.

Cox, R., McKendree, J., Tobin, R., & Lee, J. (1999). Vicarious learning from dialogue and discourse: A controlled comparison. *Instructional Science, 27*(6), 403–430.

Cready, C., Fosset, M. A., & Kiecolt, K. J. (1997). Mate availability and African American family structure in the U.S. nonmetropolitan South, 1960–1990. *Journal of Marriage and the Family, 59*, 192–203.

Cromm, J. (1998). *Familienbildung in Deutschland: Sozialdemographiche prozesse, theorie, recht und politik unter besonderer berucksichtigung der DDR.* Opladen: Westdeutscher Verlag.

Dahlerup, D. (1994). Learning to live with the state—state, market and civil society: Women's need for state intervention in East and West. *Women's Studies International Forum*, 17(2/3), 117–127.

Dalla Zuanna, G. (2004). The banquet of Aeolus. An interpretation of Italian lowest low fertility. In G. Dalla Zuanna & G. Micheli (Eds.), *Strong family and low fertility: A paradox? New perspectives in interpreting contemporary family and reproductive behaviour* (pp. 105–127). Dordrecht: Kluwer.

Dalla Zuanna, G., & Righi, A. (1999). Nascere nelle cento Italie. Comportamenti coniugali e riproduttivi nelle province italiane negli anni '80 e '90. *Argomenti no. 18*. Rome: ISTAT.

Daly, M. (1994). Comparing welfare states: Towards a gender friendly approach. In D. Sainsbury (Ed.), *Gendering welfare states* (pp. 101–117). London: Sage.

Daly, M. (1996, December). *Social security, gender and equality in the European Union*. Report to the European Commission Directorate-General V, V/5298/97-EN.

Daly, M. (2000a). A fine balance: Women's labor market participation in international comparison. In F. Scharpf & V. Schmidt (Eds.), *Welfare and work in the open economy: Diverse responses to common challenges*. New York: Oxford University Press.

Daly, M. (2000b). *The gender division of welfare*. Cambridge: Cambridge University Press.

Dechter, A. R. (2001). Comment: Potential applications and extensions for a binary choice-based social interaction framework. *Sociological Methodology*, 31(1), 107–121.

de Jong Gierveld, J., & Liefbroer, A. C. (1995). The Netherlands. In H.-P. Blossfeld (Ed.), *The new role of women. Family formation in modern societies* (pp. 102–125). Boulder, CO: Westview.

Del Boca, D., & Fornengo, G. (1992). La segregazione occupazionale. *Politiche del Lavoro*, no. 19. Milan: Franco Angeli.

Dell'Aringa, C., & Lodovici, M. S. (1996). Policies for the unemployed and social shock absorbers: The Italian experience, *South European Society and Politics*, 1, 172–197.

De Sandre, P. (1988). Quando i figli lasciano la famiglia. In E. Scabini & P. Donati (Eds.), *La famiglia 'lunga' del giovane adulto*. Milan: Vito efensiero.

De Sandre, P. (1997). La formazione di nuove famiglie. In M. Barbagli & C. Saraceno (Eds.), *Lo stato delle famiglie in Italia*. Bologna: Il Mulino.

De Sandre, P. (2000). Patterns of fertility in Italy and factors of its decline. *Genus*, 56(1/2), 19–54.

Deutsch, M., & Gerard, H. (1955). A study of normative and informational social influence upon individual judgement. *Journal of Abnormal and Social Psychology*, 51, 629–636.

Diekmann, A. (1989). Diffusion and survival models for the process of entry into marriage. *Journal of Mathematical Sociology*, 14, 31–44.

Diekmann, A. (1992). The log-logistic distribution as a model for social diffusion processes. *Journal of Scientific & Industrial Research*, 51, 285–290.

Diekmann, A., & Engelhardt, H. (1999). The social inheritance of divorce: Effects of parent's family type in post-war Germany. *American Sociological Review*, 64, 783–793.

Diewald, M. (2001). Causal understanding and the division of labour in social sciences. Experiences and prospects of life course research, special issue on longitudinal methology. *Canadian Studies in Population*, 28(2), 219–248.

Di Giulio, P., & Rosina, A. (2007). Intergenerational family ties and the diffusion of cohabitation in Italy. *Demographic Research*, 16, 441–468.

Direction Générale de l'Aménagement du Territoire, du Logement et du Patrimoine. (2002). *Housing statistics in the European Union 2002*. Liège, Belgium: University of Liège. Available at http://mrw.wallonie.be/dgatlp/HousingStat Ditch, J., Barnes, H., Bradshaw, J., Commaile, J., & Eardley, T. (Eds.). (1996). *A synthesis of national family policies 1995*. Brussels: Commission of the European Communities.

Dolado, J. J., & Jimeneo, J. F. (1997). The causes of Spanish unemployment: A structural VAR approach. *European Economic Review, 41*, 1281–1307.

Domingo i Valls, A. (1997). *La formación de la pareja en tiempos de crisis. Madrid y Barcelona, 1975–1995*. Unpublished doctoral dissertation discussed at the Universitad Nacional de Educación a Distancia, Facultad de Ciencias Politica y Sociologìa (UNED), Departamento de Sociologia II.

Donner, C. (2000). *Housing policies in the European Union. Theory and practice.* Vienna: Ernst Becvar Verlag.

Drobnič, S., Blossfeld, H.-P., & Rohwer, G. (1999). Dynamics of women's employment patterns over the family life course: A comparison of the United States and Germany. *Journal of Marriage and the Family, 61*(1), 133–146.

Duggan, L. S. (1993). Production and reproduction: Family policy and gender inequality in East and West Germany. *Dissertation Abstracts International* (UMI No.).

Duggan, L. (2003). East and West Germany policy compared: The distribution of childrearing costs. *Comparative Economic Studies, 45*(1), 63–86.

Duncan, G. J. (2000). Using panel studies to understand household behaviour and well-being. In D. Rose (Ed.), *Researching social and economic change. Household panel studies: Methods and substance.* London: Routledge.

Duncan, G. J., & Kalton, G. (1987). Issues in the design and analysis of surveys across time. *International Statistical Review, 55*(1), 97–117.

Durlauf, S. N., & Walker, J. R. (2001). Social interactions and fertility transitions. In J. B. Casterline (Ed.), *Diffusion processes and fertility transition: Selected perspectives* (pp. 115–137). Washington, DC: National Academy Press.

Duvander, A-Z E. (1999). The transition from cohabitation to marriage. *Journal of Family Issues, 20*, 698–718.

Duvander, A-Z E. (2000). *Couples in Sweden. Studies of family and work.* Edsbruk: Akademitryck AB.

Easterlin, R. A. (1975). An economic framework for fertility analysis. *Studies in Family Planning, 6*(3), 54–63.

Easterlin, R. A. (1993). *Birth and fortune*. Chicago: University of Chicago Press.

Elster, J. (1998). A plea for mechanisms. In P. Hedström & R. Swedberg (Eds.), *Social mechanisms* (pp. 45–73). Cambridge: Cambridge University Press.

England, P. (2000). Marriage, the costs of children, and gender inequality. In L. J. Waite et al. (Eds.), *Ties that bind. Perspectives on marriage and cohabitation* (pp. 320–342). New York: Aldine de Gruyter.

Erickson, B. H. (1988). The relational basis of attitudes. In B. Wellmann & S. D. Berkowitz (Eds.), *Social structures: A network approach* (pp, 99–121). New York: Cambridge University Press.

Ermisch, J. (2005). The puzzling rise in childbearing outside marriage. In A. F. Heath, J. Ermisch, & D. Gallie (Eds.), *Understanding social change* (pp. 23–53). Oxford: Oxford University Press.

Ermisch, J., & Di Salvo, P. (1997). The economic determinants of young people's household formation. *Economica, 64*, 627–644.

Ermisch, J. & Francesconi, M. (2000). Cohabitation in Great Britain: not for long, but here to stay. *Journal of Royal Statistical Society.* 163(2):153-71

Frerich, J. (1996). *Sozialpolitik. Das Spezialleistungssystem der Bundesrepublik Deutschland*, München/Wien: Oldenbourg.

Frerich, J., & Frey, M. (1996). *Handbuch der Geschchte der Sozialpolitik in Deutschland*, Band 2: Sozialpolitik in der Deutschen Demokratischen Republik, and Band 3: Sozialpolitik in der Bundesrepublik Deutschland bis zur Herstellung der Deutschen Einheit, München/Wien: Oldenbourg.

Esping-Andersen, G. (1990). *The three worlds of welfare capitalism.* New York: Princeton University Press.

Esping-Andersen, G. (Ed.). (1993). *Changing classes: Stratification and mobility in post-industrial societies.* London: Sage.

Esping-Andersen, G. (1995). Il welfare state senza il lavoro. L'Ascesa del familismo nelle politiche sociali dell'Europa continentale. *Stato e Mercato, 45,* 347–380.

Esping-Andersen, G. (1999). *Social foundations of postindustrial economies.* Oxford: Oxford University Press.

Esping-Andersen, G., & Korpi, W. (1987). From poor relief to institutional welfare states: The development of Scandinavian social policy. In R. Erikson (Ed.), *The Scandinavian model: Welfare states and welfare research* (pp. 39–74). Armonk, NY: Sharpe.

European Central Bank. (2003, March). *Structural factors in the EU housing markets.* Frankfurt: Author.

European Commission. (2000). *Employment in Europe 2000.* Luxembourg: Author.

European Mortgage Federation. (1997). *Hypostat 1986–1996.* Brussels: EC Mortgage Federation.

Fagan, C., & Rubery, J. (1996). The salience of the part-time divide in the European Union. *European Sociological Review, 12*(3), 227–247.

Farìa, V. E. & Potter, J. E. (1994, February 16–19). *The telenovela, family values and fertility change.* Paper presented at the Seminar on Values and Fertility Change, CCFIUSSP, Sion, Switzerland. Published as Farìa, V. E. & Potter, J. E. (1999). Television, telenovelas, and fertility change in Northeast Brazil. In R. Leete (Ed.), *Dynamics of values in fertility change* (pp. 252–272). Oxford: Clarendon Press.

Ferrera, M. (1993). *Modelli di solidarietà.* Bologna: Il Mulino.

Ferrera, M. (1996). The southern model of welfare in social Europe. *Journal of European Social Policy, 1,* 17–37.

Ferrera, M., & Castles, F. C. (1996). Home ownership and the welfare state: Is southern Europe different? *South European Politics and Society, 1*(2), 163–185.

Festinger, L. (1954). A theory of social comparison processes. *Human Relations, 7,* 117–140.

Festinger, L., Schachter, S., & Back, K. W. (1950). *Social pressure in informal groups.* Stanford: Stanford University Press.

Festy, P. (1980). On the New Context of Marriage in Western Europe. *Population and Development Review, 6*(2), 311–315.

Festy, P. (1985). The contemporary evolution of family formation in Western Europe. *European Journal of Population, 1*(2–3), 179–205.

Festy, P., & Prioux, F. (2002). *An evaluation of the Fertility and Family Surveys Project.* New York and Geneva: United Nations.

Finch, J., & Groves, D. (Eds.). (1983). *A labour of love: Women, work and caring.* London: Routledge.

Friedkin, N. E. (1984). Structural cohesion and equivalence explanations of social homogeneity. *Sociological Methods and Research, 12,* 235–261.

Frinking, G. (1988). Childlessness in Europe: Trends and implications. In H. Moors & J. Schoorl (Eds.), *Lifestyles, contraception and parenthood* (Vol. 17). The Hague, The Netherlands: NIDI CBGS.

Galland, O. (1986). Precarietà e modi di entrata nella vita adulta. In C. Saraceno (Ed.), *Età e corso della vita* (pp. 279–298). Bologna: Il Mulino.

Galland, O. (1997). Leaving home and family relations in France. *Journal of Family Issues, 18*(6), 645–670.

Galland, O. (2000). Entrer dans la vie adulte: Des étapes toujours plus tardives mais resserrées. *Economie et Statistique, 337–338*(7/8), 13–36.

Gambetta, D. (1998). Concatenations of mechanisms. in P. Hedström & R. Swedberg (Eds.), *Social mechanisms* (pp. 102–124). Cambridge: Cambridge University Press.

Gantz, W., Krendl, K. A., & Robertson, S. R. (1986). Diffusion of a proximate news event. *Journalism Quarterly, 63*(2), 282–287.

Gauthier, A. (1996). *The state and the family: A comparative analysis of family policies in industrialised countries*. Oxford: Clarendon Press.

Gershuny, J., Bittman, M., & Brice, J. (2005). Exit, voice, and suffering: Do couples adapt to changing employment patterns? *Journal of Marriage and Family, 67*, 656–665.

Ghidoni, M. (2002). *Determinants of young Europeans' decision to leave the parental household*. Unpublished manuscript. London: University College London. Available at http://repec.org/res2002/Ghidoni.pd Glendon, M. A. (1989). *The transformation of family law. State, law, and family in the United States and Western Europe*. Chicago: University of Chicago Press.

Glick, P. C., & Spanier, G. B. (1980). Married and unmarried cohabitation in the United States. *Journal of Marriage and the Family, 42*(1), 19–30.

Goffman, E. (1959). *The presentation of self in everyday life*. Garden City, NY: Doubleday.

Goffman, E. (1963). *Stigma*. Englewood Cliffs, NJ: Prentice-Hall.

Goffman, E. (1967). *Interaction ritual*. New York: Pantheon.

Goldsheider, F. K., & Da Vanzo, J. (1985). Living arrangements and the transition to adulthood. *Demography, 22*(4), 545–563.

Goldsheider, F. K., & Da Vanzo, J. (1989). Pathways to independent living in early adulthood: Marriage, semiautonomy, and premarital residential independence. *Demography, 26*(4), 597–614.

Goldsheider, F. K., Thornton, A., & Young-DeMarco, L. (1993). A portrait of nest-leaving process in early adulthood. *Demography, 30*(4), 683–699.

Goldsheider, F. K., & Waite, L. J. (1986). Sex differences in the entry into marriage. *American Journal of Sociology, 92*(1), 91–109.

Goldthorpe, J. H. (1996). The quantitative analysis of large-scale data-sets and rational action theory: For a sociological alliance. *European Sociological Review, 12*(2), 109–126.

González, M. J. (2002). Women's entry into motherhood in France, Sweden, East and West Germany, Spain and Italy. *FENICs Working Paper, 2*. Available at: http://www.warwick.ac.uk/ier/fenics/brussels.ht

González, M. J., Jurado, T., & Naldini, M. (Eds.). (2000). *Gender inequalities in southern Europe: Women, work and welfare in the 1990s*. London: Franck Cass.

Granovetter, M. (1973). The strength of weak ties. *American Journal of Sociology, 78*(6), 1360–1380.

Granovetter, M. (1978). Threshold model of collective behaviour. *American Journal of Sociology, 83*, 1420–1443.

Granovetter, M. (1985). Economic action and social structure: The problem of embeddedness. *American Journal of Sociology, 91*, 481–510.

Granovetter, M., & Soong, R. (1983). Threshold models of diffusion and collective behaviour. *Journal of Mathematical Sociology, 9*, 165–179.

Grasmick, H. G., & Green, D. E. (1980). Legal punishment, social disapproval and internationalisation as inhibitors of illegal behaviours. *Journal of Criminal Law and Criminology, 71*, 325–335.

Graue, E. D. (1995). Family law in Germany. In C. Hamilton & K. Standley (Eds.), *Family law in Europe*. London: Butterworths.

Greve, H. R. (1995). Jumping ship: The diffusion of strategy abandonment. *Administrative Science Quarterly, 40*, 444–473.

Greve, H. R., Strang, D., & Tuma, N. B. (1993). *Estimation of diffusion processes from incomplete populations*. Paper presented at the annual meetings of the American Sociological Association, Miami.

Greve, H. R., Strang, D., & Tuma, N. B. (1995). Specification and estimation of heterogeneous diffusion models. In P. V. Marsden (Ed.), *Sociological methodology* (pp. 377–420). New York: Blackwell.

Gualmini, E. (1998). *La politica del lavoro*. Bologna: Il Mulino.

Guerrero, T., & Naldini, M. (1996). *Is the South so Different? Italian and Spanish families in comparative perspective*. Mannheimer Zentrum für Europeische Sozialforshung, Working Paper No. 12.

Guimezanes, N. (1995). Family law in France. In C. Hamilton & K. Standley (Eds.), *Family law in Europe*. London: Butterworths.

Hakim, C. (1997). A sociological perspective on part-time work. In H.-P. Blossfeld & C. Hakim (Eds.), *Between equalisation and marginalization: Women working part-time in Europe and the United States of America* (pp. 22–70). New York: Oxford University Press

Hakim, C. (2000). *Work-lifestyle choices in the 21st century*. Oxford: Oxford University Press.

Hansen, H., & Larsen, J. E. (1993). Difference in pension savings opportunities for men and women. In S. Carlsen & J. E. Larsen (Eds.), *The equality dilemma* (pp. 91–102). Copenhagen: The Danish Equal Status Council.

Hatfield, E., Cacioppo, J. T., & Rapson, R. L. (1993). *Emotional contagion*. New York: Cambridge University Press.

Hedström, P. (1994). Contagious collectivities: On the spatial diffusion of Swedish trade unions, 1890–1940. *American Journal of Sociology, 99*(5), 1157–1179.

Hedström, P. (1998). Rational imitation. In P. Hedström & R. Swedberg (Eds.), *Social Mechanisms* (pp. 306–327). Cambridge: Cambridge University Press.

Hedström, P. (2005). *Dissecting the social: On the principles of analytical sociology*. Cambridge: Cambridge University Press.

Hedström, P., & Åberg, Y. (2002, May). *Social interaction, endogenous processes, and youth unemployment*. Paper presented at the Swedish Collegium for Advanced Studies in the Social Sciences, Stockholm.

Hedström, P., Sandell, R., & Stern, C. (2000). Mesolevel networks and the diffusion of social movements: The case of the Swedish Social Democratic Party. *American Journal of Sociology, 106*(1), 145–172.

Hedström, P., & Swedberg, R. (1996a). Social mechanisms. *ACTA Sociologica, 3*, 281–308.

Hedström, P., & Swedberg, R. (1996b). Rational choice, empirical research, and the sociological tradition. *European Sociological Review, 12*, 127–146.

Hedström, P., & Swedberg, R. (Eds.). (1998). *Social mechanisms*, Cambridge: Cambridge University Press.

Hernes, H. M. (1987). *Welfare state and women power*. Oslo: Norwegian University Press.

Hobcraft, J., Menken, J., & Preston, S. (1982). Age, period and cohort effects in demography: A review. *Population Index, 48*(1), 4–43.

Hobson, B. (1990). No exit, no voice: Women's economic dependency and the welfare state. *Acta Sociologica, 33*, 235–250.

Hochshild, A. (1989). *The second shift*. New York: Avon.

Hoem, B. (1995). Sweden. In: H.-P. Blossfeld (Ed.), *The new role of women. Family formation in modern societies* (pp. 35–55). Boulder, CO: Westview.

Hoem, J. M., & Hoem, B. (1988). The Swedish family: Aspects of contemporary developments. *Journal of Family Issues*, 9, 397–424.

Homans, G. C. (1950). *The human group*. New York: Harcourt, Brace & World.

Homans, G. C. (1961). *Social behavior. Its elementary forms*. New York: Harcourt, Brace & World.

Hornik, R., & McAnany, E. (2001). Mass media and fertility change. In J. B. Casterline (Ed.), *Diffusion processes and fertility transition: Selected perspectives* (pp. 208–239). Washington, DC: National Academy Press.

Huinink, J. (1995). *Warum noch familie?* Frankfurt am Main: Campus Fachbuch.

Huinink, J. (2000). Bildung und familienentwicklung im lebensverlauf. *Zeitschrift für Erziehungswissenschaft*, 2, 209–227.

Huinink, J., & Wagner, M. (1995). Partnerschaft, ehe und familie in der DDR. In J. Huinink, K. U. Mayer (Eds.), *Kollektiv und eigensinn, Lebensverläufe in der DDR und danach* (pp. 145–188). Berlin: Akademie Verlag.

Hullen, G. (1998). *Lebensverläufe in West- und Ostdeutschland*, Opladen: Leske Budrich.

Huston, T. L. & Geis, G. (1993). In what ways do gender-related attributes and beliefs affect marriage? *Journal of Social Issues*, 49(3), 87–106.

Iacovou, M. (1998). Young people in Europe: Two models of household formation. *ISER Working Paper* 1998–13 (pp. 212–250). Colchester: University of Essex.

Iacovou, M. (2001). Leaving home in the European Union. *ISER Working Paper* 2001–18. Colchester: University of Essex.

Iacovou, M. (2002). Regional Differences in the Transition to Adulthood. *Annuals of the American Academy of Political and Social Science*. 580:40-69

Iannelli, C., & Bonmatí, A. S. (2003). Transition pathways in Italy and Spain: Different patterns, similar vulnerability? In W. Müller & M. Gangl (Eds.), *Transitions from education to work in Europe. The integration of youth into EU labour markets* (pp. 212–250). Oxford: Oxford University Press.

ISTAT. (1999). Famiglie, abitazioni e sicurezza dei cittadini. Indagine multiscopo sulle famiglie, Anno 1998. *Informazioni* No. 36. Rome: Author.

Jenson, J. (1997). Who cares?: Gender and welfare regimes. *Social Politics*, 4, 182–187.

Jenson, J., Hagen, E., & Reddy, C. (Eds.). (1988). *Feminization of the labor force: Paradoxes and promises*. New York: Oxford University Press.

Jones, G. (1995). *Leaving home*. Buckingham: Open University Press.

Jones, S. R. G. (1984). *The economics of conformism*. Oxford: Basil Blackwell.

Jurado Guerrero, T. (1995). Legitimation durch Sozialpolitik? Die spanische beschäftigungskrise und die theorie des wohlfahrtsstaates. *Kölner Zeitschrift für Soziologie und Sozialpsychologie*, 47, 727–752.

Jurado Guerrero, T. (2001). *Youth in transition: Housing, employment, social policies and families in France and Spain*. Aldershot: Ashgate.

Kahan, D. M. (1997). Social influence, social meaning, and deterrence. *Virginia Law Review*, 83, 349–395.

Kanfer, F. H., & Marston, A. R. (1963). Human reinforcement: Vicarious and direct. *Journal of Experimental Psychology*, 65, 292–296.

Katz, E., & Lazarsfeld, P. F. (1955). *Personal influence*. Glencoe, IL: Free Press.

Kaufer, D. S., & Carley, K. M. (1993). *Communication at a distance: The effect of print on socio-cultural organization and change*. Hillsdale, NJ: Erlbaum.

Kaufer, D. S., & Carley, K. M. (1996). The influence of print on social and cultural change. *Annual Review of Applied Linguistics*, 16, 14–25.

Kaufmann, J.-C. (1995). *Trame coniugali. Panni sporchi e rapporto di coppia*. Bari: Dedalo. (Original work published 1992 as *Trame conjugale: Analyse du couple par son linge*. Paris: Nathan)

Kaufmann, J.-C. (1996). *La vita a due. Sociologia della coppia.* Bologna: Il Mulino.

Kemp, A. A. (1994). *Women's work: Degraded and devaluated.* Englewood Cliffs, NJ: Prentice Hall.

Kiernan, K. E. (1993). The future of partnership and fertility. In R. Cliquet (Ed.), *The Future of Europe's Population.* Strasbourg: Council of Europe.

Kiernan, K. E. (1999). Cohabitation in Western Europe. *Population Trends, 96,* 25–32.

Kiernan, K. E. (2000). European perspectives on family formation. In L. Waite et al. (Eds.), *Ties that bind. Perspectives on Marriage and Cohabitation* (pp. 40–58). New York: Aldine de Gruyter.

Kiernan, K. E. (2001). The rise of cohabitation and childbearing outside marriage in Europe. *International Journal of Law, Policy and the Family, 15*(1), 1–21.

Kiernan, K. E. (2002). Cohabitation in Western Europe: Trends, issues and implications. In A. Booth & A. Crouter (Eds.), *Just living together: Implications of cohabitation on families, children and social policy* (pp. 3–31). Hillsdale, NJ: Erlbaum.

Kiernan, K. E. (2004a). Redrawing the boundaries of marriage. *International Journal of Marriage and the Family, 66,* 980–987.

Kiernan, Kathleen E. (2004b). Cohabitation and divorce across nations and generations. In P. L. Chase-Lansdale, K. Kiernan, & R. Friedmann (Eds.). *The potential for change across lives and generations: Multidisciplinary perspectives.* New York: Cambridge University Press.

Klijzing, E., & Cairns, H. (2000). *On the quality of FFS event history data: Of critical importance in life course research.* GLOBALIFE Working Paper Series No. 13, Faculty of Sociology. Bielefeld: University of Bielefeld.

Klijzing, E., & Corijn, M. (Eds.). (2002). *Dynamics of fertility and partnership in Europe: Insights and lessons from comparative research.* Geneva and New York: United Nations.

Klijzing, E., & De Rose, A. (1999). Le indagini su fecondità e famiglia nel contesto internazionale: Prospettive di comparazione. In P. de Sandre, A. Pinelli, & A. Santini (Eds.), *Nuzialità e Fecondità in Trasformazione: Percorsi e Fattori di Cambiamento* (pp. 41–55). Bologna: Il Mulino.

Kohler, H.-P. (1997). Learning in social networks and contraceptive choice. *Demography, 34,* 369–383.

Kohler, H.-P. (2001). *Fertility and social interaction. An economic perspective.* Oxford: Oxford University Press.

Kohler, H.-P., Behrman, J. R., & Watkins, S. C. (2001). The density of social networks and fertility decisions: Evidences from South Nyanza District, Kenya. *Demography, 38,* 43–58.

Konietzka, D., & Kreyenfeld, M. (2002). Women's employment and non-marital childbearing: A comparison between East and West Germany in the 1990s. *Population, 57,* 441–458.

Konietzka, D., & Solga, H. (1995, September 22–25). *Two certified societies? The regulation of entry into the labor market in East and West Germany.* Paper presented at the workshop Transition in Youth: Comparisons Over Time and Across Countries, Oostvoorne, The Netherlands.

Korpi, W. (2000). Faces of inequality: Gender, class and patterns of inequalities in different types of welfare states. *Social Politics, 7*(2), 127–191.

Kravdal, O. (1999). Does marriage require a stronger economic underpinning than informal cohabitation? *Population Studies, 53*(1), 63–80.

Kreyenfeld, M. (2000). Educational attainment and first birth: East Germany before and after unification. *MPIDR Working Paper* 11. Rostock: Max Planck Institute for Demographic Research.

Kreyenfeld, M. (2003). Crisis or adaptation—reconsidered: A comparison of East and West Germany fertility patterns in the first six years after the 'wende.' *European Journal of Population*, 19, 303–329.

Kreyenfeld, M. (2004). Fertility decisions in the FRG and GDR: An analysis with data from the German fertility and family survey. *MPIDR Working Paper* 11 (Special Collection 3). Rostock: Max Planck Institute for Demographic Research.

Kuijsten, A. C. (1996). Changing family patterns in Europe: A case of divergence? *European Journal of Population*, 12, 115–143.

Kuran, T. (1995). *Private truths, public lies: The social consequences of preference falsification*. Cambridge, MA: Harvard University Press.

Kurz, K., & Blossfeld, H.-P. (Eds.). (2004). *Homeownership and social inequality in comparative perspective*. Stanford: Stanford University Press.

Kurz, K., & Steinhage, N. (2001). Globaler wettbewerb und unsicherheiten beim einstieg in den arbeitsmarkt. Analysen für Deutschland in den 80er und 90er jahren. *Berliner Journal für Soziologie*, (4):513–532.

Kurz, K., Steinhage, N., & Golsch, K. (2005). Case study Germany: Global competition, uncertainty and the transition to adulthood. In H.-P. Blossfeld et al. (Eds.), *Globalization, uncertainty and youth in society* (pp. 51–82). London: Routledge.

Laferrère, A., & Bessière, S. (2003, June 5–13). *Nest-living and nest-leaving: Does the nest matter?* Paper presented at the ESPE conference, New York.

Lazarsfeld, P. F., & Merton, R. K. (1964). Friendship as social process: A substantive and methodological analysis. In M. Berger et al. (Eds.), *Freedom and control in modern society*. New York: Octagon.

Lee, J., Dineen, F., McKendree, J., & Mayes, T. (1999). *Vicarious learning: Cognitive and linguistic effects of observing peer dialogues*. Paper presented at American Educational Research Association (AERA '99) annual meeting. Available at http://www.hcrc.ed.ac.uk/gal/vicar/VicarPapers Leridon, H. (1990). Cohabitation, marriage, separation: An analysis of the life histories of French cohorts from 1968 to 1985. *Population Studies*, 44, 127–144.

Leridon, H., & Toulemon, L. (1995). France. In H.-P. Blossfeld (Ed.), *The new role of women. Family formation in modern societies* (pp. 77–101). Boulder, CO: Westview.

Leridon, H., & Villeneuve-Gokalp. C. (1989). The new couples: Number, characteristics and attitudes. *Population (an English Selection)*, 44(1), 203–235.

Lesthaeghe, R. (1977). *The decline of Belgian fertility*. Princeton: Princeton University Press.

Lesthaeghe, R. (1992). Beyond economic reductionism: The transformation of the reproductive regimes in France and Belgium in the 18th and 19th centuries. In C. Goldscheider (Ed.), *Family structure and population policy* (pp. 1–44). Boulder, CO: Westview.

Lesthaeghe, R. (1995). The second demographic transition in Western countries: An interpretation. In K. O. Mason & vA.-M. Jensen (Eds.), *Gender and family change in industrialised countries*. New York: Oxford University Press.

Lesthaeghe, R., & Meekers, D. (1986). Value changes and the dimensions of familism in European community. *European Journal of Population*, 2, 225–268.

Lesthaeghe, R., & Neels, K. (2002). From the first to the second demographic transition: An interpretation of the spatial continuity of demographic innovation in France, Belgium and Switzerland. *European Journal of Population*, 18, 325–360.

Lesthaeghe, R., & Surkyn, J. (1988). Cultural dynamics and economic theories of fertility change. *Population and Development Review*, 14(1), 1–45.

Lesthaeghe, R., & Vanderhoeft, C. (2001). Ready, willing & able. A conceptualization of transitions to new behavioural forms. In J. B. Casterline (Ed.), *Diffusion processes and fertility transition: Selected perspectives* (pp. 240–264). Washington, DC: National Academy Press.

Leth-Sorensen, S., & Rohwer, G. (2001). Work careers of married women in Denmark. In H.-P. Blossfeld & Sonja Drobnic (Eds.), *Careers of couples in contemporary society. From male breadwinner to dual-earner families* (pp. 261–280). Oxford: Oxford University Press.

Liefbroer, A. (1991). The choice between a married or unmarried first union by young adults. A competing risks analysis. *European Journal of Population, 1,* 273–298.

Lillard, L. A. (1993). Simultaneous equations for hazards. Marriage duration and fertility timing. *Journal of Econometrics, 56,* 189–217.

Lillard, L. A., Brien, M. J., & Waite, L. J. (1995). Premarital cohabitation and subsequent marital dissolution: A matter of self-selection? *Demography, 32*(3), 437–457.

Lillard, L. A., & Waite, L. J. (1993). A joint model of marital childbearing and marital disruption. *Demography, 30*(4), 653–681.

Lister, R. (1997). *Citizenship. Feminist perspectives.* London: Macmillan.

Lorber, J., & Farrell, S. A. (Eds.). (1991). *The social construction of gender.* London: Sage.

Lorber, J. (1994). *Paradoxes of gender.* New Haven, CT: Yale University Press.

Luciano, A. (1992). Oltre le pari opportunità. Carriere femminili e maschili nelle organizzazioni complesse. *Polis,* (6)1:43–63.

MacAllister, I. (1990). Gender and the division of labour: Employment and earnings variations in Australia. *Work and Occupations, 17,* 79–99.

MacInnes, J. (2006). Work-life balance in Europe: A response to the baby bust or reward for the baby boomers? *European Societies, 8*(2), 223–249.

Mahajan, V., & Peterson, R. A. (1985). *Models for innovation diffusion.* Beverly Hills, CA: Sage.

Major, B. (1993). Gender, entitlement, and the distribution of family labor. *Journal of Social Issues, 49*(3), 141–159.

Major, B. (1994). From social inequality to personal entitlement: The role of social comparisons, legitimacy appraisals, and group membership. In M. Zanna (Ed.), *Advances in experimental social psychology* (Vol 26, pp. 293–355). New York: Academic Press.

Major, B., McFarlin, D., & Gagnon, D. (1984). Overworked and underpaid: On the nature of gender differences in personal entitlement. *Journal of Personality and Social Psychology, 47,* 1399–1412.

Manski, C. F. (1993a). Dynamic choice in social settings: Learning from the experiences of others. *Journal of Econometrics, 58*(1), 121–136.

Manski, C. F. (1993b). Identification of endogenous social effects: The reflection problem. *Review of Economics Studies, 60,* 531–542.

Manski, C. F. (2000). Economic analysis of social interactions. *Journal of Economic Perspectives, 14*(3), 115–136.

Manski, C. F. (2004). Social learning from private experiences: The dynamics of the selection problem. *Review of Economic Studies, 71*(2), 443–458.

Manting, D. (1996). The changing meaning of cohabitation and marriage. *European Sociological Review, 12,* 53–65.

Maravall, J. M., & Fraile, M. (1998). *The politics of unemployment: The Spanish experience in a comparative perspective.* Working Paper No. 14. Madrid: Instituto Juan March, Centro de Estudios Avanzado en Ciencias Sociales.

March, J. G., & Olsen, J. P. (1979). Organizational choice under ambiguity. In J. G. March & J. P. Olsen (Eds.), *Ambiguity and choice in organizations* (2nd ed., pp. 10–23). Bergen: Universitetsforlaget.

Marini, M. M. (1984). Age and sequencing norms in the transition of adulthood. *Social Forces, 63,* 229–244.

Marini, M. M. (1985). Determinants of the timing of adult role entry. *Social Science Research, 14,* 309–350.

Marin Muñoz, M. (2003). Trabajo femenino, polìtica familiar y teorìas ecónomicas. *Boletino Economico de ICE, 2774,* 5–11.

Marsden, P.V., & Friedkin, N. E. (1993). Network studies of social influence. *Sociological Methods and Research, 22,* 127–151.

Martín-García, T., & Baizán, P. (2006). The impact of the type of education and of educational enrolment on first births. *European Sociological Review, 22*(3), 259–275.

Maruani, M. (1991). La construccion social de las diferencias de sexo en el mercado. *Revista de Economia y Sociologia del Trabajo, 13/14,* 129–137.

Mayer, K. U. (1997). Notes on a comparative political economy of life courses. *Comparative Social Research, 16,* 203–226.

Mayer, K. U. (2000). Promises fulfilled? A review of 20 years of life course research. *Archives Européennes de Sociologie, 151*(2), 259–282.

Mayer, K. U. (2001). The paradox of global social change and national path dependencies. In A. Woodward & M. Kohli (Eds.), *Inclusions and exclusions in European societies* (pp. 89–110). New York: Routledge.

Mayer, K. U., & Müller, W. (1996). The state and the structure of the life course. In A. B. Sørensen, F. E. Weinert, & L.R. Sherrod (Eds.), *Human development: Interdisciplinary perspectives* (pp. 217–245). Hillsdale, NJ: Erlbaum

McAdam, D., & Rucht, D. (1993). The cross-national diffusion of movements and ideas [Special issue]. *The Annals of the American Academy of Political and Social Sciences, 528,* 56–74.

Mead, G. H. (1964). *On social psychology: Selected papers.* Chicago: University of Chicago Press.

Mead, G. H., & Miller, D. L. (Eds.). (1982). *The individual and the social self: Unpublished work of George Herbert Mead.* Chicago: University of Chicago Press.

Mead, G. H., & Morris, C. W. (Eds.). (1934). *Mind, self and society from the standpoint of a social behaviourist.* Chicago: University of Chicago Press.

Meron, M., & Courgeau, D. (2004). Home ownership and social inequality in France. In K. Kurz & H.-P. Blossfeld (Eds.), *Home ownership and social inequality in comparative perspective* (pp. 61–78). Stanford: Stanford University Press.

Merton, R. K. (1957). *Social theory and social structure.* Glencoe: The Free Press.

Miguel Castaño de, C. (1991). Tendencias y perspectivas de la participación femenina en la actividad economica. *Revista de Economia y Sociologia del Trabajo, 13/14,* 43–61.

Milgram, S., Bickman, L., & Berkowitz, L. (1969). Note on the drawing power of crowds of different size. *Journal of Personality and Social Psychology, 13,* 79–82.

Millar, J., & Warman, A. (Eds.). (1996). *Family obligations in Europe.* London: Family Policy Study Centre.

Mills, M. (1999, October 18–19). *Social interaction and the emergence of innovative demographic behaviour. An exploration of theory and methodology.* Paper presented at the Workshop on Social Interaction and Demographic Behaviour. Rostock: Max Planck Institute for Demographic Research.

Mills, M. (2000). *The transformation of partnerships. Canada, The Netherlands, and the Russian Federation in the age of modernity.* Amsterdam: Thela Thesis Population Studies.

Mills, M., & Blossfeld, H.-P. (2001, October 6–10). *Globalization and changes in the early life course.* Paper presented at the EURESCO conference European Societies or European Society? Kerkrade, the Netherlands.

Mills, M., Blossfeld, H.-P., & Klijzing, E. (2005). Becoming an adult in uncertain times: A 14-country comparison of the losers of globalization. In H.-P. Blossfeld et al. (Eds.), *Globalization, Uncertainty and Youth in Society* (pp. 423–441). London: Routledge.

Mills, M., & Trovato, F. (2000). A comparative analysis of the effect of pregnancy in cohabiting unions on formal marriage in Canada, the Netherlands, and Latvia. *United Nations Economic Commission for Europe's Statistical Journal, 17,* 1–16.

Mingione, E. (1995). Labour market segmentation and informal work in southern Italy. *European Urban and Regional Studies, 2,* 121–143.

Mingione, E. (1999). Foreword. Longitudinal research: A bridge between quantitative and qualitative research? *Quality & Quantity, 33*(3), 215–218.

Mingione, E. (2001). Il lato oscuro del welfare: Trasformazione delle biografie, strategie famigliari e sistemi di garanzia. In *Atti del convegno "Tecnologia e Società II"* (pp. 147–170). Rome: Accedemia dei Lincei.

Montgomery, M. R., & Casterline, J. B. (1993). The diffusion of fertility control in Taiwan: Evidence from pooled cross-section time-series models. *Population Studies, 47*(3), 457–479.

Montgomery, M. R., & Casterline, J. B. (1996). Social learning, social influence, and new models of fertility. *Population and Development Review, 22*(Suppl.), 151–175.

Morán Carta, M. P. (1991). Las mujeres y el empleo en España 1987–90. *Revista de Economia y Sociologia del Trabajo, 13/14,* 88–103.

Moscovici, S. (1985). Social influence and conformity. In G. Lindzey & E. Aronson (Eds.), *Handbook of social psychology* (pp. 347–412). New York: Random House.

Moscovici, S., & Personnaz, B. (1980). Studies in social influence. *Journal of Experimental Social Psychology, 16,* 270–282.

Mulder, C. H., & Manting, D. (1994). Strategies of nest-leavers: 'Settling down' versus flexibility. *European Sociological Review, 10*(2), 155–172.

Müller, W., & Wolbers, M. H. J. (2003). Educational attainment in the European Union: Recent trends in qualification patterns. In W. Müller & M. Gangl (Eds.), *Transitions from education to work in Europe. The integration of youth into EU labour markets* (pp, 23–62). Oxford: Oxford University Press.

Myers, D. J. (1997). Racial rioting in the 1960s: An event history analysis of local conditions. *American Sociological Review, 62,* 94–112.

Myers, D. J. (2000). The diffusion of collective violence: Infectiousness, susceptibility, and mass media networks. *American Journal of Sociology, 106,* 173–208.

Naldini, M. (2003). *The family in the Mediterranean welfare states.* London: Frank Cass.

Nazio, T., & Blossfeld, H.-P. (2003). The diffusion of cohabitation among young women in West Germany, East Germany and Italy. *European Journal of Population, 19,* 47–82.

Nazio, T., & MacInnes, J. (2007). Time stress, well-being and the double burden. In G. Esping-Andersen (Ed.), *Family formation and family dilemmas in contemporary Europe* (pp. 155–184). Barcelona: FBBVA.

Newcomb, T. (1943). *Personality and social change: Attitude formation in a student community.* New York: Holt.

Nilsson, K., & Strandh, M. (1999). Nest leaving in Sweden: The importance of early educational and labor market careers. *Journal of Marriage and the Family, 61*(4), 1068–1079.

O'Connor, J. S. (1993). Gender, Class and citizenship in the comparative analysis of welfare state regimes: Theoretical and methodological issues. *British Journal of Sociology, 44*(3), 501–518.

O'Connor, J. S. (1996). From women in the welfare state to gendering welfare state regimes. *Current Sociology*, *44*(2), 1–132.

OECD. (1999). *Classifying educational programmes: Manual for ISCED-97 implementation in OECD countries*. Paris: OECD Publishing: Centre for Educational Research and Innovation.

Olstner, I. (1994). Independence and dependency. Options and constrains for women over the life course. *Women's Studies International Forum*, *17*(2/3), 129–139.

Olstner, I. (2001). Cohabitation in Germany. Rules, reality and public discourses. *International Journal of Law, Policy and the Family*, *15*, 88–101.

Olstner, I., & Lewis, J. (1995). Gender and the evolution of European social policies. In P. Pierson & S. Leibfried (Eds.), *Fragmented social policy* (pp. 1–40). Washington, DC: The Brooking Institution.

Ongaro, F. (2001). Transition to adulthood in Italy. In M. Corijn & E. Klijzing (Eds.), *Transitions to adulthood in Europe* (pp. 173–207). Dordrecht: Kluwer.

Oppenheimer, V. K. (1977). The sociology of women's economic role in the family. *American Sociological Review*, *42*(3), 387–406.

Oppenheimer, V. K. (1988). A theory of marriage timing. *American Journal of Sociology*, *94*(3), 563–589.

Oppenheimer, V. K. (1994). Women's rising employment and the future of the family in industrial societies. *Population and Development Review*, *20*(2), 293–342.

Oppenheimer, V. K. (1997a). Women's employment and the gain to marriage: The specialisation and trading model. *Annual Review of Sociology*, *23*, 431–453.

Oppenheimer, V. K. (1997b). Men's career development and marriage timing during a period of rising inequality. *Demography*, *34*(3), 311–330.

Oppenheimer, V. K. (2000). The continuing importance of men's economic position in marriage formation. In L. J. Waite et al (Eds.), *Ties That Bind* (pp. 283–301). New York: Aldine de Gruyter.

Orloff, A. S. (1993). Gender and the social rights of citizenship: The comparative analysis of gender relations and welfare states. *American Sociological Review*, *58*(3), 303–328.

Orloff, A. S. (1996). Gender in the welfare state. *Annual Review of Sociology*, *22*, 251–278.

Orloff, A. S. (2002, June 7–8). *Gender equality, women's employment: Cross-national patterns of policy and politics*. Paper presented at the workshop Welfare, Work and Family: Southern Europe in Comparative Perspective, Badia Fiesolana (FI).

Palloni, A. (1999, December 17). *Demographic analysis: New theories, new models and new data*. Working paper presented at the Giornata di Studio—Demografia: Presente e Futuro, Padova University, and Società Italiana di Statistica, Padova, Italy. Now available as *Center for Demography and Ecology (CDE) working Paper*, 2000–01, University of Wisconsin-Madison.

Palloni, A. (2001). Diffusion in sociological analysis. In John B. Casterline (Ed.), *Diffusion processes and fertility transitions: Selected perspectives* (pp. 66–114). Washington, DC: National Academy Press.

Palme, J. (1990). *Pension rights in welfare capitalism: The development of old-age pensions in 18 OECD countries 1930 to 1985*. Stockholm: Swedish Institute for Social Research Dissertation Series No. 14.

Peinado, A. (1991). Analisis de las diferencias salariales por sexo. *Revista de Economia y Sociologia del Trabajo*, *13/14*, 104–113.

Phillips, D. P. (1974). The influence of suggestion on suicide: Substantive and theoretical implications of the Werther effect. *American Sociological Review*, *3*, 340–354.

Picchio, A. (1992). Il lavoro di riproduzione, questione centrale nell'analisi del mercato del lavoro. *Politiche del Lavoro*, *19*, Milano: Franco Angeli.

212   References

`段

Pinelli, A., & De Rose, A. (1995). Italy. In: H.-P. Blossfeld (Ed.), *The new role of Women. Family formation in modern societies* (pp. 174–190). Boulder, CO: Westview.

Pitcher, B. L., Hamblin, R. L., & Miller, J. L. L. (1978). The diffusion of collective violence. *American Sociological Review, 43,* 23–35.

Polavieja, J. G. (2003). *Estables y precarios: Desregulación laboral y estratificación social en España (1984–1997).* Madrid: Siglo XXI/Centro de Investigaciones Sociológicas.

Pötter, U., & Blossfeld, H.-P. (2001). Causal inference from series of events. *European Sociological Review, 17*(1), 21–32.

Prinz, C. (1995). *Cohabiting, married, or single.* London: Avebury.

Quadagno, J. (1988). Women's access to pensions and the structure of eligibility rules. *Sociological Quarterly, 29,* 541–558.

Rafóls Esteve, J. (1998). Ciclo económico y accesibilidad de la vivienda en España. In R. Vergés Escuìn (Ed.), *El precio de la vivienda y la formación del hogar* (pp. 85–98). Barcelona: Centro de Cultura Contemporánia de Barcelona.

Reed, H., Briere, R., & Casterline, J. (Eds.). (1999). *The role of diffusion processes in fertility change in developing countries. Report of a workshop.* Committee on Population, National Research Council. Washington, DC: National Academy Press.

Rehrer, D. S. (1998). Family ties in Western Europe: Persistent contrasts. *Population and Development Review, 24*(2), 203–234.

Reinhard, S. C., & Horwitz, A. V. (1995). Caregiver burden: Differentiating the content and consequences of family caregiving. *Journal of Marriage and the Family, 57*(3), 751–762.

Rindfuss, R. R., & Van den Heuvel, A. (1990). Cohabitation: A precursor to marriage or an alternative to being single? *Population and Development Review, 16*(4), 703–726.

Roca, E. (1995). Family law in Spain. In C. Hamilton & K. Standley (Eds.), *Family law in Europe.* London: Butterworths.

Rogers, E. M. (1985). *Diffusion of innovations* (4th ed.), New York: The Free Press.

Rogoff Ramsøy, N. (1994). Non-marital cohabitation and change in norms: the case of Norway. *Acta Sociologica, 37*(1):23-37.

Rohwer, G., & Pötter, U. (1998). *Transition data analysis (TDA) manual.* Available at http://www.stat.ruhr-uni-bochum.d Rosekrans, M., & Hartup, W. (1967). Imitative influences of consistent and inconsistent response to a model on aggressive behavior in children. *Journal of Personality and Social Psychology, 7,* 429–434.

Rosenberg, D. J. (1991). Shock therapy: GDR women in transition from a socialist welfare state to a social market economy. *Signs, 17,* 129–151.

Rosenfeld, R. A., & Birkelund, G. E. (1995). Women's part-time work: A cross-national comparison. *European Sociological Review, 11*(2), 111–134.

Rosina, A. (2001, December 1–2). *Questa unione informale non s'ha da fare. Matrimonio e famiglia: Un binomio indissolubile in Italia.* Paper presented at the seminar La Bassa Fecondità tra Costrizioni Economiche e Cambio di Valori, Florence.

Rosina, A., & Fraboni, R. (2004). Is marriage losing its centrality in Italy? *Demographic Research, 11,* 149–172.

Ross, C. E., & Mirowsky, J. (1996). Economic and interpersonal work rewards: Subjective utilities of men's and women's compensation. *Social Forces, 75*(1), 223–246.

Rossi, G. (1997). The nestlings. Why young adults stay at home longer: The Italian case. *Journal of Family Issues, 18,* 627–644.

Roussel, L. (1992). The family in Western Europe: Divergences and convergence. *Population, 47*(1), 133–152.

Roussel, L., & Festy, P. (1978). *Recent developments in attitudes and behaviour regarding the family in the member states of the Council of Europe.* Paris: INED.

Rubery, J., & Fagan, C. (1995). Gender segregation in societal context. *Work, Employment & Society, 9*(2), 213–240.

Sainsbury, D. (1994). Women's and men's social rights: Gendering dimensions of welfare states. In D. Sainsbury (Ed.), *Gendering welfare states* (pp. 150–169). London: Sage.

Saldeen, Å. (1995). Family law in Sweden. In C. Hamilton, K. Standley, & David Hodson (Eds.), *Family law in Europe.* London: Butterworths.

Saraceno, C. (1987a). Le politiche del ciclo di vita. In L. Balbo (Ed.), *Time to care.* Milan: Franco Angeli.

Saraceno, C. (1987b). Division of family labour and gender identity. In A. Showstack Sasson (Ed.), *Women and the state. The shifting boundaries of public and private* (pp. 191–206). London: Hutchinson.

Saraceno, C. (1988). Le strutture di genere della cittadinanza. *Democrazia e Diritto, 28*(1), 273–295.

Saraceno, C. (1992). Donne e lavoro o strutture di genere del lavoro? *Polis, 1,* 5–22.

Saraceno, C. (1993). Elementi per un'analisi delle trasformazioni di genere nella società contemporanea e delle loro conseguenze sociali. *Rassegna Italiana di Sociologia, 34*(1), 19–56.

Saraceno, C. (1994). The ambivalent familism of the Italian welfare state. *Social Politics, 1,* 60–82.

Saraceno, C. (1997). Family change, family policies and the restructuring of welfare. In *OECD Social Political Studies:* No. 21. *Family, Market and Community* (pp. 81–100), Paris: OECD.

Saraceno, C. (2003a). La conciliazione di responsabilità familiari e attività lavorative in Italia: Paradossi e equilibri imperfetti. *Polis,* 17(2):99–228.

Saraceno, C. (2003b). *Mutamenti della famiglia e politiche sociali in Italia* (2nd ed.). Bologna: Il Mulino.

Schelling, T. C. (1978). *Micromotives and macrobehavior.* New York: Norton.

Schneider, D. J. (1988). *Introduction to social psychology.* New York: Harcourt Brace Jovanovich.

Selden, R. W. (1992). Standardising data in decentralised educational data system. In *The OECD International Education Indicators. A Framework for Analysis* (pp. 107–114). Paris: OECD.

Seltzer, J. A. (2004). Cohabitation in the United States and Britain: Demography, kinship, and the future. *Journal of Marriage and Family,* 66(4):921–28.

Sen, A. K. (1990). Gender and cooperative conflicts. In Irene Tinker (Ed.), *Persistent inequalities* (pp. 123–149). Oxford: Oxford University Press.

Sennet, R. (2001). *L'Uomo flessibile. Le conseguenze del nuovo capitalisno sulla vita personale.* Milan: Feltrinelli.

Settersten, R. A. Mayer, K.-U. (1997). The measurement of age, age structuring, and the life course. *Annual Review of Sociology.* 23:233-61

Shavit, Y., & Blossfeld, H.-P. (Eds.). (1993). *Persistent inequality.* Boulder, CO: Westview.

Sheiwe, K. (1994). German pension insurance, gendered times and stratification. In D. Sainsbury (Ed.), *Gendering welfare states* (pp. 132–149). London: Sage.

Shelton, B. A., & John, D. (1993). Does marital status make a difference? Housework among married and cohabiting men and women. *Journal of Family Issues, 14,* 401–420.

Sherif, M. (1936). *The psychology of social norms.* New York: Harper.

Sherif, M., & Sherif, C. (1964). *Reference groups*. New York: Harper & Row.

Sigle-Rushton, W., & Perrons, D. (2006). Employment transitions over the life cycle: a statistical analysis. *EOC working paper series*, No. 46.

Simó Noguera, C., Castro Martín, T. & Bonmatí, A. S. (2005). The Spanish case. The Effects of the globalization process on the transition to adulthood In H.-P. Blossfeld et al. (Eds.), *Globalization, uncertainty and youth in society* (pp. 375–402). London: Routledge.

Simó Noguera, C., Golsch, K., & Steinhage, N. (2000). Entry into first parenthood in Spain and the process of globalisation. In *GLOBALIFE Working Paper Series* No. 8, Faculty of Sociology. Bielefeld: University of Bielefeld.

Slemrod, J. (Ed.). (1992). *Why people pay taxes: Tax compliance and enforcement*. Ann Arbor: University of Michigan Press.

Solga, H., & Konietzka, D. (1999). Occupational matching and social stratification. *European Sociological Review*, 15(1), 25–47.

Sorensen, A., & H. Trappe (1995). The persistence of gender inequality in earnings in the German Democratic Republic. *American Sociological Review*, 60, 398–406.

Soule, S. A. (1997). The student divestment movement in the United States and tactical diffusion: The Shantytown protest. *Social Forces*, 75(3), 855–882.

Statistisches Bundesamt. (2001). *Leben und arbeiten in Deutschland. Ergebnisse des Mikrozensus 2000*. Wiesbaden: Author.

Steele, F. A., Kallis, C., & Heather, J. (2006). The formation and outcomes of cohabiting and marital partnerships in early adulthood: The role of previous partnership experience. *Journal of the Royal Statistical Society: Series A (Statistics in Society)*, 169(4), 757–779.

Steele, F. A., Kallis, C., Goldstein, H., & Joshi, H. (2005). The relationship between childbearing and transition from marriage and cohabitation in Britain. *Demography*, 42(4), 647–673.

Steiner, V., & Wrohlich, K. (2004). Household taxation, income splitting and labor supply incentives—a microsimulation study for Germany. *CESifo Economic Studies*, 50(3), 541–568.

Stone, L. (1977). *The family, sex and marriage in England 1500–1800*. New York: Harper & Row.

Strang, D. (1990). From dependency to sovereignty: An event history analysis of decolonization. *American Sociological Review*, 55, 846–860.

Strang, D. (1991). Adding social structure to diffusion models: An event history framework. *Sociological Methods and Research*, 19(3), 324–353.

Strang, D.,& Meyer, J. W. (1993). Institutional conditions for diffusion. *Theory and Society*, 22, 487–512.

Strang, D., & Soule, S. A. (1998). Diffusion in organisations and social movements: From hybrid corn to poison pills. *Annual Review of Sociology*, 24, 265–290.

Strang, D., & Tuma, N. B. (1993). Spatial and temporal heterogeneity in diffusion. *American Journal of Sociology*, 99(3), 614–639.

Strohmeier, K. P., & Kuijsten, A. (1997). Family life and family policies in Europe: An introduction. In F.-X. Kaufmann, A. Kuijsten, H.-J. Schulze, & K. P. Strohmeier (Eds.), *Family life and family policies in Europe* (pp. 1–11). Oxford: Clarendon Press.

Surkyn, J., & Lesthaeghe, R. (2004). Value orientations and the second demographic transition (SDT) in northern, western, and southern Europe: An update. *Demographic Research*, 3(3), 45–86.

Szydlik, M. (1994). Incomes in a planned and a market economy: The case of the German Democratic Republic and the 'former' Federal Republic of Germany. *European Sociological Review*, 10(3), 199–217.

Thévenon, O. (2003). Welfare state regimes and female labour supply: A comparison between France, Germany, Italy, the Netherlands, Spain and the United Kingdom. *FENICs Working Paper.*

Thiessen, V., Rohlinger, H., & Blasius, J. (1994). The 'significance' of minor changes in panel data: A correspondence analysis of the division of household tasks. In M. Greenacre & J. Blasius (Eds.), *Correspondence analysis in the social sciences* (pp. 252–266). London: Academic Press.

Thomson, E., & Colella, U. (1992). Cohabitation and marital stability: Quality or commitment? *Journal of Marriage and the Family, 54*(2), 259–267.

Thornton, A. (1991). Influence of the marital history of parents on the marital and cohabitational experiences of children. *American Journal of Sociology, 96*(4), 868–894.

Thornton, A., Axinn, W. G., & Hill, D. H. (1992). Reciprocal effects of religiosity, cohabitation and marriage. *American Journal of Sociology, 98*(3), 682–651.

Timoteo, M. (1995). Family law in Italy. In C. Hamilton & K. Standley (Eds.), *Family law in Europe.* London: Butterworths.

Tosi, A. (1990). Italy. In W. Van Vliet (Ed.), *International handbook of housing policies and practices* (pp. 195–220). New York: Greenwood Press.

Tosi, A. (1994). *La casa: Il rischio e l'esclusione—rapporto IRS sul disagio abitativo in Italia.* Milan: Franco Angeli.

Toulemon, L. (1997). Cohabitation is here to stay. *Population, 9,* 11–46.

Trappe, H. (1995). *Emanzipation oder Zwang? Frauen in der DDR zwischen beruf, familie un sozialpolitik.* Berlin: Akademie Verlag.

Trappe, H., & Rosenfeld, R. A. (1998). A comparison of job-shifting patterns in the former East Germany and the former West Germany. *European Sociological Review, 14,* 343–368.

Trappe, H., & Rosenfeld, R. A. (2000). How do children matter? A comparison of gender earnings inequality for young adults in the former East Germany and the former West Germany, *Journal of Marriage and the Family, 62,* 489–507.

Trost, J. (1978). A renewed social institution: Non-marital cohabitation. *Acta Sociologica, 21,* 305–315.

Trost, J. (1979). *Unmarried cohabitation.* Västerås, Sweden: International Library.

Tudge, J. R. H., & Winterhoff, P. A. (1993). Vygotsky, Piaget & Bandura: Perspectives on the relations between the social world and cognitive development. *Human Development, 36,* 61–81.

Ungerson, C. (1997). Social politics and the commodification of care. *Social Politics, 4*(3), 362–381.

Van de Kaa, D. J. (1987). Europe's second demographic transition. *Population Bulletin, 42*(1), 1–38.

Van Knippenberg, D. (2000). Group norms, prototipicality and persuasion. In T. D. Hogg & M. Hogg (Eds.), *Attitudes, behaviour, and social context. The role of norms and group membership* (pp. 157–170). London: Erlbaum.

Villeneuve-Gokalp, C. (1991). From marriage to informal union: Recent changes in the behaviour of French couples. *Population (an English Selection), 3,* 81–111.

Villeneuve-Gokalp, C. (2000). Les jeunes parent toujours au meme age de chez leurs parents. *Economie et Statistique, 337–338*(7/8), 61–80.

Waite, L. J., Bachrach, C., Hindin, M., Thomson, E., & Thornton, A. (Eds.). (2000). *Ties that bind. Perspectives on marriage and cohabitation.* New York: Aldine de Gruyter.

Wan, C. K., Jaccard, J., & Ramey, S. L. (1996). The relationship between social support and life satisfaction as a function of family structure. *Journal of Marriage and the Family, 58*(2), 502–513.

Watkins, S. C. (1991). *From province into nations: Demographic integration in Western Europe 1870–1960.* Princeton: Princeton University Press.

Winkler, G. (Ed.). (1990). *Frauenreport 90*. Berlin: Verlag Die Wirtshaft.

Wright, E., Baxter, J., & Birkelund, G. E. (1995). The gender gap in workplace authority. *American Sociological Review, 60,* 407–435.

Wu, Z. (2000). *Cohabitation. An alternative form of family living.* Oxford: Oxford University Press.

Xie, Y., Raymo, J., Goyette, K., & Thornton, A. (2001). *Economic potential and entry into marriage and cohabitation.* Paper presented at the 2001 annual meeting of the Population Association of America.

Yamaguchi, K. (1991). *Event history analysis.* London: Sage.

Yeandle, S. (1996). Work and care in the life course: Understanding the context for family arrangements. *Journal of Social Policy, 25*(4), 507–527.

Yeandle, S. (1999). Social quality in everyday life: Changing European experiences of employment, family and community. *European Journal of Social Quality, 1*(1/2), 90–108.

Zighera, J. (1992). Nota sobre la diferenciación por edad y sexo de la jornada semanal de trabajo y de su reciente evolución. *Revista de Economía y Sociología del Trabajo, 15/16,* 28–30.

Author Index

Subject Index